Perspectives on Development in the Middle East and North Africa (MENA) Region

Series Editor

Almas Heshmati, Jönköping University, Jönköping, Sweden

This Scopus indexed book series publishes monographs and edited volumes devoted to studies on the political, economic and social developments of the Middle East and North Africa (MENA). Volumes cover in-depth analyses of individual countries, regions, cases and comparative studies, and they include both a specific and a general focus on the latest advances of the various aspects of development. It provides a platform for researchers globally to carry out rigorous economic, social and political analyses, to promote, share, and discuss current quantitative and analytical work on issues, findings and perspectives in various areas of economics and development of the MENA region. Perspectives on Development in the Middle East and North Africa (MENA) Region allows for a deeper appreciation of the various past, present, and future issues around MENA's development with high quality, peer reviewed contributions. The topics may include, but not limited to: economics and business, natural resources, governance, politics, security and international relations, gender, culture, religion and society, economics and social development, reconstruction, and Jewish, Islamic, Arab, Iranian, Israeli, Kurdish and Turkish studies. Volumes published in the series will be important reading offering an original approach along theoretical lines supported empirically for researchers and students, as well as consultants and policy makers, interested in the development of the MENA region.

Goran M. Muhamad

Reducing Natural Resource Dependency for Economic Growth in Resource Rich Countries

Goran M. Muhamad
Economics and Finance
University of Kurdistan Hewler
Erbil, Iraq

Economic Research Center (ERC)
Soran University
Erbil, Kurdistan Region, Iraq

ISSN 2520-1239 ISSN 2520-1247 (electronic)
Perspectives on Development in the Middle East and North Africa (MENA) Region
ISBN 978-981-99-3639-7 ISBN 978-981-99-3640-3 (eBook)
https://doi.org/10.1007/978-981-99-3640-3

© The Editor(s) (if applicable) and The Author(s), under exclusive license to Springer Nature Singapore Pte Ltd. 2023

This work is subject to copyright. All rights are solely and exclusively licensed by the Publisher, whether the whole or part of the material is concerned, specifically the rights of translation, reprinting, reuse of illustrations, recitation, broadcasting, reproduction on microfilms or in any other physical way, and transmission or information storage and retrieval, electronic adaptation, computer software, or by similar or dissimilar methodology now known or hereafter developed.
The use of general descriptive names, registered names, trademarks, service marks, etc. in this publication does not imply, even in the absence of a specific statement, that such names are exempt from the relevant protective laws and regulations and therefore free for general use.
The publisher, the authors, and the editors are safe to assume that the advice and information in this book are believed to be true and accurate at the date of publication. Neither the publisher nor the authors or the editors give a warranty, expressed or implied, with respect to the material contained herein or for any errors or omissions that may have been made. The publisher remains neutral with regard to jurisdictional claims in published maps and institutional affiliations.

This Springer imprint is published by the registered company Springer Nature Singapore Pte Ltd.
The registered company address is: 152 Beach Road, #21-01/04 Gateway East, Singapore 189721, Singapore

To
My wife Hayat and our lovely daughters
Liva, Lahy and Lani!

Preface

This empirical study attempts to examine the reduction of natural resource revenue dependency in resource rich countries. Such countries experience lower economic growth due to high volatility in commodity prices, reduction in accountability, undermining of the competitiveness of other economic sectors and weak power of institutions. The analysis is based on an identified gap in the literature regarding whether and how private sector development and public sector development affect the degree of dependency on resource revenue in natural resource rich countries. Much of the previous empirical studies on resource curse is related to resource dependency and economic growth. On one hand, previous studies have not examined the importance of private sector development and public sector development in reducing the danger of resource curse. On the other, attention has been paid to the relationship between institutional quality and natural resource dependency. While this might be true for non-economic determinants, in general the economic determinants are not broadly addressed.

This book studies the interaction between private and public sector development with dependency on natural resources, specifically exploring whether the two diversified factors lead to a decrease in the degree of dependency, which is important for economic growth. Economic diversification is viewed as a long-term solution to the high economic dependency from natural resources.

The analysis of the book will help to shed light on private sector development, public services sector privatisation and a taxation system to diversify sources of income, with the objective to reduce dependency on natural resources extraction. In doing so, an unbalanced panel data of 110 countries of different types and levels of natural resource dependency and different political systems covering the period 1990–2017 is employed. Accordingly, two models, static and dynamic adjustment models, are established to examine the abovementioned relationships as a system of interdependent equations. The dynamic flexible adjustment model and the better performance of system of equations made a key difference compared to the other estimation models.

The results conclude that economic diversification to reduce resource revenue dependency of natural resource rich countries can be achieved through public sector development. The public sector can be developed to lead diversification either through the privatisation of public services, or through the development of a national taxation system. Nevertheless, beside the effect of the diversified factors, institutional quality and human development improve the performance of economic diversification to reduce natural resource dependency. Therefore, countries that experienced improvement on institutions and human capacity have adjusted faster towards less dependency. This result is critical for the resource rich countries to focus on diversifying the economy, and hence avoid the resource curse.

The significance of this book is vital to a group of interests related to the study in the market, namely, public policymakers, the private sector, the law maker and the scholars. It also guides the new private entrants who might be investing in such countries.

The book is organised as follows; chapter 1 of the book presents a general overview of the book including problem of natural resource dependency and the way the present study investigates to reduce the degree of dependency. Chapter 2 provides a summary of the previous studies surrounding the relationship between private sector development, public sector privatisation, taxation and the reduction of natural resource dependency. Chapter 3 introduces the methodology of the study, and the empirical specifications, namely the dynamic adjustment model and its adjustment speed. Chapter 4 continues to then describe the data for estimation. Several variables related to the dependent and independent are selected due to their relevance based on literature and data availability. Several new variables are computed for the analysis of the study using various methods of computations. Chapter 5 presents the results according to the procedure stated in chapter 3. It includes the presentation of the results organised by the research questions set out in chapter 1. Chapter 6 presents the overall summary, hypothesis tests and policy implication of the study.

Erbil, Iraq   Goran M. Muhamad

Acknowledgements

I would like to acknowledge my gratitude to Dr Nabaz T. Khayyat and Professor Almas Heshmati for their valuable support. Their insightful advice and guidance have been influential in the preparation and completion of this book.

My sincere gratitude to my parents, who firmly establish in me a sense of moral and ethical thinking. I remain eternally grateful for their marvellous upbringing.

I would like to acknowledge my gratitude to Taylor & Francis Group to accept reproducing of the below article in the content of the current book.

Goran M. Muhamad, Almas Heshmati & Nabaz T. Khayyat (2020) The Dynamics of Private Sector Development in Natural Resource Dependent Countries, *Global Economic Review, 49:4, 396–421*, DOI: https://doi.org/10.1080/1226508X.2020.1821745

© 2020 The Author(s). Published by Informa UK Limited, trading as Taylor & Francis Group

Contents

1 **Overview of the Book** 1
   1.1 Introduction 1
   1.2 Problem of Natural Resource Dependency 5
   1.3 Research Aims and Objectives 6
   1.4 Research Questions and Hypotheses 7
   1.5 Significance of the Study 9
   1.6 The Book Design and Organisation 10
   1.7 Summary 12
   Bibliography 12

2 **Economic Diversification to Reduce Natural Resource Dependency in the Literature** 15
   2.1 Introduction 15
   2.2 Natural Resource Dependency in Resource Rich Countries 16
   2.3 Why Is Natural Resource Dependency Reduction Important? 22
   2.4 The Effects of Economic Diversification on Resource Dependency 25
       2.4.1 The Private Sector Development 28
       2.4.2 Investment in Human Development and Infrastructure 31
       2.4.3 The Public Sector Development 34
   2.5 Successful Cases of Economic Diversifications Policies 40
   2.6 Critics of the Previous Literature 43
   2.7 Summary 44
   Bibliography 45

3 **Methodology and Empirical Specifications** 55
   3.1 Introduction 56
   3.2 Econometric of Panel Data Estimation 56
   3.3 Empirical Specifications 58
       3.3.1 The Speed of Adjustment 58
       3.3.2 Flexible Dynamic Adjustment Model 60
       3.3.3 System of Equations 61

		3.4	Model Specification	62
			3.4.1 The Static Model	62
			3.4.2 The Dynamic Flexible Adjustment Model	62
			3.4.3 The System of Equations	65
		3.5	Summary	68
		Bibliography		69
4	**Data Presentation and Analysis**			**73**
	4.1	Introduction		73
	4.2	Data Presentation		74
		4.2.1	Data Sources	74
		4.2.2	Sampling Strategy	75
		4.2.3	The Dependent and Independent Variables	79
		4.2.4	County Classification	83
		4.2.5	Validation and Multicollinearity Results	83
		4.2.6	Countries Heterogeneity and Variance Heteroskedasticity	84
		4.2.7	Summary Statistics	87
	4.3	Data Analysis, Model Specification, Estimation and Testing		89
		4.3.1	Static vs Dynamic Models	90
		4.3.2	Single Equation vs. System of Equations Estimations	92
	4.4	Summary		93
	Bibliography			94
5	**Presentation of Results**			**97**
	5.1	Introduction		97
	5.2	Results of Private Sector Development		98
		5.2.1	Determinants of Optimal Private Sector Development (PSD)	98
		5.2.2	The Speed of Adjustment Values	103
	5.3	Privatisation Effect Results		110
		5.3.1	Determinant of Optimal Privatisation	110
		5.3.2	The Speed of Adjustment Values	114
	5.4	The Result of Taxation Effects		120
		5.4.1	Determinant of Optimal Taxation	120
		5.4.2	The Speed of Adjustment Values	124
	5.5	Results of Natural Resource Dependency Reduction		130
		5.5.1	Factors Affecting the Reduction of Dependency	131
		5.5.2	The Speed of Adjustment Values	136
	5.6	Summary		143
	Bibliography			147

6	**Overall Summary, Hypotheses Tests and Policy Implications**		155
	6.1 Introduction		155
	6.2 The Research Questions and Hypotheses Test		156
	6.2.1 The Research Questions		156
	6.2.2 Hypotheses Testing		157
	6.3 Summary of Results		159
	6.4 Policy Implications		164
	6.5 Final Conclusion and Contributions to the Literature		165
	6.5.1 Final Conclusion		165
	6.5.2 Contributions to the Literature		166
	6.6 Limitations and Recommendations for Further Research		167
	Bibliography		168
Appendix 1: Country Classification and Coefficient Correlations			171
Appendix 2: Single Equation Model			179
Appendix 3: The Determinants of Speed of Adjustment			185
Appendix 4: Country Mean Indicator Values			189

About the Author

Dr. Goran M. Muhamad is a well-experienced economist having a series of academic qualifications including B.Sc./Postgraduate Diploma/M.Sc./and Ph.D. in Economics. He received his M.Sc. in Economic Development and Policy Analysis at the University of Nottingham, United Kingdom, and his Ph.D. in Economics at the University of Kurdistan Hewler. He has a professional experience in academia, consultancy and management positions in various industries. His research is internationally recognised focusing on a diversified range of economics subjects particularly Natural Resource Economics, Private Sector Development, Environmental Economics, Development Economics and Post-conflict Affected Area.

Author's Publications:

Journal Articles

1. Environmental effects of entrepreneurship indices on ecological footprint of croplands and grazing lands in the economy, at Journal of Cleaner Production, 414, (2023), pages 137550, DOI: https://doi.org/10.1016/j.jclepro.2023.137550
2. Private Sector Development Analysis in Post-Conflict Kurdistan Region of Iraq. At UKH Journal of Social Science 6(2), 19–32 in 2022, DOI: https://doi.org/10.25079/ukhjss.v6n2y2022.pp19-32
3. Economic Freedom's Spatial Effects on the Ecological Footprints of Cropland, Forest Products, and Grazing Land in Asian-Pacific Countries, at *Journal of Environmental Management 316, (2022), pages 115274*, DOI: https://doi.org/10.1016/j.jenvman.2022.115274
4. Aid in the Development of Kurdistan Region of Iraq, Economic Research Forum (ERF), available at Aid in the development of the Kurdistan region of Iraq - Economic Research Forum (ERF)
5. Dependency on Natural Resources and Diversification of Economies in MENA, available at: https://theforum.erf.org.eg/2021/06/27/dependency-natural-resources-diversification-economies-mena/

6. How to Reduce the Degree of Dependency on Natural Resources? *Resources Policy 72, (2021), pages 102047,* DOI: https://doi.org/10.1016/j.resourpol.2021.102047 © 2021 The Authors. Published by Elsevier Ltd. This is an open access article under the CC BY license (http://creativecommons.org/licenses/by/4.0/).
7. The Dynamics of Private Sector Development in Natural Resource Dependent Countries at *Global Economic Review, 49(4), (2020) 396–421,* DOI: 10.1080/1226508X.2020.1821745 © 2020 The Author(s). Published by Informa UK Limited, trading as Taylor & Francis Group

Books
1. The Economic Impact of the Kurdish Genocide Process (2010) (Kurdish Language)
2. The Demonstration in Kurdistan Region between Riots and Democracy (2005) (Kurdish Language, Co-author).

Abbreviations

3SLS	Three Stage Least Square
DF	Degree of Freedom
EIA	Energy Information Administration
FDI	Foreign Direct Investment
FGLS	Feasible Generalised Least Square
FMIL	Full Information Maximum Likelihood
GDP	Gross Domestic Product
GMM	Generalised Method of Moments
GNI	Gross National Income
HDI	Human Development Index
ICT	Information and Communication Technology
MSE	Mean Square Error
OECD	Organisation for Economic Co-operation and Development
OLS	Ordinary Least Square
OPEC	Organisation of the Petroleum Exporting Countries
PCA	Principal Component Analysis
PPP	Private Public Partnership
PSD	Private Sector Development
R&D	Research and Development
RMSE	Root Mean Square Error
SOEs	State Owned Enterprises
SUR	Seemingly Unrelated Regression
UNDP	Untied Nation Development Programme
WBD	World Bank Dataset
WDI	World Development Indicators

List of Figures

Fig. 1.1	Annual privatisation revenue in million US dollar (*Source* Privatisation Barometer [2019], author's own construction)	3
Fig. 2.1	Private sector development engagement in economic growth (*Source* International Corporation and Development 2019)	29
Fig. 5.1	Mean of observed and optimal of PSD by year	108
Fig. 5.2	Mean of observed and optimal of privatisation by year	119
Fig. 5.3	Mean of observed and optimal of taxation by year	129
Fig. 5.4	Mean of observed and optimal of dependency reduction by year	141

List of Tables

Table 1.1	Private investment share of GDP (%) compared to development indicators	2
Table 2.1	A review of the selected existing literature on resource rich economies	21
Table 2.2	A review of the selected existing literature on PSD	32
Table 2.3	A review of the selected literature on public sector development	35
Table 4.1	Definition of variables (WBD; World Bank Database, UNDP; United Nations Development Programme)	76
Table 4.2	Correlation coefficient of PCA for institutional quality	78
Table 4.3	Correlation coefficient of PCA for credit to the private sector	78
Table 4.4	Correlation coefficient for PCA for infrastructure	78
Table 4.5	List of computed variables	80
Table 4.6	Common indicators to measure natural resource dependency	82
Table 4.7	Pearson correlation coefficient of dependency model	85
Table 4.8	Heterogeneity among the country groups—analysis of variance	86
Table 4.9	Summary statistics of the variables	88
Table 4.10	Static vs. dynamic models	91
Table 4.11	Different values between single and system of equations estimations	93
Table 5.1	Static and dynamic model parameters estimates (PSD)	99
Table 5.2	Mean of speed of adjustment by time period	104
Table 5.3	Mean of speed of adjustment by income group	104
Table 5.4	Mean of speed of adjustment by private sector size	105
Table 5.5	Mean of speed of adjustment by degree of dependency	105
Table 5.6	Development of mean indicators of PSD by year	107
Table 5.7	Country mean value of PSD	108

Table 5.8	Static and dynamic model parameter estimates (privatisation)	110
Table 5.9	Mean adjustment speed of privatisation by time period	115
Table 5.10	Mean adjustment speed of privatisation by income group	115
Table 5.11	Mean adjustment speed of privatisation by private sector size	116
Table 5.12	Mean adjustment speed of privatisation by degree of dependency on natural resources	117
Table 5.13	Development of mean indicator of privatisation by year	118
Table 5.14	Country mean value of privatisation	120
Table 5.15	Static and dynamic model parameter estimate (taxation)	121
Table 5.16	Mean adjustment speed of taxation by time period	125
Table 5.17	Mean adjustment speed of taxation by income group	126
Table 5.18	Mean value of taxation by private sector size	126
Table 5.19	Mean value of taxation by degree of dependency	127
Table 5.20	Development of mean indicator of taxation by year	128
Table 5.21	Mean indicator of taxation by country	129
Table 5.22	Static and dynamic model parameter estimate (dependency)	132
Table 5.23	Mean value of resource dependency reduction by time period	136
Table 5.24	Mean value of dependency reduction by income group	137
Table 5.25	Mean value of dependency reduction by private sector size	138
Table 5.26	Mean value of dependency reduction by degree of dependency	138
Table 5.27	Development of mean indicator of dependency reduction by year	140
Table 5.28	Mean of dependency reduction by country	142
Table 6.1	Hypotheses test among the estimated models	157
Table 6.2	Country Adjustment in Comparison to Human Development and Governance Indicators	162
Table 6.3	Country Level Adjustment towards Dependency Reduction	163
Table A.1	Country classification	171
Table A.2	Pearson correlation coefficients (PSD)	175
Table A.3	Pearson correlation coefficients (privatisation)	176
Table A.4	Pearson correlation coefficients (taxation)	177
Table A.5	Static and dynamic model parameters estimates (PSD)	179
Table A.6	Static and dynamic model parameter estimate (privatisation)	181
Table A.7	Static and dynamic model parameter estimate (taxation)	182
Table A.8	Static and dynamic model parameters estimates (dependency)	183
Table A.9	The determinants of speed of adjustment (PSD)	185

List of Tables

Table A.10	The determinants of speed of adjustment for privatisation	186
Table A.11	The determinants of speed of adjustment (taxation)	187
Table A.12	The determinants of speed of adjustment (dependency reduction)	187
Table A.13	Country mean indicator value of PSD	189
Table A.14	Country mean indicator values of privatisation	192
Table A.15	Country mean indicator values of taxation	194
Table A.16	Country mean indicator values of dependency	196

Chapter 1
Overview of the Book

Abstract This chapter provides a general introduction to the book. It outlines the problems of natural resource dependency and the importance of economic diversification in overcoming those problems. Then, it provides aims and objectives set out for this book to investigate the factors that possibly contribute to economic diversification as a long-term solution to the high economic dependency on natural resources. Private sector development and public sector reforms including privatisation and taxation may lead to this diversification. To achieve the objectives set out previously, this book attempts to examine the topic empirically by finding answers to several main research questions. The analysis is based on an identified gap in the literature regarding whether and how private sector development and public sector development affect the degree of dependency on resource revenue in natural resource rich countries. This research applies the dynamic flexible adjustment model to identify the adjustment behaviour of private sector development, the privatisation of public services and the development of national taxation system in natural resource rich countries over time. The findings suggest that the development of the public sector including privatisation and the development of a national taxation system are effective factors in reducing the degree of dependency on natural resource revenue. The significance of this subject is vital to a group of interests related to the study in the market, namely, public policymakers, the private sector, the law maker and the scholars. It also guides the new private entrants who might be investing in such countries.

Keywords Economic diversification · Natural resource economic dependency · Private sector development · Public sector development (Privatisation and Taxation)

1.1 Introduction

The lack of economic diversification has been observed in many natural resource rich countries. Frankel (2012) and Schoneveld and Zoomers (2015) reported that resource dependency and lack of diversification impacted natural resource economies through

Table 1.1 Private investment share of GDP (%) compared to development indicators

Indicators\periods	1990–1996	1997–2003	2004–2010	2011–2017
Private sector investment (% of GDP)	6.064	7.028	8.262	7.837
Unemployment rate (% of total labour force)	5.735	6.190	5.697	5.524
Tax revenue (% of GDP)	24.816	25.819	24.57	24.795
Annual growth rate (GDP growth annual %)	2.452	2.980	3.030	2.811

Source WDI (2018), author's own construction

the production of currency revaluations, trade balance fluctuations, labour market insecurities and by undermining the competitiveness of other economic sectors. As such, these factors lead to macroeconomic instability. Economic diversification is viewed as a long-term solution to the high economic dependency on natural resources. This diversification can be achieved through both private sector development (PSD) and public sector development.

Private sector development affects the degree of resource revenue dependency by contributing to the economic growth of natural resource rich countries. The private sector has actively engaged in expanding productions, job creations and welfare gains of developing countries (International Corporation and Development, 2019). Therefore, PSD is seen as a driver of inclusive growth and job creation, and thus its impact on economic and social well-being is observed.

Theoretically, the development of the private sector is related to the poor performance of the public sector. Issues surrounding efficiency and effectiveness of the public sector in natural resource rich countries are major factors behind the poor performance of this sector. The critical factor behind the movement from public enterprises to privatisation is poor performance of public sector (Boycko et al., 1996; Kay & Thompson, 1986; Mohan, 2001). In essence, the public sector can be developed to lead diversification either through privatisation of public services providing firms with reduced public financing (development[1]) of those services, or through development of a national taxation system that reduces the government's dependency on revenue from natural resources.

Table 1.1 shows the world's private investment growth from 1990 to 2017 compared to additional key development indicators. Private sector data seem consistent with decreasing unemployment rates and increasing revenue in the form of government taxes. Moreover, the relative effectiveness of the private sector largely remains when it appears as a pair of parallel trends to annual growth rate.

The privatisation of state-owned enterprises (SOEs) in natural resource rich countries provides substantial revenues for the government which may lead to stabilise

---

[1] For example, China has adopted a privatisation policy to develop its state-owned enterprises since 1978 (Wang & Chen, 2011). In addition, the global trend of water services and airport reform are the most notable examples of the development of public firms, see Gillen (2011), Lieberherr and Truffer (2015), and Molinos-Senante and Sala-Garrido (2015).

1.1 Introduction

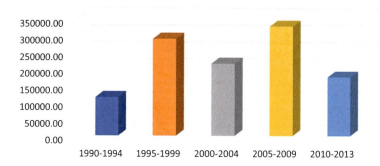

Fig. 1.1 Annual privatisation revenue in million US dollar (*Source* Privatisation Barometer [2019], author's own construction)

fiscal policy. Therefore, many countries have developed privatisation to deepen economic reforms and increase private investment in public enterprises as well as to increase the private sector's engagement with economic activities (Nhema, 2015). For example, Zimbabwe in Sub-Saharan Africa employed reform models of outright privatisation, commercialisation and leasing and management contracts.

There has been a strong tendency worldwide towards privatising SOEs, and thus, increasing various sources of government revenue. Figure 1.1 shows the annual revenue that governments have received from privatisation from 1990 to 2013, in which the privatisation cumulative value exceeds 1,129 billion US dollars of revenue for the governments (Privatisation Barometer, 2019).[2] As indicated by Megginson and Netter (2001, p. 326) 'this revenue has come to governments without raising taxes or cutting other government services'. Thus, the lure of revenue received from selling the SOEs speeds up the privatisation process as well as widening privatisation policy.

The private sector may provide a normal rate of return to the resource wealth[3] countries in the form of taxes. Therefore, taxation provides relatively long-lasting economic stability to reduce long-term resource revenue volatility and strengthen accountability in natural resource rich countries, thereby enhancing economic growth. Taxation is a significant government fiscal policy instrument to mobilise revenue and promote economic growth (Odhiambo & Olushola, 2018).

Economic diversification of natural resource rich countries is vitally important but not easy to attain. Countries dependent on natural resources derive a high share of fiscal revenues from the natural resource sector including oil, natural gas, minerals and other natural resources. Natural resource rents account for 7% of world GDP, amounting more than four trillion US dollars per year (Mishrif & Al Balushi, 2018). These rents had an adverse impact on economic growth (Van der Ploeg, 2011;

---

[2] Different sources and different database were checked for up to date data for privatisation cumulative value, it was not available.

[3] Resource rich countries or resource wealth countries will be used throughout the manuscript interchangeably.

Venables, 2016), in which these features are well-known in the literature as the 'resource curse' or the so-called 'paradox of plenty' (Adams et al., 2019). This curse refers to a negative correlation between resource abundance and economic growth (Badeeb et al., 2017; Frankel, 2012; Venables, 2016). While it is proven that natural resource rich countries may not derive economic growth (Arezki & Van der Ploeg, 2011; Ji et al., 2014), average growth rates in resource rich countries are slower than resource poor countries (Badeeb et al., 2017; Smith, 2015). This is despite there being a number of natural resource rich countries that have never experienced development (Frankel, 2012). Countries suffer from the curse, for example, are Nigeria, Sudan, Cameron, Iraq, Ecuador and Venezuela.

Diversification can be achieved in every sector of the economy. Natural resource rich countries, that are dependent on resource revenue, may have more secure revenue to stabilise fiscal policy from the following sources: private sector development, selling state-owned enterprises across the privatisation process and imposing effective taxation on the private sector and its employees. These factors may lead to diversification in natural resource rich countries through the following:

The private sector may contribute to the growth of resource rich countries by leading the backward and forward linkage from resource commodity to manufacturing. Then, the private sector may provide a normal rate of return to the resource-dependent countries in the form of taxes or other linked investments. Thus, natural resource rich countries may demonstrate a stable fiscal policy from more secure revenues in selling SOEs across the privatisation process and more revenues from taxes.

Taxation provides relatively long-lasting economic stability to reduce long-term resource revenue volatility and strengthen accountability, thereby enhancing economic growth.

The privatisation of SOEs in natural resource rich countries may deepen economic reforms and increase private investment in public enterprises. This provides a large revenue for the government as well as increasing the engagement of the private sector in economic activities.

Through increased efficiency in managing natural resources, both private sector and public sector development might involve reducing the threat of violence and instability in natural resource rich economies. These outcomes, consequently, lead to greater efficiency of resource management, more diverse revenues and economic growth.

The current study examines the importance of various factors of diversification in reducing the degree of dependency on natural resource revenues. The aim is to quantitatively examine the diversified factors of the economy to reduce dependency on natural resources. This diversification can take place in every sector of the economy. The private and public sectors lead the diversification through private sector development, and privatisation of public services, or through the development of a national taxation system.

The theories of the political economy of industrialisation, natural resource dependency, privatisation and taxation are used to deal with the abovementioned dependency reduction policies. The literature evaluating the effects of private and public sector development on natural resource dependency reduction is not developed, and much of the literature on natural resource dependency is related to resource dependency and economic growth (See for example Badeeb et al., 2017; Havranek et al., 2016; Sachs & Warner, 2001).

The empirical model used in this research is a dynamic flexible adjustment model which accounts for private sector development, privatisation of public services and the development of a taxation system. A combination of the three different policy measures is expected to reduce resource revenue dependency. This study, then, constructs a relationship between private sector development and natural resource dependency on one side, and on the other between public sector development and natural resource dependency in natural resource rich countries.

The data used in this study are annual data of aggregate country level. It is obtained from the World Bank World Development Indicators (WDI). It is an unbalanced panel data which includes a large sample of 110 natural resource producers in developed, developing and emerging countries of different sizes and of different political systems observed from 1990 to 2017. The full list of variables related to dependent variables and vectors of explanatory variables are determined by the data availability and their relevance based on the literature.

1.2 Problem of Natural Resource Dependency

Resource rich countries that are dependent on resource revenues are suffering from revenue insecurity as commodity prices are highly volatile, in particular, energy commodities, such as oil and gas, in turn, the public revenue from these sources is also considered highly volatile. Ghura and Pattillo (2012) found that instability in fiscal revenue causes procyclical government spending that further leads to volatility in public spending. This volatility in revenue, as stated by (Mejía Acosta, 2013), widens the gap between the citizens' expectation of economic opportunities to improve their living conditions and actual government spending. Therefore, governments are not protecting the well-being of their citizens (Darby, 2010).

In addition to the price volatility, another explanation for decreased economic growth, in naturally resource rich countries, is a reduction in accountability. Studies have found that considerable revenue from natural resource rents reduces the government's need to tax its citizens, thereby minimally taxed populations may demand less accountability (Cabrales & Hauk, 2011; Jensen & Wantchekon, 2004; Ross, 2001). As a result, as Collier (2010), Collier and Hoeffler (2009) and McGuirk (2013) discovered, a reduction in accountability leads to lower economic growth.

Volatilities in commodity prices which make countries vulnerable to external shocks, are a major factor causing the severe economic and debt crises faced by many resource rich countries that experienced resource dependency between the 1980s and 1990s (Nabli & Arezki, 2012; Nissanke, 2011; Von Haldenwang & Ivanyna, 2018). Therefore, Hendrick and Crawford (2014), Pagano and Hoene (2010) and Shi and Tao (2018) suggest the promotion of revenue diversification to reduce revenue volatility, and as a result of the suggested policy, less vulnerable economies become those which are the most sufficiently diversified (Afonso, 2013; Odhiambo & Olushola, 2018).

There has been growing recognition in the literature that privatisation and private sector development play a significant role in economic wealth and job creation, and the support of government revenue through taxes and duties. This is due to the fact that the private sector and its employees are the providers of most taxes, thereby achieving income diversification (Nhema, 2015; Popoola, 2016). Furthermore, taxation is a significant way to derive long-lasting economic stability (Afonso, 2013; Odhiambo & Olushola, 2018; Von Haldenwang & Ivanyna, 2018) to reduce the volatility resulting from natural resource dependency as well as of strengthening government accountability (Eubank, 2012; Odhiambo & Olushola, 2018) and hence, fostering economic growth.

1.3 Research Aims and Objectives

Natural resources are considered essential factors in the development process. They are also significant factors in the production process as the need for energy is globally increased. The United States (US) energy information administration (EIA) predicts that energy consumption will increase universally by 50% between 2018 and 2050 (EIA, 2019). This intensity in the use of energy may lead to increased relative fiscal dependency on resource extraction. As such, there will be a vicious cycle linking natural resources with fiscal dependency on resource revenues.

The aim of this study is to investigate the factors that possibly contribute to the reduction of the degree of dependency on natural resources. Economic diversification is viewed as a long-term solution for the high revenue dependency, the curse of the natural resources and the inefficient institutional structure. Diversification can take place in both public and private sectors and in each of the economic sectors.

Diversification in the private sector refers to private sector development and the generation of new sources of incomes which reduce government burden in the provision of services. Diversification in public sector revenues can be achieved through the privatisation of public services providing firms with reduced public financing of those services (Huizinga & Nielsen, 2001; Lieberherr & Truffer, 2015; Molinos-Senante & Sala-Garrido, 2015; Wang & Chen, 2011). Another alternative public sector diversification method is through the development of a national taxation system and tax base that reduces the regional governments dependence on revenues from natural resources (Afonso, 2013; Besley & Persson, 2013; Odhiambo & Olushola, 2018).

The objective of this book is to evaluate the relationship between private sector development and public sector development with dependency on natural resources. This is to identify the leading factors of private sector development, privatisation and taxation in natural resource rich countries that aid to reduce the danger of the resource curse (details are provided in Chapter 2).

1.4 Research Questions and Hypotheses

Further objectives of this study are as follows:

1. To examine the role of private sector development and public sector development in natural resource rich countries over the period 1990–2017 to enable an in-depth analysis of whether these developments may reduce the degree of dependency on resource revenue extractions as a basis for further empirical analysis (Chapter 4). This examination will contribute to the existing empirical literature on private and public sector development in natural resource rich countries.
2. To examine the effect of private sector development on the degree of dependency on resource revenues in natural resource rich countries. The outcome of this examination can inform policy to defeat the problem of revenue volatility and thereby lead to macroeconomic stability in natural resource rich countries (Chapter 4).
3. To empirically identify the leading factors contributing to private sector development, privatisation, and taxation (macroeconomic variables) in natural resource rich countries which may aid the reduction of the degree of dependency on resource revenues. The analysis will be extended to assess the impact of non-economic factors of institutional quality and political stability on natural resource dependence (Chapter 3). This is important for diversification policy and future development in resource rich countries.
4. To comprehensively evaluate the impacts of public sector development on reducing the degree of dependency on resource revenue in natural resource rich countries through two examinations. First, to examine the effect of public sector privatisation on the degree of dependency on resource revenue in natural resource rich counties, and second, to examine whether a national taxation system causes less dependency on resource revenue in natural resource rich countries. The outcomes of these examinations may help to assess what policies are specifically needed based on countries' characteristics to enhance diversification and therefore economic growth.
5. To examine how natural resource rents from oil and gas affect economic diversification in natural resource rich countries. The findings may support specific diversification policies, for example in development of the private sector.
6. To examine the effect of human development in leading the diversified factor of private sector development. Most importantly, the examination is extended to analyse the impact of human development in reducing the degree of dependency on natural resources. The outcome provides assistance in deriving solid policy recommendations towards improving human development.

1.4 Research Questions and Hypotheses

To achieve the objectives set out previously, this research attempts to examine the topic empirically by finding answers to several main research questions. The analysis is based on an identified gap in the literature regarding whether and how private sector development and public sector development affect the degree of dependency on resource revenue in natural resource rich countries.

This book studies the interaction between private and public sector development with dependency on natural resources, specifically exploring whether the two diversified factors lead to a decrease in the degree of dependency, which is important for economic growth. The results will help to shed light on private sector development, public services sector privatisation and a taxation system to diversify sources of income, with the objective to reduce dependency on natural resources extraction. Accordingly, two models, static and dynamic adjustment models, are established to examine the following research questions and test hypotheses empirically:

- RQ_1: How does private sector development affect the degree of dependency on resource revenues in natural resource rich countries?
- RQ_2: How does public sector development affect the degree of dependency on resource revenue extractions?

  Those questions were further broken down into two sub-research questions to measure the effect of public sector privatisation and taxation system.

  - RQ_{21}: How does public sector privatisation affect the degree of dependency on natural resources in resource rich countries?
  - RQ_{22}: How does a national taxation system result in less dependency on resource revenues in natural resource rich countries?

- RQ_3: How do natural resource rents from oil and gas affect economic diversification factors of PSD, privatisation and taxation in natural resource rich countries?
- RQ_4: How does institutional quality affect the degree of dependency on natural resources in resource rich countries?
- RQ_5: Does human development affect the degree of dependency on natural resources in resource rich countries?

For research question RQ_1, the null hypothesis is:

$H_{RQ_{1_0}}$: There is a positive impact of PSD in reducing the degree of dependency on natural resource revenues.

For research question RQ_2, the null hypotheses are:

$H_{RQ_{21_0}}$: Public sector privatisation affects the degree of dependency in natural resource rich countries.

$H_{RQ_{22_0}}$: A national taxation system reduces the degree of resource revenue dependency in natural resource rich countries.

For research question RQ_3, the null hypotheses are:

$H_{RQ_{31_0}}$: Natural resource rents from oil and gas positively affect private sector development in natural resource rich countries.

$H_{RQ_{32_0}}$: Natural resource rents from oil and gas do not promote public sector privatisation in natural resource rich countries.

$H_{RQ_{3_{30}}}$: Natural resource rents from oil and gas have negative effect on national taxation system in natural resource rich countries.

For research question RQ_4, the null hypothesis is:

$H_{RQ_{4_0}}$: Natural resource dependency reduction relies on the quality of institutions.

For research question RQ_5, the null hypothesis is:

H_{RQ_5}: Human development does positively affect natural resource dependency reduction.

1.5 Significance of the Study

A comprehensive review of the literature and the creation of a panel database of representative sample of countries will lead to specification and estimation of the system of models estimated with advanced estimation methods. The use of multidimensional indices and the generation of results and their analysis helps to shed light on the private sector development, public services sector privatisation and taxation system to diversify the sources of income with the objective to reduce dependency on natural resources extraction.

This research introduces three diversification factors to study natural resource economic dependency reduction. First, it will explore the relationship between private sector development and natural resource rents. Second, it explores the relationship between public sector development including privatisation and taxation with natural resource dependency. Finally, it will investigate whether the diversified factors of private sector development and public sector development in natural resource dependent countries reduce dependency on natural resource revenues.

The significance of this subject is vital to a group of interests related to the study in the market, namely, public policymakers, the private sector, the law maker and the scholars. It also guides the new private entrants who might be investing in such countries.

The public policymakers of the natural resource rich countries will benefit from this book through the identification of factors that promote diversification, which may lead to the reduction of dependency on resource revenue in natural resource rich countries. Furthermore, public policymakers may introduce these factors into existing programmes of diversification of income to reduce the degree of resource revenue dependency.

The law maker or regulator from natural resource wealth countries may benefit from this study as they may be able to introduce new forms of revenue generation with reference to, for instance, the privatisation of SOEs, and the development of a national taxation system. The development of an appropriate analytical framework to identify the key macroeconomic factors affecting private sector development and public sector development in natural resource wealth countries provides further and is imperative to address key recommendations on how government policies can stimulate private and public sector development that will in turn boost economic diversification of natural resource rich countries.

This book can also benefit those entering the private sector and business in these natural resource rich countries by reviewing the determining factors of development such as institutional quality, human development and other factors that lighten the speed of adjustment of the private sector. Furthermore, this study may provide information on business environments that aid the development of business strategies, such as the availability of loans and credit to the private sector.

Finally, the outcome of the book can add to the body of literature surrounding this topic in numerous ways. Firstly, the creation of a large database of aggregate country-level data for resource rich countries would enable future analyses to take place. Secondly, this research employs a dynamic flexible adjustment model including various determinants of diversification, such as private sector development and public sector development, namely, privatisation and taxation. The purpose of estimating this model is to examine the diversified factor of private sector development and public sector development in reducing the degree of dependency on resource revenues in natural resource rich countries from 1990 to 2017. So far, no systematic empirical study has been conducted regarding resource revenue dependency reduction. Researchers may find particularly a model that has not been used in the study of private sector development, public sector development and natural resource dependency reduction. Finally, adjustment models will be specified in which country and time-specific policy factors determining the speed of adjustment are identified. This sheds light on the importance of taking into account the adjustment cost in a study of economic diversification.

1.6 The Book Design and Organisation

The theoretical literature is reviewed in Chapter 2 and deals with resource revenue reduction, including the political economy of industrialisation, natural resource dependency, privatisation and taxation. This chapter provides a summary of the literature on the relationship between private sector development, public sector privatisation and taxation with dependency on natural resource revenue extraction. The literature review chapter includes a critical discussion of recent developments attempting to address the best appropriate economic analysis with reference to natural resource wealth economies. It also contains a revision of relevant and current studies pertaining to this book. It is divided into sections which include literature on private sector development, privatisation and taxation in the context of natural resource dependency.

Overall, this chapter provides a comprehensive summary of the theoretical and empirical literature upon which natural resource economies can be diversified by building the theoretical determination of privatisation, taxation and the economic diversification in natural resource rich countries and tested empirically. The literature review chapter concludes with theoretical gaps in, and critics to, the literature of

1.6 The Book Design and Organisation

those models and the need for further understanding of the relationship between the diversified factor of private and public sector development with natural resource revenue dependency.

Chapter 3 introduces methodology of the study and the main empirical specification, namely the dynamic adjustment model and its adjustment speed, and system of equations to establish a relationship between natural resource rents, private sector development, privatisation of public sector and taxation.

This chapter discusses the econometric issues with the estimation of panel data, system of equations and dynamic adjustment model. In doing so, the chapter discusses country heterogeneity and simultaneity effects related to the panel data. Then, the issues of the econometric model specification, model estimation and testing the speed of adjustment of the diversified factors towards optimal level are elaborated. In this regard, the effectiveness of various policies, including openness policy, subsidy policy, investment policy and interest rate policies has been examined, in stimulating private sector and public sector development in natural resource rich countries. Finally, the potential effect of resource type, in particular, oil and gas revenue in fostering the adjustment speed of the diversified factor of private sector development, privatisation and taxation is also investigated in this chapter to address RQ_3.

Chapter 4 continues to introduce the description of data. In the elaboration of the data source, types and collection procedure, attention has been paid to the complementary role of non-economic factors, including governance, political instability and institutional quality, along with traditional factors, in determining diversified factors of private and public sector development. The chapter covers a variety of variables so as to identify the most important factors influencing private sector development, privatisation and taxation in the context of natural resource rich countries. The late section introduces specification, estimation and testing of the methodology of the study to justify the chosen model between the traditional static model, the dynamic model, dynamic flexible adjustment model and system of equations. Then the chapter continues to provide detailed analyses and results in four main parts including (1) a comparison between the static and dynamic models and single equation versus system of equations, (2) determinants of optimal dependent variables, (3) the mean value of adjustment speed.

Chapter 5 includes the analysis and presentation of the results, which includes four empirical analyses. Further results will be presented for (i) the analysis of the relationship between the dynamic of private sector development in natural resource rich countries to answer the RQ_1, (ii) measuring the relationship between privatisation and resource revenue dependency to answer RQ_{2_1}, (iii) the effect of taxation on natural resource revenue dependency to answer RQ_{2_2} and (iv) the analysis of private and public sector development and diversification of income to reduce dependency on natural resources answer to RQ_4. The empirical analysis will be based on the dynamic flexible adjustment model of system of equations due to the value advantage over other models.

Chapter 6 presents the conclusion of the study by summarising the estimated models, testing the hypotheses and discussing the implications of the results. Furthermore, the study provides limitations, policy recommendations and suggestions for future research in the context of natural resource rich countries are provided.

1.7 Summary

The resource rich countries that depend on natural resources, derive almost all revenue from resource rents sourced oil, natural gas, minerals and other natural resources. This revenue generation is labelled as the curse of natural resources. This curse is transmitted to the economy in different ways, mainly through macroeconomic channels. As such, while this dependency on one side is impeding the effort to diversify income generations, on the other side leads to negative economic growth.

This quantitative research examines the importance of various factors of diversification in reducing the degree of dependency on natural resource revenues. The aim is to examine the diversified factors of the economy to reduce dependency on natural resources. This diversification can take place in every sector of the economy. The private and public sectors which are dynamic and innovative can lead diversification respectively either through private sector development, and privatisation of public services, or through development of a national taxation system.

This research applies the dynamic flexible adjustment model to identify the adjustment behaviour of private sector development, the privatisation of public services and the development of national taxation system in natural resource rich countries over time. The models are estimated as a system of four interdependent equations accounting for endogeneity and simultaneity effects, thus a combination of the three different policy measures is expected to reduce dependency on revenues from natural resources.

A comprehensive review of the literature and the creation of a panel database of representative samples of countries covering periods after the main privatisation waves will lead to specification and estimation of the system of models estimated with advanced estimation methods. The use of multidimensional indices and generation of results may shed light on private sector development, public services sector privatisation and a taxation system to diversify the sources of income with the objective to reduce dependency on natural resources extraction.

Bibliography

Adams, D., Adams, K., Ullah, S., & Ullah, F. (2019). Globalisation, governance, accountability and the natural resource 'curse': Implications for socio-economic growth of oil-rich developing countries. *Resources Policy, 61*, 128–140.

Bibliography

Afonso, W. B. (2013). Diversificaiton toward stability? The effect of local sales taxes on own source revenue. *Journal of Public Budgeting, Accounting & Financial Management, 25*(4), 649–674.

Arezki, R., & Van der Ploeg, F. (2011). Do natural resources depress income per capita? *Review of Development Economics, 15*(3), 504–521.

Badeeb, R. A., Lean, H. H., & Clark, J. (2017). The evolution of the natural resource curse thesis: A critical literature survey. *Resources Policy, 51*, 123–134.

Besley, T., & Persson, T. (2013). Taxation and development. In *Handbook of public economics* (Vol. 5, pp. 51–110). Elsevier.

Boycko, M., Shleifer, A., & Vishny, R. W. (1996). A theory of privatisation. *The Economic Journal, 106*(435), 309–319.

Cabrales, A., & Hauk, E. (2011). The quality of political institutions and the curse of natural resources. *The Economic Journal, 121*(551), 58–88.

Collier, P. (2010). The political economy of natural resources. *Social Research, 77*(4), 1105–1132.

Collier, P., & Hoeffler, A. (2009). Testing the neocon agenda: Democracy in resource-rich societies. *European Economic Review, 53*(3), 293–308.

Darby, S. (2010). *The transparency and accountability initiative—Natural resource governance strategic summary*. London.

EIA. (2019). *International Energy Outlook with projections to 2050*. https://www.eia.gov/outlooks/ieo/pdf/ieo2019.pdf

Eubank, N. (2012). Taxation, political accountability and foreign aid: Lessons from Somaliland. *Journal of Development Studies, 48*(4), 465–480.

Frankel, J. A. (2012). *The natural resource curse: A survey of diagnoses and some prescriptions* (HKS Faculty Research Working Paper Series RWP12-014). John F. Kennedy School of Government, Harvard University.

Ghura, D., & Pattillo, C. (2012). *Macroeconomic policy frameworks for resource-rich developing countries*. https://www.imf.org/external/np/pp/eng/2012/082412.pdf

Gillen, D. (2011). The evolution of airport ownership and governance. *Journal of Air Transport Management, 17*(1), 3–13.

Havranek, T., Horvath, R., & Zeynalov, A. (2016). Natural resources and economic growth: A meta-analysis. *World Development, 88*, 134–151.

Hendrick, R., & Crawford, J. (2014). Municipal fiscal policy space and fiscal structure: Tools for managing spending volatility. *Public Budgeting & Finance, 34*(3), 24–50.

Huizinga, H., & Nielsen, S. B. (2001). Privatisation, public investment, and capital income taxation. *Journal of Public Economics, 82*(3), 399–414.

International Corporation and Development (ICD). (2019). *Economic growth: Private sector development*. Retrieved 23 January 2019, from https://ec.europa.eu/europeaid/sectors/economic-growth/private-sector-development_en

Jensen, N., & Wantchekon, L. (2004). Resource wealth and political regimes in Africa. *Comparative Political Studies, 37*(7), 816–841.

Ji, K., Magnus, J. R., & Wang, W. (2014). Natural resources, institutional quality, and economic growth in China. *Environmental and Resource Economics, 57*(3), 323–343.

Kay, J. A., & Thompson, D. J. (1986). Privatisation: A policy in search of a rationale. *The Economic Journal, 96*(381), 18–32.

Lieberherr, E., & Truffer, B. (2015). The impact of privatisation on sustainability transitions: A comparative analysis of dynamic capabilities in three water utilities. *Environmental Innovation and Societal Transitions, 15*, 101–122.

McGuirk, E. F. (2013). The illusory leader: Natural resources, taxation and accountability. *Public Choice, 154*(3–4), 285–313.

Megginson, W. L., & Netter, J. M. (2001). From state to market: A survey of empirical studies on privatization. *Journal of Economic Literature, 39*(2), 321–389.

Mejía Acosta, A. (2013). The impact and effectiveness of accountability and transparency initiatives: The governance of natural resources. *Development Policy Review, 31*(S1), s89–s105.

Mishrif, A., & Al Balushi, Y. (2018). *Economic diversification in the gulf region, Volume II: Comparing global challenges*. Springer.

Mohan, T. R. (2001). Privatisation: Theory and evidence. *Economic and Political Weekly, 36*(52), 4865–4871.

Molinos-Senante, M., & Sala-Garrido, R. (2015). The impact of privatization approaches on the productivity growth of the water industry: A case study of Chile. *Environmental Science & Policy, 50*, 166–179.

Nabli, M. M. K., & Arezki, M. R. (2012). *Natural resources, volatility, and inclusive growth: Perspectives from the Middle East and North Africa* (Vol. 111). International Monetary Fund.

Nhema, A. G. (2015). Privatisation of public enterprises in developing countries: An overview. *International Journal of Humanities and Social Science, 5*(9), 247–256.

Nissanke, M. (2011). *Commodity markets and excess volatility: Sources and strategies to reduce adverse development impacts*. Common Fund for Commodities. http://www.common-fund.org/data/documenten/CFC-Nissanke-CommodityMarketVolatility_Feb_2011.pdf

Odhiambo, O., & Olushola, O. (2018). Taxation and economic growth in a resource-rich country: The case of Nigeria. In J. Iwin-Garzynska (Ed.), *Taxes and taxation trends*. IntechOpen.

Pagano, M. A., & Hoene, C. (2010). States and the fiscal policy space of cities. In B. Michael, B. David, & Y. Joan (Eds.), *The property tax and local autonomy* (pp. 243–284). Puritan Press Inc.

Popoola, O. O. (2016). Privatization of public enterprises in Nigeria: Critical success factors. *Journal of Law, Policy and Globalization, 49*, 85.

Privatisation Barometer (PB). (2019). *Privatisation cumulative value*. Retrieved 22 January 2019, from http://www.privatizationbarometer.com/database.php

Ross, M. (2001). Does oil hinder democracy? *World Politics, 53*(3), 325–361.

Sachs, J. D., & Warner, A. M. (2001). The curse of natural resources. *European Economic Review, 45*(4–6), 827–838.

Schoneveld, G., & Zoomers, A. (2015). Natural resource privatisation in Sub-Saharan Africa and the challenges for inclusive green growth. *International Development Planning Review, 37*(1), 95–118.

Shi, Y., & Tao, J. (2018). 'Faulty' fiscal illusion: Examining the relationship between revenue diversification and tax burden in Major US cities across the economic cycle. *Local Government Studies, 44*(3), 416–435.

Smith, B. (2015). The resource curse exorcised: Evidence from a panel of countries. *Journal of Development Economics, 116*, 57–73.

Van der Ploeg, F. (2011). Natural resources: Curse or blessing? *Journal of Economic Literature, 49*(2), 366–420.

Venables, A. J. (2016). Using natural resources for development: Why has it proven so difficult? *Journal of Economic Perspectives, 30*(1), 161–184.

Von Haldenwang, C., & Ivanyna, M. (2018). Does the political resource curse affect public finance? The vulnerability of tax revenue in resource-dependent countries. *Journal of International Development, 30*(2), 323–344.

Wang, L. F., & Chen, T.-L. (2011). Mixed oligopoly, optimal privatization, and foreign penetration. *Economic Modelling, 28*(4), 1465–1470.

WDI. (2018). *Natural resource contribution to GDP*. Retrieved 23 January 2019, from World Bank.

Chapter 2
Economic Diversification to Reduce Natural Resource Dependency in the Literature

Abstract The resource curse refers to a negative correlation between natural resource dependence and economic growth. This phenomenon is labelled 'the paradox of plenty'. It was previously viewed that the size and variety of natural resources resulted in a rapid development. However, this conventional wisdom has been challenged, with arguments arising to address the disadvantages of dependence on natural resources. This chapter outlines the problem of natural resource dependency along with providing relevant theories in relation to economic diversification to reduce natural resource dependency. A summary of the previous studies surrounding the relationship between private sector development, public sector privatisation, taxation and the reduction of natural resource dependency is provided. Previous studies have approached the problem of natural resource dependency in various ways. The majority of empirical studies were focused on measuring the relationship between natural resource abundance and economic growth or the importance of institutional quality in overcoming natural resource dependency. This reviewed chapter is related to diversification strategies concerned with the importance of diversified factors of private sector development, and/or public sector development, in reducing the danger of resource curse in resource rich countries.

Keywords Resource curse · Economic diversification · Private sector development · Public sector privatisation · Taxation · Natural resource dependency reduction

2.1 Introduction

This literature review chapter entails a critical discussion of recent developments, attempting to address appropriate economic analysis with reference mainly to natural resource rich economies. It also contains a revision of relevant and current studies pertaining to the book.

The problem of natural resource dependency is also addressed, followed by discussion of ways to reduce this dependency in natural resource rich countries. The theoretical foundation of the book will focus on the effects of economic diversification of private sector development, privatisation and taxation to reduce natural resource dependency.

The reason why natural resource dependency reduction is important is that a high degree of dependency on natural resource revenue will be unable to stabilise for a long period of time, due to volatility in the price of resources and their commodities. As such, the promotion of revenue diversification is suggested. Indonesia is an example of successful defeat of the issue of resource dependency through economic diversification and industrialisation.

The chapter concludes with identification of the theoretical gap and critics to the literature and provides recommendations for further research for understanding the relationship between the diversified factor of private and public sector development in countries with natural resource revenue dependency.

Overall, this chapter provides a comprehensive summary of the theoretical and empirical literature, building the theoretical determination of privatisation, taxation and the economic diversification in natural resource rich countries, by studying reviews of books, peer reviewed journal articles, organisational reports, research papers and several academic websites.

2.2 Natural Resource Dependency in Resource Rich Countries

Natural resource rich countries derive a high share of fiscal revenue from the natural resources related sectors accounts for 7% of world GDP. Annually, this revenue amounts more than four trillion US dollars (Mishrif & Al Balushi, 2018). Previously, the size and variety of natural resources were viewed as a source of rapid development.

The importance of natural resource wealth in stimulating industrialisation of countries has been discussed. The development theorist Walter Rostow (1990) explained how the abundance of natural resources helped to transfer several countries from underdeveloped to industrial developed economies. Countries such as Australia, the United States and Britain are for example.

However, arguments arise to challenge this conventional wisdom by addressing the disadvantages of dependence on natural resources. It is well known in the literature that natural resource dependency, in the long term, has a negative impact on economic growth (Frankel, 2012; Van der Ploeg, 2011; Venables, 2016). While some studies find a correlation between natural resource abundance and economic growth, resource rich countries develop at a slower rate compared with less fortunate ones (Badeeb et al., 2017; Smith, 2015).[1]

---

[1] Earlier studies found the same result such as Rodriguez and Sachs (1999) and Sachs and Warner (2001).

2.2 Natural Resource Dependency in Resource Rich Countries

This phenomenon is labelled 'the paradox of plenty'. Despite the variety of resources, there are a number of natural resource rich countries that have never experienced development. Frankel (2012) exemplifies several African resource rich countries that experience low life quality, even though they are fortunate in natural resources such as oil, diamond and other minerals.

The resource endowment effects on socio-economic development are studied as a paradox of plenty of natural resources mainly oil, natural gas and minerals, in which, these features are well-known in the literature as the 'resource curse'[2] (Adams et al., 2019).

The resource curse refers to a negative correlation between natural resource dependence and economic growth (Badeeb et al., 2017; Frankel, 2012; Venables, 2016). This curse is transmitted to the economy in different ways, mainly through macroeconomic channels 'the Dutch Disease', political economy, corruption, rent seeking, less accountability and democracy' and conflict or civil war (Badeeb et al., 2017; Boutilier, 2017).

Political and economic theories state the creation of additional challenges due to dependency on natural resource revenues which can be highlighted as the political and economic aspect of the resource curse.

Theoretically, one of the feature of the natural resource wealth countries, particularly oil wealth, is that their governments are less tied to citizens, thereby become or remain authoritarian over the past years. This feature strengthens the tendency towards authoritarianism, and in turn it weakens the level of democracy and accountability (Cammett et al., 2019).

Political theory suggests that natural resources distort politicians' behaviour and those who come to power. The windfall revenues from resource rents may motivate politicians who rule governments either to seize power through coercive strategies or constrict electoral participation. Carreri and Dube (2017) empirically test for this effects and find that natural resources undermine democracy by distorting elections. Accordingly, Iraq, Nigeria and Burma are examples of those countries that their electoral democracy is undermined due to natural resources wealth and the intervention of armed actors in electoral politics.

Those countries that derive a high share of fiscal revenue from the natural resource rents experience lower economic growth due to a reduction in accountability (Cabrales & Hauk, 2011; Collier, 2010; McGuirk, 2013). While it has been proven that the size of natural resources may undermine accountability, the existence of accountability has been addressed to experience development (Collier, 2010; Collier & Hoeffler, 2009; McGuirk, 2013).

Cabrales and Hauk (2011), Jensen and Wantchekon (2004), and M. Ross (2001) find that the size of fiscal revenue from natural resources causes a major decline in tax revenue in resource rich countries. Thus, the governments need to tax its citizens decline, and thereby low tax populations expect to demand less accountability. As such, a reduction in accountability has been determined the cause of lowering economic growth (Collier & Hoeffler, 2009).

---

[2] This phenomenon was first labelled by Richard Auty (1993).

Badeeb et al. (2017) propose two distinct and overlapping explanations for the resource curse, both economic and political. Economically, the negative long-term economic growth of natural resources is linked to Dutch disease, and the volatility of commodity prices. Volatilities in commodity prices which make countries vulnerable to external shocks, represent a major factor behind the severe economic and debt crises faced by many commodity-dependent countries between the 1980s and 1990s (Nabli & Arezki, 2012; Nissanke, 2011; Von Haldenwang & Ivanyna, 2018).

The economic effect of 'Dutch disease' is related to three economic sectors: the natural resources sector, the non-resource traded goods sector and the non-traded goods sector.

Macroeconomic instability through depreciating real exchange rates and crowding out manufacturing is another outcome of commodity price volatility.[3] Schoneveld and Zoomers (2015) and Weber (2014) identify multiple effects of this instability. Accordingly, increased demand from the commodity boom would raise the price of non-tradable goods and services which are vulnerable to the swing of real exchange rates. With this appreciation in real exchange rate, 'spending effect' would decline the competitiveness of other sectors such as exports, and thus seriously harm long-term productivity growth (Van der Ploeg, 2011).

The effects of commodity price volatility pose a major threat to the development of manufacturing through the 'resource movement effect'. This leads to increased movement of manpower from the traded goods sector into the non-traded sector, leading to more benefits in the latter sector (Schoneveld & Zoomers, 2015; Weber, 2014). It is believed that this would derive de-industrialisation in the non-resource traded goods sector, and thereby cause a decline in manufacturing productivity (Frankel, 2012; Ismail, 2010). Sachs and Warner (2001) found earlier that resource rich countries failed to grow their manufacturing sectors between 1970 and 1990.

Previous studies mostly linked natural resource revenue dependency in resource rich economies to revenue volatility and growth (see for example: Crivelli & Gupta, 2014; IMF, 2013). The effects of the world market price of resource commodity lead to higher volatility in public revenue. The fiscal revenue in natural resource rich countries is based on the extractive sector; mainly oil, natural gas, minerals and other natural resources. Prices of these commodities are mostly highly volatile, this is particularly true for energy commodities, such as oil and gas.

This dependency of fiscal revenue on resource commodities in resource rich countries causes relative insecurity in revenue generation. Venables (2016) addressed the extended issues that are a result of commodity price volatility such as unpredictable resource revenue. Ghura and Pattillo (2012) found that instability in fiscal revenue causes procyclical government spending that further leads to volatility in public

---

[3] Van der Ploeg (2011) provides wider understanding on resource rent effect of real exchange rate.
Accordingly, the effect of resource rent on either appreciation or depreciation of real exchange rate is associated with the fixed exchange rate or floating exchange rate. Another explanation for this change is that it relates to the capital intensive of either the traded sector or non-traded sector. If the nontraded sector is more capital intensive compare to the traded sector, the relative supply of nontraded goods depreciates the real exchange rate. However, resource boom induces appreciation of the real exchange rate through the growth of nontraded sectors and shrinking of the traded sector.

2.2 Natural Resource Dependency in Resource Rich Countries

spending. This impedes the core of state development and reduces economic growth (Frankel, 2012; Nabli & Arezki, 2012). Studies such as Frankel (2012), Venables (2016) and Von Haldenwang and Ivanyna (2018) explain this impediment, arguing that extractive sector resources often crowd out the competitiveness of other sectors, this is referred to as 'Dutch disease', and leads to a smaller tax base, and thereby less diverse economies.

Furthermore, the market of natural resource-dependent countries has less discipline, due to weak institutional quality. The economy of natural resource rich countries that have a high degree of dependency on resource revenue is characterized by weak governance, weak law enforcement, thin capital market and poor market structure (Ghura & Pattillo, 2012; Venables, 2016; Weber, 2014). As such, these economies are not stable, which could thus impose unnecessary costs on resource rich governments.

Natural resource management is associated with the danger of the resource curse. Nissanke (2011) claims that the high price volatility in resource rich countries raises difficulties for them in managing their economies. Inefficiency in managing natural resources is a considerable difficulty faced by resource rich countries as a result of price volatility (Nissanke, 2012). This inefficiency leads to market instability, which in turn increases uncertainty that further hinders an effective economic development (Badeeb et al., 2017). Natural resource management, according to Venables (2016), starts with the successful use of resources, which involves complex multiple stages from discovering to developing.

The natural resource branch of research looks at the effects of natural resource wealth on political instability or conflicts. The volatility in resource revenue as stated by Mejía Acosta (2013), widens the gap between the citizens' expectation of economic opportunities to improve their living conditions and actual government spending. This sheds light on the sensitivity of resource rich countries to violent conflict. Therefore, the well-being of citizens is not protected by their natural resource-dependent governments (Darby, 2010). Fearon (2004) who theorised the duration of civil war, proposes that because of the inefficiency of resource rich governments in redistributing resource wealth revenue to citizens, conflicts arise with insurgent groups. Consequently, this motivates the rebel groups to establish self-generated resource revenue independent of state (Dal Bó & Dal Bó, 2011; Ross, 2012).

Corruption and rent seeking are another aspect of the resource curse. Corruption is seen as a consequence of poor governance and less accountability in natural resource rich countries which may harm the economic performance of the resource-dependent governments. In studying the relationship between corruption, natural resources and economic growth, Erum and Hussain (2019) find that corruption impedes economic growth of natural resource rich countries.

As for the rent seeking, a large body of literature has focused on explaining resource curse in producing rent seeking (Arezki & Van der Ploeg, 2011; Ogwang et al., 2019; Van der Ploeg, 2010). Rent seeking is unproductive activities of accumulating large wealth on the expense of others especially during a resource boom (Asher & Novosad, 2018). Natural resource boom creates the potential of increasing rent seeking and even corruption in those countries because of the low quality of institutions and less accountability. As a result, rent seeking may contribute to decline in the productivity of the public sector as well as reducing the level of democracy (Busse & Gröning, 2013; Ross, 2001).

Despite all these political and economic effects of resource curse, here is a debate in the literature about the existence of the curse. Whereas James (2015), Norrbin et al. (2008) and Smith (2015) continue to challenge the existence of this curse, a large body of the literature such as Adams et al. (2019), S. Bhattacharyya and Collier (2013), Frankel (2012) and Venables (2016) are convincing of the real existence of the curse. However, according to S. Bhattacharyya and Hodler (2014), Van der Ploeg (2011) and Venables (2016) these features depend on country-specific conditions such as institutional quality and the management of natural resources (Nissanke, 2012; Williams, 2011).

Natural resource dependency has significant implications for the level of economic growth in resource rich countries. Frankel (2012) and Von Haldenwang and Ivanyna (2018) considered possible causes of long-lasting economic instability in natural resource-abundant countries, that necessarily lead to lower economic growth: (1) the price of resources and their commodities are volatile, which are also subject to the countries conditions to the world markets; (2) natural resources are exhausted, it could therefore be dead-end sector; (3) institutional quality is very weak in natural resource rent, in particular in oil rich countries; (4) such resource-dependent countries are sensitive to civil war; (5) volatility in commodity prices could impose unnecessary costs on resource-dependent governments, and as a result of world market decline in commodity prices, would derive excessive macroeconomic instability through the depreciation of real exchange rates and the crowding out manufacturing; and (6) natural resource revenue management tends to be poor in such resource-dependent countries (Williams, 2011). These factors, which are harming economic growth, turn the blessing of natural resources into a curse.

Ait-Laoussine and Gault (2017) identified further factors that impeded the achievement of diversification in natural resources rich countries especially oil exporters, including inconsistency of government policies, leaving long-term commitment to diversification to face short-term oil price volatility, weak governance and lack of transparency and inadequate public support for the diversification process.

A summary review of the literature most relevant to this section of the book is presented in Table 2.1 and includes methodologies and findings.

2.2 Natural Resource Dependency in Resource Rich Countries

Table 2.1 A review of the selected existing literature on resource rich economies

No.	Author/year	Methodology	Findings
1	Frankel (2012)	Literature survey	Six channels of causation of natural resource curse are proposed. (1) long-term trends in world prices; (2) price volatility; (3) permanent crowding out of manufacturing; (4) autocratic institutions; (5) anarchic institutions; and (6) cyclical Dutch Disease
2	Ji et al. (2014)	Classical growth model was applied on panel data to distinguish between stock and flow measures of resource reserve	Resource abundance has a positive effect on economic growth at the provincial level in China in the existence of institutional quality
3	Venables (2016)	Dependency was assessed by the percentage of natural resources in fiscal revenue and exports, based on IMF countries classification of rich resources with a focus on low-income countries	A negative correlation between resource rents and the saving rates
4	Havranek et al. (2016)	The meta-analysis methods to examining the effect of natural resources on economic growth are used	The findings suggest three factors in explaining the differences in natural resource impact on the economy: (1) an interaction between natural resources and institutional quality, (2) controlling for the level of investment activity, and (3) distinguishing between different types of natural resources
5	Badeeb et al. (2017)	Literature survey	The negative effects of natural resource on economic growth particularly working through factors closely associated with growth in the developing countries

(continued)

Table 2.1 (continued)

No.	Author/year	Methodology	Findings
6	Hayat and Tahir (2019)	The study investigates the impact of natural resources' volatility on economic growth. Using data from 1970 to 2016 by employing the autoregressive distributed lag (ARDL) cointegration approach	A significant positive relationship between the natural resource and economic growth for the economy of the United Arab Emirates (UAE) and Saudi Arabia. Nevertheless, the volatility of natural resources has a significant negative impact on the economic growth of Oman, UAE and Saudi Arabia economies

Source Author's own construction, 2020

2.3 Why Is Natural Resource Dependency Reduction Important?

There is reason to believe that a natural resource rich economy with a high degree of dependency on resource revenue will be unable to stabilise for a long period, due to volatility in the price of resources and their commodities. Studies such as Hendrick and Crawford (2014), Pagano and Hoene (2010), and Shi and Tao (2018) suggest the promotion of revenue diversification as an enhancement to reduce revenue volatility, and as a result of this policy, less vulnerable economies will become those which are the most sufficiently diversified (Afonso, 2013; Odhiambo & Olushola, 2018).

In this regard, policies to support, for example, private sector development, public sector development and reforms, would lead to more diversification in the economy. The private sector can lead the backward and forward linkage from resource commodity to manufacturing, thereby accelerating the industrialisation of resource revenue-dependent countries. S. Sinha et al. (2001) claim that strong links between private businesses across sectors which are spread geographically improve complementary needs that contribute to economic diversification. Chile and Malaysia, for instance, have used this linkage as a starting point for wider economic development including, but not limited to, manufacturing development (Morris et al., 2012). Turkey is another example demonstrating that the private sector moved into the industrial sector, while the state concentrated on the production of intermediate commodities as inputs for the private sector (Agartan, 2017).

Manufacturing leads the economic transformation of many emerging and developing countries such as China, Botswana, Malaysia and Vietnam. This transformation increases the productivity of private firms by providing quality products to the domestic market, raising the share of industry in regional markets and accumulating experiences with technology, management and marketing (Dinh et al., 2012). Such policies, for instance in China, have encouraged a movement in the primary drivers

2.3 Why Is Natural Resource Dependency Reduction Important?

of trade and growth (Farooki & Kaplinsky, 2013). Then, local and regional markets have significantly increased (Reiner & Staritz, 2013).

Farooki and Kaplinsky (2013) argue about the significance of industrialisation and manufacturing production in creating job opportunities, especially low and medium technology-based jobs, that are more likely labour-intensive sectors. Accordingly, industrialisation policy contributes to social progress by generating high skill employment, resulting in well-paid jobs and increased opportunities.

Van der Ploeg (2011) exemplifies four out of 65 resource rich developing countries that successfully managed to overcome the problem of natural resource dependency, these countries are Botswana, Indonesia, Malaysia and Thailand. The commendable achievement of the latter three Asian countries, according to Van der himself, was due to economic diversification and industrialisation policies. Industrialisation, indeed, is the engine of sustainable economic growth in contemporary economy (Cantore et al., 2017; Su & Yao, 2017).[4]

Natural resource rich countries may have more secure revenue to stabilise their fiscal policy from selling state owned enterprises (SOEs) across the privatisation process, as well as taxing the private sector and its employees. Privatisation has been developed to increase private investment in public enterprises, thereby leading to increased engagement of the private sector in economic activities (Nhema, 2015). Therefore, the privatisation process raises substantial cash for governments and develops the remaining public enterprises by improving cost inefficiency (Bennett & La Manna, 2012; Bjorvatn & Eckel, 2011). Recently Saudi Arabian oil company is offered to be partially privatised to diversify the heavily oil-dependent economy (Nasser, 2019).

Inefficient management of the economy is one of the largest causes of privatisation. Therefore, the main goals of privatisation are to increase efficiency and improve economic performance (Estrin & Pelletier, 2018; Kay & Thompson, 1986; Pheko, 2013). Venables (2016) discussed the value that the private sector may contribute to natural resource management and national economy in resource rich countries in two ways. First, the private sector is competent in providing the distinguished sizable technical expertise needed for such complexity. Second, if this involvement is based on a regulatory and fiscal regime, the private sector would provide a normal rate of return to the resource-dependent countries, in the form of taxes or other linked investments.

This return, in the way of taxes, for instance, increases and diversifies the revenue of the government. The tax system plays a significant role in deriving long-lasting economic stability to reduce the volatility resulting from natural resource dependency as well as strengthening accountability (Afonso, 2013; Odhiambo & Olushola,

---

[4] According to the Kaldor's law of economic growth, economic growth has a notable link with manufacturing productions. Kaldor presents three major laws; (1) manufacturing growth has a close relationship with the growth of productions in an economy, (2) the growth of productivity in the manufacturing sector is associated with production growth in this sector which is not true in other sectors such as services and Agriculture, (3) there is a positive linkage between productivity growth in an economy and manufacturing output. See Nicholas (1966).

2018; Von Haldenwang & Ivanyna, 2018). These values consequently lead to greater efficiency of resource management and then economic growth.

In order to defeat natural resource dependency, a resource rich government is required to involve the private sector in managing natural resources. Private sector development might involve reducing the threat of violence in natural resource rich economies. The effectiveness of the private sector in efficient management of the resources may reduce the risk of political instability and conflict in these countries. Therefore, the management of natural resources may be improved. As many resources remain underexplored and unexploited, the private sector is a potential provider of technical expertise that is required from discovering to developing (Venables, 2016).

Furthermore, the importance of transparency in managing resources is critical. A. Williams (2011) has confirmed the benefit of better resource management. Natural resource revenue transparency in particular is important to diminish resource curse threats. Williams believes that it is the absence of revenue transparency that causes poor economic growth, rather than dependency on natural resources itself.[5] Resource revenue transparency can be achieved through quality institutions and good governance (Mejía Acosta, 2013). Thus, the improvement in natural resource management has developed the term of natural resource governance.[6]

Further importance of natural resource dependency reduction relates to the reduction of social-environmental problems in societies. For instance, countries that improve the rate of resource productivity may not have human rights issues related to land grabbing. Land is an indispensable resource for practicing several human rights namely the right to life, food, housing, development and property rights. However, conflicts arise in respect with the enjoyment of those rights. The lack of adequate legislative and property rights in some countries might facilitate land grabbing. Tura (2018) exemplifies the Ethiopian land law that does not guarantee the rights of the land users. This has caused the ethnic group land users to exclude the enjoyment of some of those rights especially vulnerable smallholders. Nevertheless, sustainable use of natural resources might discourage such a land grabbing through having other source of revenue and financing the development projects.

Natural resource dependency reduction is also in line with reducing the possibility of human-made natural resources including floods, landslides, bad air quality and forest fires. Natural resource revenue has critical environmental implications especially in relation to new resource discoveries and thereby causing to destruct the environment. Ulucak and Khan (2020) expose the developing countries' drastic destruction of natural resources in the search for new resource discoveries. As such, the ecological footprint of natural resource rents has been observed (Ahmed et al., 2020; Alvarado et al., 2021).

---

[5] For a broader picture on the effect of transparency on economic growth, see A. Williams (2011).

[6] The term Natural-Resource Governance is used to improve transparency and accountability in natural resources management, by setting several strategies starting from licensing and exploration to generation and allocation of resource revenues, and the involvement of all the societies agents in the process in general entailing governments, private companies, nongovernmental organisations, the media and civil society (Mejía Acosta, 2013).

The contribution of oil and gas is highly appreciated to environmental degradation because energy is inevitable input in the production of goods and services. This has resulted in producing high levels of CO_2 emission, contributing to climate change, disrupting the environment and holding humankind at critical risk of irreversible harm. The environmental effect of energy consumption level has been investigated. The findings confirm that energy consumption reduces environmental quality (Majeed et al., 2021; Mamkhezri et al., 2022; Usman et al., 2021). Therefore, economic diversification to reduce resource revenue dependency of natural resource rich countries can reduce social-environmental problems in societies, improves the quality of environment and thereby prevent the environmental health for the next generation.

2.4 The Effects of Economic Diversification on Resource Dependency

Natural resource rich countries with a high degree of dependency on resource revenues are in danger of being locked into a natural resource-dependent cycle. This cyclical dependency on resource revenues would retard economic growth. Nevertheless, economic diversification would provide macroeconomic stability which is a critical issue in resource rich economies (Farooki & Kaplinsky, 2014; Hendrick & Crawford, 2014; Shi & Tao, 2018).

Economic diversification has long been related to macroeconomic stability and economic growth sustainability. The diversification process tends to alter the economic structure of natural resource rich countries, from a single commodity to diverse commodities; economic diversification is possible when a country has various sources of income that are not directly connected to each other (Shayah, 2015).

Therefore, economic diversification of natural resource rich countries is a tool for better governance which contributes to job creation, increased revenue, reduced corruption and improvement in the institutional quality of countries (Albassam, 2015).

Economic diversification of resource rich countries can be achieved through industrialisation. In essence, the private sector may contribute to diversify the economy through leading the backward and forward linkages from resource commodity to manufacturing and further linkages to other economic sectors. The significance of this linkage had been promoted by one of the pioneers of development economics Albert Hirschman. Hirschman (1981) proposed three types of linkages from resource commodities to industrialisation: fiscal linkages, consumption linkages and production linkages.

Fiscal linkages in the forms of money transfer from the resource commodity sectors in the form of corporate taxes, royalties and taxes on employee incomes, are hard to continue, as resource rich countries have a low ability to tax, weak capability to invest efficiently and productively, and suffer from weak institutions and lack of transparency (Besley & Persson, 2014; Crivelli & Gupta, 2014).

Consumption linkages, in the form of resource commodity rents would lead to raised demand for the output of other sectors. However, the extractive sector resources often crowd out the competitiveness of other sectors, leading to a smaller tax base, and thereby less economic activities (Frankel, 2012; Venables, 2016; Von Haldenwang & Ivanyna, 2018).

Finally, the most feasible linkages between resource commodities and manufacturing, according to Hirschman (1981) are production linkages. The linkages are both backward and forward from the resource sector in which the former is upstream, meaning production is inputted into the commodities sector, and the latter, which is downstream, means processing commodities (Ebert & La Menza, 2015).

Hirschman argued that production linkages provide great potential for industrial development, but the scale and technological intensity of production would affect it (Hirschman, 1981). Studies on the backward and forward linkage from resource commodity to manufacturing in eight African countries concluded that the resource commodity sector needs input and produces output as intermediate products for other sectors (Ebert & La Menza, 2015; Morris et al., 2011).

In support of Hirschman's arguments, Ben Hammouda et al. (2006), and Singh et al. (2018) discuss the importance of industrialisation in diversification strategies. Industrial production can improve international integration and competition in the national economy such as the first generation of emerging economies, in which they are now the most dynamic regions in international trade due to their high share of industry in GDP.

Investment is another determining factor of diversification. From the experience of emerging countries, Ben Hammouda et al. (2006) and Singh et al. (2018) suggest that the contribution of private sector investment to the economy leads to high growth and increased productivity of new economic sectors. This contribution occurred through industrial policy, foreign trade and investment.

Accordingly, the experience of the emerging economies shows that an increase in private investment in manufacturing production translates into diversification of national productive capacity. It can be argued that there is an interdependence between the private sector and economic diversification. Therefore, private sector development raises the diversification of the economy, and thereby economic diversification depends on the level of private sector development (Ekpo et al., 2014).

Private sector investment can lead to the availability of new technologies, greater competition and improved productivity between the new economic sectors required for economic diversification (Singh et al., 2018; Williams et al., 2015). This consequently results in increased exports and an improved level of international integration for emerging economies. For instance, the evolution of China's export structure in the rise of the private sector led to a 0–39% increase in export between 1995 and 2013 (Lardy, 2014).

It has been proven that the private sector is an engine of economic growth, but to be considered a driver of economic diversification, it has to meet criteria

2.4 The Effects of Economic Diversification on Resource Dependency

including economic efficiency, competition and competitiveness, flexibility, responsiveness and financial sustainability (Sinha et al., 2001). Undoubtedly, sustainable growth requires diversified economic structures that reduce dependency on primary commodities (Albassam, 2015).

The private sector may provide a normal rate of return to the dependent countries in the form of taxes or other kinds of investment which in turn would promote economic diversification. Thus, taxation is another way of promoting diversification in natural resource rich countries. Farooki and Kaplinsky (2014) argue the importance of increasing the direct taxing of the private sector surplus during the resource commodities boom. For instance, during the global oil boom between 2005 and 2008, the total corporate taxes paid to government increased by 55%. However, introducing new taxes must not distort economic incentives that might deteriorate the investment environment and then economic growth. A sharp rise in taxes, otherwise, would increase illicit trade which leads to loss of revenue (Mansour, 2015).

Ekpo et al. (2014) show that successful diversification of the economy would require the collaboration of the public and private sectors of the economy. In essence, Schulpen and Gibbon (2002) claimed that while the private sector generates economic growth, governments have to provide the background conditions for this to occur; the government has to play a constructive role in order for the private sector to develop further. Whereas the government must play a crucial role in developing an active private sector, the private sector itself must lead those activities that had traditionally been led by the government (Tanzi, 2011). For example, where the private sector in Turkey moved into the industrial sector, the government focused on intermediate commodities production as inputs for the private sector (Agartan, 2017).

Economic diversification, unlike natural resource dependency where a single commodity is the main source of income in the economy, is a process in which a large and growing number of different outputs are produced by more than one sector. Antonova et al. (2018) define the diversification process as a driver of changing the economic structure from a single industry to a diverse one. Shayah (2015) defines this process as diversification of markets for export or the diversification of the source of income by foreign investment. Therefore, diversification can improve the economic performance of the resource rich countries by reducing volatility, generating other sources of revenue and contributing to economic growth (Afonso, 2013; Shi & Tao, 2018).

However, economic diversification is not only deriving development, but is also positively associated with several issues in natural resource rich economies. Bjorvatn et al. (2012) and Busse and Gröning (2013) claim that economic diversification has a positive impact on political stability, social development and institutional quality. For illustration, studies have identified the effect of natural resource rents in less diversified economies on raising political instability in particular in fairing conflict and civil war (Badeeb et al., 2017; Dal Bó & Dal Bó, 2011; Ross, 2012).

Another outcome of low levels of economic diversification in natural resource rich countries that have dependency on resource revenues is the association of resource rents with corruption. Badeeb et al. (2017), Boutilier (2017) and Sachs and Warner (2001) argue that the effects of resource rent that are transmitted into the economy through macroeconomic channels include corruption, rent seeking and less accountability. For instance, Busse and Gröning (2013) in a study exploring the effect of natural resources in less diversified economies on a governance indicator of developing and developed countries from 1984 to 2007, found natural resource export had an increasing effect on corruption.

Economic diversification, therefore, can be a long-term solution to the high economic dependency from natural resource revenue extractions which can be achieved in every sector of the economy. This diversification can take place in both the private and public sectors of the economy.

2.4.1 The Private Sector Development

Diversification of the private sector refers to private sector development, and generation of new sources of income, which reduce government burden to provide services. PSD refers to a range of strategies aimed at strengthening the private sector to promote economic growth, sustainability, employment opportunities and improve the welfare of people (Di Bella et al., 2013; Lin et al., 2011).

The private sector has been developed since the onset of the economic liberalisation in the 1980s. The liberalisation policy placed the private sector in the stage of development in which, deriving economic growth and development of manufacturing were the main aims of this policy (Cook, 2006; Haouas et al., 2002). The idea behind the development of the private sector according to Toye (1993), was the development policy of the 1970s that challenged Keynesianism. Accordingly, economic development can be achieved within an economic system that freely operates with minimal intervention from the government.

Private sector development plays a key role in growth, employment and improved well-being. As presented in Fig. 2.1, the PSD incentivises people to invest in skill acquisition which provides them with more job opportunities. Through competitiveness and access to finance, it supports not only the diversification of the economy, but also diversifying revenues via generating increased tax revenues, thus it grants further funding for the government (International Corporation and Development, 2019).

Countries apply different models to enhance the contribution of the private sector in job creation and economic growth. For instance, in Turkey, the reform to enhance performance of the public enterprises led to the introduction of privatisation (Agartan, 2017). Accordingly, Turkey received privatisation to focus on two sets of corrective measures; the problem of the unsatisfactory performance of state economic enterprises and reshaping the public sector role in both the level and the scope of public expenditure. The private sector, consequently, expanded capital market growth and the additional revenue resulted in a reduction of national debt and the budget deficit of the public enterprises. In addition, Malaysia launched private–public partnership

2.4 The Effects of Economic Diversification on Resource Dependency

Private Sector Development

Infrastructure Development

Improved Governance → Private Sector Development ← Capacity Building

Competitiveness ← Private Sector Development → Access to Finance

Regulatory Reform — Business Development Services

Fig. 2.1 Private sector development engagement in economic growth (*Source* International Corporation and Development 2019)

(PPP) as an initial step to privatisation. Private sectors were provided with the opportunities to run public services, reducing public expenditure and increasing the revenue and physical assets of the government (Singaravelloo, 2017).

The worldwide growth of SOEs privatisation increased the annual revenue governments received. Privatisation Barometer (2019) reports that the cumulative value governments earned from privatisation exceeds 1,129 billion US dollars between 1990 and 2013. As such, the rapid expansion of the privatisation process resulted from the lure of revenue from selling SOEs (Megginson & Netter, 2001). Thus, since the development of the private sector in the 1980s, the share of private investment in the global economy has increased. However, the aggregate share of the private sector is much larger in industrialised countries than in resource rich countries.[7]

The political economy of industrialisation has been a key concern of development in natural resource wealth economies. It argues important factors that the government can focus on to foster industrial development that include structural change, endogenous technological progress and the role played in the economy by investment, saving and export (Storm, 2017). Accordingly, it is the government's task to create a condition for the private sector to lead innovation and economic diversification through providing infrastructure development and funding research and development (R&D) (Wade, 2014).

Atherton and Smallbone (2013) argue that opening the economy to the private sector should not be a process led by governments. Rather the government should provide conditions in which the private sector is able to grow. In this regard, S. Sinha et al. (2001) categorise a group of factors schematically into macro, meso and micro factors, in which to be effective, it has to be multi-sectoral and multi-disciplinary, integrated with other interventions. Therefore, they are essential to understanding how the private sector develops.

---

[7] Privatisation Barometer (2019) provides a wider picture on the size of privatisation across countries.

The macro factors that affect the development of the private sector are the economic system and policies, political system and governance and the social and cultural context. According to S. Sinha et al. (2001), the economic system, whether centrally planned, state-dominant or market driven is an important factor for determining effective economic policies. The economic policy of governments, as described by Adelina-Geanina (2011), includes systems for setting levels of taxation, government budgets and interest rates as well as the labour market and national ownership.

In the business environment, a tax regime significantly affects the development of the private sector in operational decisions. Klemm and Van Parys (2012) believe that tax incentives foster a favourable business climate for private investment, and thus businesses produce jobs and economic prosperity. However, for tax incentives to be effective in improving the economy they should be targeted (Koven & Lyons, 2003). For instance, tax incentives are targeted to attract a certain type of investment in developed countries, but for the small economies of Hong Kong, Lebanon and Mauritius tax incentives are given to all sectors. The outcome of the incentives subsequently depends on the purpose of the tax incentive either for attracting investment projects or high-added value (Cristina & Marcel, 2012).

Most empirical literature on the effect of tax on the private sector focuses on the relationship between tax incentives and foreign direct investment (FDI). For example, a study by Klemm and Van Parys (2012) found that a decrease of 10% in corporate tax is associated with an increase in FDI between 0.33 and 4.5% of GDP. This explains the significance of tax incentives in attracting FDI.

Political systems and governance including business legislation, market regulation and the rule of law often affect economic systems and policies (Kirkpatrick, 2014). Generally, governments regulate the environment in which businesses operate. To a large extent, however, the type of regulations that rule the business activity and the market operation are affected by the governance and its quality of institutions (Sinha et al., 2001). Therefore, the role of institutions is of paramount importance in the development of private sector.

S. G. Banerjee et al. (2006), Berkowitz et al. (2015) and Vining and Weimer (2016) argue about the effect of government institutions on the private sector through the provision of property rights, the operation of effective capital market and the rule of law.[8] Good governance is emphasised as a condition for the private sector to achieve and deliver more equitable results.[9]

In addition to the abovementioned environment for private sector development, S. Sinha et al. (2001) claim that the private sector develops as a result of opportunities for access to international markets; the extent to which the government intervenes in the market (deregulation); and the success of privatisation and private–public

---

[8] Acemoglu and Robinson (2012) provide evidence that institutions matter for development. Institutions are explained as possibly the main factor why some nations thrive while others stagnate.

[9] A good governance is defined "as a government's ability to make and enforce rules, and to deliver services, regardless of whether that government is democratic or not" (Fukuyama, 2013, p. 3).

partnerships in enhancing ownership of commercial businesses and contributing to the provision of public services.

Theories about the private sector have referenced specific objectives of privatisations. Kay and Thompson (1986) and Mohan (2001) state the major motivations behind privatisation to be one or more of the following; (1) to promote increased efficiency or improved economic performance; (2) to expand revenue for the governments; (3) to reduce the role of the government in the economy by limiting interventions and promoting more private initiatives; and (4) to advance capital market development through broader share ownership. There is a trade-off between each one of these objectives and there might be conflict over time (Kay & Thompson, 1986).

The private sector theory argues several logical reasons in favour of privatisation. Mikesell (2013) and Tanzi (2011) claim that about the changing role of the governments in response to privatisation; privatisation may reduce the government's role in the economy. Privatisation of SOEs also provides large revenue to the government (Mikesell, 2013), and firms that completely privatise are more productive than partially privatised firms (Brown et al., 2019). Megginson and Netter (2001) believe that the attractive lure of revenue from selling SOEs is one reason that global privatisation has rapidly taken place.

Mohan (2001) emphasised requirements for the effectiveness of the private sector which affect the design of privatisation such as incentive structure, public objective of privatisation, efficiency and the degree of state intervention in regulation, taxes and macroeconomic management. Atherton and Smallbone (2013) argue that opening the economy to the private sector starts with conditions the government provides to the private sector to grow. According to Mohan (2001), privatisation is effective once associated with competition or deregulation.

The private sector is seen to bring efficiency when accompanied with competition. Institutional and regulation quality mechanise corporate governance in a capital market. Then, private sector development comes to action in monitoring post-privatisation performance with developing strategies to help improve the performance of the privatised sector.

A summary review of the literature most relevant to this subsection of the book is presented in Table 2.2 and includes methodologies and findings.

2.4.2 Investment in Human Development and Infrastructure

A review of the literature related to economic diversification strategies in resource rich countries reveals a dynamic relationship between human development and economic growth, and investment and economic growth. While there are two-way relationships between both human development and economic growth on one side and investment and economic growth on the other side, herewith attention has been paid to human development and investment as drivers of economic growth (Rivera, 2017).

Human development, which is defined as the ability to promote and enhance the capabilities of individuals that enables them to lead longer, healthier and fuller lives,

Table 2.2 A review of the selected existing literature on PSD

No	Author/year	Methodology	Findings
1	Ramamurti (2000)	A dynamic multilevel econometric model was used to investigate firm, industry and country determinants of privatisation	Countries in a macroeconomic crisis are likely to privatise SOEs, the change in ownership alone is likely to improve firm-level performance, and the industry shows little dynamism
2	Sinha et al. (2001)	A three-stage process of evaluation of private sector development is used	Country analysis and strategy documents should integrate PSD support into the overall programme of development assistance. • Issues of the relationship between the factors that affect the private business sector need to be better understood. • Inter-departmental co-operation on delivering PSD support is limited and should be strengthened
3	Klemm and Van Parys (2012)	Spatial econometrics techniques were used to investigate whether incentives are used as a tax tool for competitiveness, and dynamic panel data based on tax reaction were used to analyse the effect of tax incentives on attracting investment	Low level of taxation was associated with boosting gross private fixed capital formation
4	Atherton and Smallbone (2013)	Case studies to determine challenges, opportunities, conditions and constraints of PSD	Lack of capacity and expertise within local government affect having effective frameworks for private sector development. Lack of a dedicated budget publicly funded private sector limits stimulating the emergence of private business
5	Brown et al. (2019)	Econometrics of firm-level panel data with fixed effect was used to classify private ownership into domestic and foreign before and after privatisation	A significant contribution of privatisation was found on manufacturing productivity growth in Ukraine

Source Author's own construction, 2020

has been identified as the core objective of development (Mehrotra & Gandhi, 2012; Suri et al., 2011).

Theoretically, economic development literature related to all growth models including classic, neo-classic and growth theory considered human development as a determinant of economic growth (Suri et al., 2011). Empirically, evidence shows that sustainable growth requires long-lasting human development improvement (Suri et al., 2011). Therefore, the change in human capital investment might affect the growth level.

Natural resource rich countries derive a high share from natural resources which can be used to finance human development. As such, the larger rents driven from natural resources may be an advantage for resource rich countries to improve the country's level of human development. A study confirms the significance of the availability of finance to invest in human capital. Popov (2014) found that lack of access to finance is associated with significantly lower investment in human capital in job-training and education.

China is one of the fastest growing economies. The growth rate on average has been 10% since the end of the 1970s. Human capital accumulation has been marked as one of the most crucial factors in the growth of the Chinese economy. A study of the determinants of growth in China over the period 1991–2010 found that the growth rate positively correlated with the investment rate in physical capital and human capital (Su & Liu, 2016). Similarly, Akinyemi (2011) found that the business landscape in Rwanda due to human development policy has become one of the fastest environment in the world to start a business.

The level of human capital development largely identifies labour quality and the population's innovative capacity which can be affected by countries' social spending, income level and competitiveness across and within countries. Empirical evidence suggests that the rate of social expenditure and the distribution of income are critical factors of human development on a country level (Suri et al., 2011). Thus, the social spending ratio to invest in human capital has been substantially increasing. Jalles (2019) studied 45 developing countries from 1982 to 2012 focusing on government social spending and found that social expenditure has generally been cyclical over time in developing economies.

The competitiveness of countries might explain why the social expenditure of many countries has followed a cyclical pattern. An empirical study by Hickman and Olney (2011) examined the impact of globalisation on the domestic labour market for low-skilled workers and found that globalisation leads to improved human development in the United States. Nevertheless, while the determinants of human development identify labour quality and the innovative capacity of a country's population as important, human capital development is generally regarded as a significant determinant of economic growth.

With regard to investment in infrastructure, countries that have a high level of infrastructure investments may experience economic growth. Economic literature and its driven policies generally view economic growth as investment. However, sufficient levels of infrastructure investment are a driver of economic growth.

While, public sector investment in infrastructure is viewed as the main precursor of business sector profitability and efficiency, on the level of economy, infrastructure investment can reduce the cost of production, expanding input productivity factors and smoothing the business cycle (Ansar et al., 2016). With regard to the cost efficiency of the business sector, Donaldson (2018) studied trade flow between 45 regions in India, and found that although infrastructure investment in railroads increased trade flows, trade costs and interregional price gaps were reduced. A further example is in China where infrastructure investment has recorded a positive effect on economic growth (Chen et al., 2013; Newman, 2011).

Nevertheless, empirical research shows that it is not always the case that infrastructure investment has a positive effect on economic growth. Ansar et al. (2016) contradicted previous literature by finding that unproductive debt-financed investment projects would cause debt accumulation and financial market insecurity through distortionary monetary expansion, and thereby contribute to economic fragility. Ansar and others marked poor management of the infrastructure projects and a lower level of higher quality infrastructure investments as essential factors that caused this fragility.

X. Jiang et al. (2017) differentiated the impact of infrastructure projects on economic growth at national and provincial levels and different results were found. These differences are associated with several factors mainly economic development policy, the size and the level of the projects and central government's reform policies.

While long-lasting improvement in human development and a high level of infrastructure investments are required for economic growth, it is proportional neither to the human development nor to infrastructure investment.

2.4.3 The Public Sector Development

The lack of economic diversification in several natural resource rich countries recorded an adverse impact on economic growth (Badeeb et al., 2017; Venables, 2016). Therefore, natural resource rich countries that are highly depending on natural resource revenues, require a long-term solution to this dependency from natural resources, and thereby economic diversification seems to be highly significant. Diversification in public sector revenues can be achieved through privatisation of SOEs and taxation system.

The public sector can be developed to lead diversification, either through privatisation of public services, providing firms with reduced public financing of those services, or through development of national taxation system that reduces the regional governments dependency on revenue from natural resources.

Table 2.3 summarised the most relevant studies on public sector development.

Privatisation as an Engine for Economic Diversification

Privatisation is the transfer of ownership by a deliberate sale of state-owned enterprises to the private sector to improve the performance of the industries concerned (Boubakri & Saffar, 2019; Estrin & Pelletier, 2018; Nhema, 2015).

Due to the effects of privatisation on the cost of government finances and changes in ownership arrangement, it is defined as a dynamic phenomenon (Nhema, 2015; Yarrow, 1999). Although the areas of public interest which become privatised are

2.4 The Effects of Economic Diversification on Resource Dependency

Table 2.3 A review of the selected literature on public sector development

No	Author/year	Methodology	Findings
1	Wang and Chen (2011)	Cost function and inverse demand function	Governments to increase the degree of privatisation along with increasing proportion of domestic ownership of multinational firms. Furthermore, an increase in domestic ownership of multinational firms raises all domestic private firms' profit and social welfare
2	Bjorvatn and Eckel (2011)	Qualitative method: deals with privatisation strategies for developing countries facing different types of investors by analysing both the investment strategies of the firms and the privatisation strategies of the host governments	The findings show that there may be an incentive to privatise by selling the state-owned firm to a local investor at a lower price in order to achieve a more competitive post-privatisation market structure
3	Haidar (2012)	Regression analysis	The results show that business regulatory reforms are good for economic growth; every regulatory reform of business environment is associated with a 0.15% increase in GDP growth rate
4	Besley and Persson (2014)	A Benchmark Model to investigate the relationships between taxation and economic development	Provide analysis for the forces that derive the relationship between taxation and economic development
5	Hendrick and Crawford (2014)	A system of two equations estimated with panel data is used	The results show that internal fiscal structure and external fiscal policy of municipal governments can be used in managing spending volatility
6	Odhiambo and Olushola (2018)	A multiple linear regression model by employing Ordinary least square (OLS) is used to capture the relationship between taxation and economic growth	The findings reveal that taxation has a significant impact on Real GDP growth rates in Nigeria. However, the proportion of tax contribution to the growth rate falls short of the optimal level in terms of the volume of economic activities and total value of output, as well as the country's potential for revenue generation

Source Author's own construction, 2020

varied, and each sector may apply different methods,[10] the sale of SOEs is not subject to domestic or foreign private investors.[11]

---

[10] See Estrin and Pelletier (2018) for understanding the methods of privatisation.

[11] Selling assets during privatisation to foreign or domestic investors is controversial, see Bjorvatn and Eckel (2011) and M. H. Lin and Matsumura (2018) for wider discussion.

Privatisation has substantially increased since the adoption of economic liberalisation worldwide in the 1980s. Nellis (1998) exhibited a massive number of medium- and large-scale privatised firms from 1980 to 1991, where 60,000 were in transition economies and about 6800 were in non-transition economies. Kurlantzick (2012) reported that between 2004 and 2009, 250 private companies appeared on the Forbes list of the world's largest corporations, while 120 state-owned companies fell off it.

A study ranked the type of state enterprises in Organisation for Economic Co-operation and Development (OECD) countries, showing that half of SOEs were in transportation, telecommunication, finance, power generation, manufacturing, mining and other energy industry sectors (Christiansen, 2011). In Sub-Saharan Africa, Schoneveld and Zoomers (2015) reported the privatisation of 1,107 enterprises between 1988 and 2008 where 60% of the total value was in natural resource-based industries.

Privatisation, which continues to be a significant player in many parts of the world, is a policy issue in developing countries that needs to be addressed (Wang & Chen, 2011). A number of countries have developed privatisation in the process of economic reforms in public enterprises, as well as increasing the engagement of the private sector in economic activities (Nhema, 2015). Privatisation in natural resource-dependent countries, especially oil economies, raises cash for governments, in particular, during periods of time where oil prices are low. Nevertheless, economic diversification remains elusive; these revenues enable only limited economic diversification (Ait-Laoussine & Gault, 2017).

Different theorists have defended the importance of privatisation mainly through political theory, the competence theory and the microeconomic theory (Boycko et al., 1996; Pelikan, 1993; Winiecki, 2013). The microeconomic theory considers the sale of state-owned enterprises where two strands of literature focus on whether the government should completely or partially privatise SOEs (Chang & Ryu, 2015). While it is assumed that completely privatised firms exclusively consider their profit, partially privatised firms care to maximize their profits as well as social welfare (Chang & Chen, 2015; Chen, 2017; Wang & Chen, 2010).

Theoretically, one of the critical factors behind the movement from public to privatisation is poor performance of public enterprises (Boycko et al., 1996; Kay & Thompson, 1986; Mohan, 2001). However, the key political objective of privatisation is to downsize the state (Spulber, 2006), and create drastic change in the economic sector of a country (Popoola, 2016), despite having a variety of government objectives for privatisation.

As emphasised by Estrin and Pelletier (2018), Mohan (2001), Nhema (2015) and Pheko (2013), the objective of privatisation is to encompass one or more of the following in various parts of the economy (1) to promote increased efficiency, (2) to increase revenue for the government, (3) to reduce the government expenses in the economy, (4) to promote a wider share of private ownership and capital market development, (5) to improve social welfare (Chen, 2017; Wang & Chen, 2010), (6) to rationalize public finances, (7) to generate new investment (Nhema, 2015) and finally (8), to provide the opportunity to introduce competition (Parker & Kirkpatrick, 2005). As such, these objectives commit to diversify the economy.

2.4 The Effects of Economic Diversification on Resource Dependency

A large body of literature has demonstrated that private enterprises are more efficient than public enterprises (Bai et al., 2009; Bjorvatn & Eckel, 2011; Megginson & Netter, 2001). T.-L. Chen (2017) and Wang and Chen (2010) reviewed multiple studies showing the significantly higher performance of private provision of firms relative to public enterprises by reducing its inefficiency-related costs, which then leads to an improvement of social welfare.

In addition, the current privatisation of SOEs would develop the remaining public enterprises. Studies have shown that once privatisation occurs, a state-owned enterprises cost inefficiency is improved (Bennett & La Manna, 2012; Bjorvatn & Eckel, 2011).

Theoretically, there are well-recognised factors which contribute to the successful outcomes of privatisation; one is a high degree of competition, and the other is institutional and regulatory capacity (Mohan, 2001). The private sectors are subject to government regulations, institutional framework, taxes and macroeconomic management to ensure a well-functioning capital market. These factors have been identified as preconditions for privatisation (Estrin & Pelletier, 2018; Mohan, 2001).

Theories of the private sector consider the interaction between competitiveness of the market and the performance of the private sector; market competition is key to private sector performance (Kay & Thompson, 1986; Kuczynski, 1999; Yarrow, 1999). However, private sector performance in the economy of natural resource rich countries requires improvements in infrastructure and regulatory systems. Poor infrastructure causes higher costs to private sector activities (Leke et al., 2017).

As for the regulatory system, private sector activity requires rules that establish property rights, stability, flexible macro policies and a good business regulatory environment. Haidar (2012) and Klapper et al. (2011) argue about the regulatory reform of the governments to strengthen the private sector. Accordingly, the governments have to implement comprehensive reform in macro-stabilisation policies, price liberalisation, privatisation and openness policy in trade-barrier reductions, and thereby, the private sector will contribute to the growth of the economy. For example, a study by Haidar (2012) found that every regulatory reform of a business environment is associated with a 0.15% increase in GDP growth rate. In many resource rich countries, however, these regulatory reforms remain limited.

The government's role in the development of the private sector, particularly in a business regulatory environment, has been emphasised. Tanzi (2011) discussed the changing role of the state in the economy; the government has to play only a regulatory role; the private sector should then shoulder the burden in areas that have traditionally been the responsibility of the government.

However, the private sector's role in the improvement of economic efficiency refocuses the role of governments in the economy. For example, a study has shown that once the private sector became a powerful competitor in the market it significantly contributed to changing the production structure and product output in China's dynamic economic environment. As a result, private firms left little space for state-owned companies to make profits. The private sector's productivity is improved, and hence this gradually improved economic efficiency (Fung et al., 1999). Privatisation of state-owned enterprises strengthened market forces and increased competition, and thereby reshaped the role of the state in the economy (Schulpen & Gibbon, 2002; Tanzi, 2011). This engagement of the private sector into the economy would relatively strengthen economic diversification.

The Role of Taxation on Natural Resource Dependency Reduction

Taxation can be used as a tool to increase revenue diversification in any economy, especially for the natural resource rich countries. However, although the level of reliance on taxes in resource rich countries differs, there is generally a low level of revenue generated by taxation (Keen, 2013).

Literature such as Besley and Persson (2014); Odhiambo and Olushola (2018) and Von Haldenwang and Ivanyna (2018) claim that countries which have greater access to other forms of revenue, generate lower levels of taxation. A. D. Jensen (2011) found that adding a 1% natural resource rent to total revenue is associated with lowering the share of taxation by 1.4% in GDP.

It is claimed that the resource rich countries have a relatively low domestic tax revenue, due to substantial resource revenues from natural resources and poor tax capacity. Reform in tax revenue in natural resource rich countries is challenging due to weak diversification in revenues, weak institutions in tax capacity and the high reliance on natural resource revenues (Bastagli, 2015; McGuirk, 2013).

Evidence shows that resource rich countries neglect the development of non-resource taxation. A study covering 20 'resource intensive' countries finds a negative relationship between revenues from natural resources and non-resource revenues; every 1% increase in resource revenues lowers non-resource revenues by up to 0.12% of GDP (Crivelli & Gupta, 2014).

Generally, there is a positive correlation between tax size and income, implying that the higher the income, the greater the tax revenue in the economy is. However, Besley and Persson (2014) found a negative correlation between tax size and income in the high-income oil-dependent states of Bahrain, Kuwait and Oman. It was proven that substantial revenues from natural resource rents reduce the government's need for taxing citizens (Cabrales & Hauk, 2011). For instance, a recent study of total tax revenue as a share of GDP indicates that the total tax revenues of countries such as Cuba, France, Denmark, Norway[12] and Sweden, are higher than 30%, while in countries such as Libya and Saudi Arabia, taxes account for less than 2% of national income (Esteban & Roser, 2019).

The reason for less taxation in these resource rich developing countries as argued by Besley and Persson (2014), Crivelli and Gupta (2014) and Fenochietto and Pessino (2013) is related to the economic structure that suffers from weak institutions and lack of diversification. The structure of the economy is associated with the size of both the shadow economy and the business scale. Economies that have a larger

---

[12] Norway, with strong and accountable institutions, is a special case which enjoys both abundance of natural resources and a high tax rate.

2.4 The Effects of Economic Diversification on Resource Dependency

informal sector and smaller businesses scale are hard to tax (Besley & Persson, 2014; Venables, 2016).

The power of tax in resource-dependent countries is determined by several factors, mainly the public sector quality of institution, including tax capacity and rule of law. In such situations, the level of taxation relies on the administrative capacity of the state (Besley & Persson, 2014). Collier (2010) offers an administrative structure and fiscal capacity of a state to develop efficient taxation. Besley and Persson (2014) also suggest the capacity of the state to provide goods and services, and in supporting a market economy to influence the tax effect. Consequently, low levels of taxation and weaker quality of institutions are purported to lead to a lower level of economic growth in resource-abundant countries.

The low level of domestic tax revenue in resource rich countries is associated with accountability. According to Badeeb et al. (2017), Boutilier (2017) and Sachs and Warner (2001) accountability is one of the main channels through which resource curse is transmitted into the economy of resource rich countries, which in turn impedes economic growth. Accountability is a necessary force to derive economic development, but tax level and taxation capacity of resource rich economies lower the demand for this accountability (McGuirk, 2013; Odhiambo & Olushola, 2018).

As indicated earlier, the large revenues from natural resource rents reduce the government's need to tax its citizens, thereby low-taxed populations may demand less accountability (Cabrales & Hauk, 2011; Jensen & Wantchekon, 2004; Ross, 2001). Consequently, this reduction in accountability leads to lower economic growth in the resource rich countries (Collier & Hoeffler, 2009).

However, taxation can translate into accountability in which citizens and the private sectors engage with state actors in a tax bargaining process. Literature discusses the role of taxation in securing accountability. Brautigam et al. (2008) argue the importance of taxation as a social contract to increase representation in and scrutiny of the government. Accordingly, a representative state emerged as a result of the tax bargaining process between the governments that need other revenues such as taxes to survive inter-state conflicts, and citizens who agree to taxation in exchange for government accountability.

Several studies have investigated the power of taxation in deriving political accountability. T. Bernstein and Lu (2008) found evidence of the relationship between tax structure and accountability in China. Mahon (2005) found that increases in government dependency on tax revenues are followed by increases in democratic indicators. More recently,[13] Eubank (2012) discovered the relationship between tax structure and strengthening accountability in Somaliland. Paler (2013) finds from a public awareness campaign in Indonesia that taxation increased accountability in the way of monitoring and anti-incumbent political actions.

There is reason to believe that a natural resource-dependent economy will be unable to stabilise for a long time. According to Afonso (2013), Odhiambo and Olushola (2018) and Von Haldenwang and Ivanyna (2018), taxation, which is a

---

[13] Contemporary studies paid less attention to the study of taxation and political accountability.

significant government instrument of fiscal policy to mobilise revenue, is an important method to derive long-lasting economic stability. This in turn reduces the volatility resulting from natural resource dependency and strengthens government accountability (Eubank, 2012; Odhiambo & Olushola, 2018), and fostering economic growth.

Nevertheless, defining a proper or optimal level of taxation is controversial among economists. The optimal taxation theory suggests that a tax system must be applied to augment citizens' social welfare conditions (Mankiw et al., 2009). Taxing natural resources is not as beneficial as traditional tax revenue (Ross, 2012) and Barma et al. (2011) consider the enforcement of a progressive tax[14] based on profit as the best way to achieve economic growth.

2.5 Successful Cases of Economic Diversifications Policies

Natural resource rich countries have incentives to diversify their economies. Nevertheless, economic diversification in such countries is challenging, due to the fact that the resource-dominant sector is often poorly related to the rest of the economy, the so-called 'Dutch disease effects' (Frankel, 2012; Sekwati, 2010). However, there are some countries that have successfully defeated the problem of dependency on natural resource revenue. Van der Ploeg (2011) exemplifies four out of sixty-five resource rich developing countries (Botswana, Indonesia, Malaysia and Thailand) that successfully overcame the problem of resource dependency through economic diversification and industrialisation policies. Acemoglu et al. (2002) and Van der Ploeg (2011) identified further countries which successfully diversified their economy including Australia, Canada, the United States, New Zealand, Iceland, Norway and Botswana.

Botswana is the first Sub-Saharan African country with relatively strong political and economic that has graduated from resource dependence. Its relative dependency on natural resources has decreased from 3.8% in 2010 to only 1% of GDP in 2017 (WDI, 2018). Factors that enhance economic diversification include strong institutions, public investment, political stability and investment in human development capital.

Both the developmental state theory and the core of development economics emphasise institutional change as part of structural change as a requirement of economic development (Hillbom, 2011). Good institutions and good governance are seen to be fundamental for economic development. Robinson (2013) explains the economic success of Botswana by the historical development of its institutions. Botswana's institution was inherited from Tswana state. Then, the legacy of Tswana helped to determine national institutions without evolving into conflict in other institutions in most African countries. The governance indicators of Botswana are relatively improved; the country on average from 2004 to 2018 has been ranked 69th

---

[14] While type of taxation is not considered of this study, it is recommended for further studies to investigate appropriate tax revenue policy of natural resource wealth countries.

2.5 Successful Cases of Economic Diversifications Policies

for the quality of governance and 84th for political stability and absence of violence among all countries (WGI, 2020).

Sebudubudu (2010) argues about the effect of institutions in Botswana's development. Accordingly, good governance positively impacted stability and thus facilitated development. Politically, Botswana has experienced free democratic elections since its independence in 1966. It has enjoyed a relatively long period of stability in which no coups were attempted, or civil wars occurred. This stability, indeed, is crucial for both empowering institutions and economic development.

Further factors that contribute to Botswana's success is public investment. It is suggested that resource rich countries improve their efficiency measures of public investment, which may expand fiscal capacity to invest in infrastructure. Botswana, for example, has emphasised quality public investment projects (Gylfason & Nganou, 2016) in which, according to Van der Ploeg (2011), long-term investment exceeded 25% of GDP.

Highest investment in education which led to improvements in human development contributed to the development of Botswana with relatively strong political and economic institutions (Acemoglu et al., 2002). Good governance has been marked as a necessary factor in a country's human development progress; 'countries that perform better in governance tend to do well in human development' (Sebudubudu, 2010, p. 258). Sebudubudu explained how Botswana's good governance not only affected the political environment, but also the education system of the country and human development performance. Botswana has invested heavily in human capital through expanding educations. The government adopted an education strategy which involved extensive provision of education to all by allocating on average 25% of the annual budget since 1977. As such, Botswana scored more than 70% in economic opportunities and human development which is an outstanding performance compared to other developing countries (Sebudubudu, 2010).

The identified factors that contributed to the remarkable success of Botswana were good policies of public investment in human capital and infrastructure, quality institutions and democracy (Gylfason & Nganou, 2016; Van der Ploeg, 2011). Botswana which ranked the world's highest rate of economic growth in Sub-Saharan African rich resources over the past 50 years, is marked as Africa's richest country in terms of the purchasing power of its per capita gross national income (GNI) (Gylfason & Nganou, 2016) with an average GDP growth exceeding 4% (Van der Ploeg, 2011). As such, these factors caused Botswana to graduate from the least developed countries in 2017.

Natural resource rich countries such as Australia, Canada, the United States, New Zealand, Iceland, Norway and Botswana have strong institutions (Acemoglu et al., 2002; Van der Ploeg, 2011). However, weak institutions relating to the natural resource sector as explained by Auzer (2017) and Van der Ploeg (2011) would produce rent seeking, corruptions, crime and a weakened diversification strategy.

In Norway, the essential factors determining the success of economic diversification towards less dependency on natural resources include, but are not limited to; strong institutions, manufacturing strategy and market friendly policy for business. Norway benefited from well-developed institutions to turn natural resources into a blessing rather than a curse. It is the world's second largest natural gas exporter after Russia, despite oil expansion since 1971. For some time, Norway has been enjoying productive activities with positive outcomes for the rest of the economy with an absence of rent seeking and corruption. One reason for this is that it has benefited from having reasonably well-performing institutions for a while. For example, Norway benefited from having strong governance with an average rank of 96.4 in the last 20 years, while this rate in recent years improves to 98[15] (WGI, 2020). Evidence suggests that natural resources in countries with quality institutions contribute to economic growth (Mehlum et al., 2012).

Further factors that contributed to reduce the degree of dependency on natural resources in Norway are the market friendly policies to develop businesses. At first, Norway has benefited from natural resource rents to develop higher human capital which in turn with relatively strong institutions the direct negative impact of natural resource on growth was offset (Van der Ploeg, 2011). It is thus important to accelerate different policies towards market development such as labour market policy, bank and financial development, taxation and other policies. Consequently, in a higher degree of financial development country such as Norway, macroeconomic volatility is offset which is the main channel delivering the natural resource curse (Van der Ploeg, 2011). Regarding the fiscal reaction function of the Norwegian government, the national taxation system is subjected to the pension bill within public spending rather than hydrocarbon revenue (Harding & van der Ploeg, 2009).

Furthermore, Norway has experienced critical growth of manufacturing and the rest of the economy compared to other natural resource rich countries. The 'Dutch Disease' effect of the natural resource boom would crowd out the competitiveness of the other sector. As such, manufacturing production and its industrial sector would be drowned out through the adverse effects of both resource movement and spending effects (Frankel, 2012). However, in Norway the energy boom was used as an intermediate input to the manufacturing production process. Then, in return, the manufacturing sector provided the opportunities for domestic capital goods to be used in the energy sector (Hutchison, 1994).

A further example of a successful defeat of the issue of resource dependency comes from Indonesia, a resource rich country in Asia that has achieved a low degree of resource revenue dependency through economic diversification and industrialisation. The initial stages of development were led by the government. The Indonesian national government's pro-growth economic policies that changed the public and private sectors role, contributed to diversify exports. The government provided credit to the private sector for some manufacturing production (Gylfason & Nganou, 2016). Then, the private or public–private parties played a fundamental role in further funding for such development; the private sector has taken over some of the roles that had been traditionally attributed to the Indonesian government (Dieleman, 2011).

The private sector operates within the rules and regulations in the development process of Indonesia. It has contributed to a visible development through investments

---

[15] The data sources estimation is based on percentile rank among all countries ranging from 0 (lowest) to 100 (highest) rank.

in industrialisation, banks and real estate developments (Firman & Fahmi, 2017; Shaban & James, 2018). This contributed to diversify the Indonesian economy by declining the degree of dependency on petroleum export from 40.1% in 1977 to 7.4% by 2014 and expanding the share of manufactured goods from 2.3 to 40.2% within the same period (Ait-Laoussine & Gault, 2017). This led Indonesia to have a value advantage among the Organisation of the Petroleum Exporting Countries (OPEC) members with lowest petroleum export with productive manufacturing sector. As a result, Indonesia has witnessed visible economic growth with an average of 7% annually (Dieleman, 2011).

The review of abovementioned successful countries which overcame dependency on natural resources, reveals that diversification strategies towards less dependency on natural resources took place via a number of channels. These include the commitment of the private sector, political stability, strong institutions, public investment to improve infrastructure, investment in human development and manufacturing production.

2.6 Critics of the Previous Literature

From the literature, it is found that theories which deal with the political economics of industrialisation, natural resource dependency, privatisation and taxation, are applied to explain the dependency reduction policies of diversification discussed in the previous sections. Much of the empirical literature on the resource curse cited in this book are related to natural resource curse and economic growth (see for example: Badeeb et al., 2017; Havranek et al., 2016; Ji et al., 2014). So far, there is no empirical investigation studying the change in the degree of dependency on natural resources in response to private sector development and/or public sector development.

Previous studies have approached the problem of natural resource dependency in various ways. The majority of empirical studies were focused on measuring the relationship between natural resource abundance and economic growth (Arezki & Van der Ploeg, 2011; Badeeb et al., 2017; Venables, 2016). Furthermore, a large body of the natural resource studies were focused on the importance of institutional quality in overcoming natural resource dependency. While some scholars argue that institutional qualities are to be blamed (Bhattacharyya & Hodler, 2014; Cabrales & Hauk, 2011; Havranek et al., 2016; Ji et al., 2014), others blame the management of natural wealth for the emergence of the resource curse (Auzer, 2017; Williams, 2011). While this might be true for non-economic determinants, in general, the economic determinants are not broadly addressed.

A review of theoretical literature associated with privatisation provides several review articles, covering the main effects and conclusions. However, the private sector theory hitherto is not matured. Its empirical evidence is mostly driven from three types of research; case studies, cross sectional comparisons of performance between the private and public sector and statistical evaluation of firms before and after privatisation. Although the reviewed research has identified the determinants of promoting the private sector, there is no clear explanation of how exactly the private sector develops in the previous studies.

Research has mostly studied privatisation on the micro level. For example, Doh et al. (2004) and Marcelin and Mathur (2015) investigated the institution-level, firm-level and project-level factors that affect private versus state ownership. Others study the effects of country characteristics (Henisz et al., 2005; Ramamurti, 2003), selling assets during privatisation to foreign or domestic investors, (Bjorvatn & Eckel, 2011; Lin & Matsumura, 2018), the methods of privatisation (Estrin & Pelletier, 2018; Kurtishi-Kastrati, 2013) and privatisation and the change in government ownership (Inoue et al., 2013; Vaaler & Schrage, 2009).

Studies reviewed that are related to diversification strategies in resource rich countries have not been concerned with the importance of diversified factors of private sector development, and/or public sector development, in reducing the danger of resource curse. Although literature has identified diversification as a tool for turning natural resource curse into blessing, methodologically there were no model specifications to express the reduction of natural resource dependency. Previous studies have focused almost entirely on either natural resources and economic growth and/or on diversification and income growth rather than the relationship between economic diversification and resource dependency reduction.

For example, a key shortcoming of the natural resource literature is the lack of clear understanding of the role of the private sector in diversifying the economy of the resource rich countries. Few case studies have addressed the effect of the private sector in diversifying resource-based economies such as Cammett et al. (2019) and Shayah (2015), though, they did not measure the relationship between the private sector and resource dependency reduction or relative reduction in the degree of dependency. Neither resource dependency nor privatisation literature has examined diversification sourcing from private sector development to reduce the degree of dependency on resource revenue.

2.7 Summary

Dependency on natural resources comes from a single commodity in which its price is volatile and results in vulnerability of the resource rich countries to external shocks. One of the serious outcomes of this vulnerability is producing macroeconomic instability in which it would retard economic growth. However, economic diversification of private sector development and public sector development can be a long-lasting solution to reduce the degree of dependency on natural resources.

Economic diversification was linked to macroeconomic stability and sustainability in economic growth. In essence, industrialisation was viewed as the best tool to diversify the economy of the natural resource rich countries. Industrial diversification can be led by the private sector in the so-called 'production linkages' from resource commodity to manufacturing. In addition to reducing the degree of dependency on natural resources, taxation was recommended as another factor in promoting diversification. Taxation not only generates diversified revenue, but also strengthens accountability and the governance of the natural resource rich countries, and thus stimulates economic growth.

However, in order to successfully diversify, the government of natural resource economies should provide a positive background condition such as regulatory reform, infrastructure development and improved institutional capacity. As such, these policies will adjust the structure of the economy of natural resource rich countries.

A review of the literature related to economic diversification strategies in resource rich countries concludes that a dynamic relationship exists between human development and economic growth, and investment and economic growth. The reviewed research on human development and investment as inputs to the economic growth suggests that long-lasting improvement in both human development and a high level of infrastructure investments would derive economic diversification, and thereby economic growth.

Several countries which have successfully overcome the problem of dependency on natural resources were reviewed. It can be concluded that diversification strategies towards less dependency on natural resources in these countries took place through the commitment of the private sector, political stability, strong institutions, public investment to improve infrastructure, investment in human development and manufacturing production.

The theories of political economy of industrialisation, natural resource dependency, privatisation and taxation were used to deal with the abovementioned dependency reduction policies of diversification. A review of the economic literature associated with diversification strategies in resource rich countries has not approached the change in the degree of dependency on natural resource in response to private sector development and/or public sector development. Therefore, this research seeks to investigate the effect of private sector development, privatisation and taxation on reducing the degree of dependency on natural resources.

Bibliography

Acemoglu, D., Johnson, S., & Robinson, J. A. (2002). An African success story: Botswana. *SSRN Electronic Journal*. https://doi.org/10.2139/ssrn.290791

Acemoglu, D., & Robinson, J. A. (2012). *Why nations fail: The origins of power, prosperity, and poverty*. Crown Books.

Adams, D., Adams, K., Ullah, S., & Ullah, F. (2019). Globalisation, governance, accountability and the natural resource 'curse': Implications for socio-economic growth of oil-rich developing countries. *Resources Policy, 61*, 128–140.

Adelina-Geanina, I. (2011). Monetary policy and economic policy. *Journal of Knowledge Management, Economics and Information Technology, 1*(2), 1–20.

Afonso, W. B. (2013). Diversification toward stability? The effect of local sales taxes on own source revenue. *Journal of Public Budgeting, Accounting & Financial Management, 25*(4), 649–674.

Agartan, K. (2017). Beyond politics of privatisation: A reinterpretation of Turkish exceptionalism. *Journal of Balkan and near Eastern Studies, 19*(2), 136–152.

Ahmed, Z., Asghar, M. M., Malik, M. N., & Nawaz, K. (2020). Moving towards a sustainable environment: The dynamic linkage between natural resources, human capital, urbanization, economic growth, and ecological footprint in China. *Resources Policy, 67*, 101677.

Ait-Laoussine, N., & Gault, J. (2017). Nationalisation, privatisation and diversification. *The Journal of World Energy Law & Business, 10*(1), 43–54.

Akinyemi, B. (2011). An assessment of human resource development climate in Rwanda private sector organizations. *International Bulletin of Business Administration, 12*(1), 66–78.

Albassam, B. A. (2015). Economic diversification in Saudi Arabia: Myth or reality? *Resources Policy, 44*, 112–117.

Alvarado, R., Tillaguango, B., Dagar, V., Ahmad, M., Işık, C., Méndez, P., & Toledo, E. (2021). Ecological footprint, economic complexity and natural resources rents in Latin America: Empirical evidence using quantile regressions. *Journal of Cleaner Production, 318*, 128585.

Ansar, A., Flyvbjerg, B., Budzier, A., & Lunn, D. (2016). Does infrastructure investment lead to economic growth or economic fragility? Evidence from China. *Oxford Review of Economic Policy, 32*(3), 360–390.

Antonova, I. S., Bannova, K. A., & Solomahina, E. (2018). Diversification indexes: Arrangement and application possibility for company towns. *The European Proceedings of Social & Behavioural Sciences (EpSBS), 35*, 43–54.

Arezki, R., & Van der Ploeg, F. (2011). Do natural resources depress income per capita? *Review of Development Economics, 15*(3), 504–521.

Asher, S., & Novosad, P. (2018). Rent-seeking and criminal politicians: Evidence from mining booms. *SSRN*. https://doi.org/10.2139/ssrn.2812315

Atherton, A., & Smallbone, D. (2013). Promoting private sector development in China: The challenge of building institutional capacity at the local level. *Environment and Planning C: Government and Policy, 31*(1), 5–23.

Auty, R. (1993). *Sustaining development in mineral economies: The resource curse thesis*. Routledge.

Auzer, K. A. (2017). *Institutional design and capacity to enhance effective governance of oil and gas wealth: The case of Kurdistan region*. Springer.

Badeeb, R. A., Lean, H. H., & Clark, J. (2017). The evolution of the natural resource curse thesis: A critical literature survey. *Resources Policy, 51*, 123–134.

Bai, C.-E., Lu, J., & Tao, Z. (2009). How does privatisation work in China? *Journal of Comparative Economics, 37*(3), 453–470.

Banerjee, S. G., Oetzel, J. M., & Ranganathan, R. (2006). Private provision of infrastructure in emerging markets: Do institutions matter? *Development Policy Review, 24*(2), 175–202.

Barma, N., Kaiser, K., Le, T. M., & Viñuela, L. (2011). *Rents to riches? The political economy of natural resource-led development*. The World Bank.

Bastagli, F. (2015). *Bringing taxation into social protection analysis and planning*. Overseas Development Institute. http://www.odi.org/sites/odi.org.uk/files/odi-assets/publicationsopinion-files/9717.pdf

Ben Hammouda, H., Karingi, S., Njuguna, A., & Sadni Jallab, M. (2006). *Diversification: Towards a new paradigm for Africa's Development*. United Nations Economic Commission for Africa.

Bennett, J., & La Manna, M. (2012). Mixed oligopoly, public firm behavior, and free private entry. *Economics Letters, 117*(3), 767–769.

Berkowitz, D., Lin, C., & Ma, Y. (2015). Do property rights matter? Evidence from a property law enactment. *Journal of Financial Economics, 116*(3), 583–593.

Bernstein, T., & Lu, X. (Eds.). (2008). *Taxation and coercion in rural China*. Cambridge University Press.

Besley, T., & Persson, T. (2014). Why do developing countries tax so little? *Journal of Economic Perspectives, 28*(4), 99–120.

Bhattacharyya, S., & Collier, P. (2013). Public capital in resource rich economies: Is there a curse? *Oxford Economic Papers, 66*(1), 1–24.

Bibliography

Bhattacharyya, S., & Hodler, R. (2014). Do natural resource revenues hinder financial development? The role of political institutions. *World Development, 57*, 101–113.

Bjorvatn, K., & Eckel, C. (2011). Strategic privatisation in developing countries. *Review of Development Economics, 15*(3), 522–534.

Bjorvatn, K., Farzanegan, M. R., & Schneider, F. (2012). Resource curse and power balance: Evidence from oil-rich countries. *World Development, 40*(7), 1308–1316.

Boubakri, N., & Saffar, W. (2019). State ownership and debt choice: Evidence from privatisation. *Journal of Financial and Quantitative Analysis, 54*(3), 1313–1346.

Boutilier, R. G. (2017). Raiding the honey pot: The resource curse and weak institutions at the project level. *The Extractive Industries and Society, 4*(2), 310–320.

Boycko, M., Shleifer, A., & Vishny, R. W. (1996). A theory of privatisation. *The Economic Journal, 106*(435), 309–319.

Brautigam, D., Fjeldstad, O.-H., & Moore, M. (2008). *Taxation and state-building in developing countries: Capacity and consent*. Cambridge University Press.

Brown, J. D., Earle, J. S., Shpak, S., & Vakhitov, V. (2019). Is privatisation working in Ukraine? New estimates from comprehensive manufacturing firm data, 1989–2013. *Comparative Economic Studies, 61*(1), 1–35.

Busse, M., & Gröning, S. (2013). The resource curse revisited: Governance and natural resources. *Public Choice, 154*(1–2), 1–20.

Cabrales, A., & Hauk, E. (2011). The quality of political institutions and the curse of natural resources. *The Economic Journal, 121*(551), 58–88.

Cammett, M., Diwan, I., & Leber, A. (2019). *Is oil wealth good for private sector development?* (Economic Research Forum Working Paper 1299).

Cantore, N., Clara, M., Lavopa, A., & Soare, C. (2017). Manufacturing as an engine of growth: Which is the best fuel? *Structural Change and Economic Dynamics, 42*, 56–66.

Carreri, M., & Dube, O. (2017). Do natural resources influence who comes to power, and how? *The Journal of Politics, 79*(2), 502–518.

Chang, W. W., & Chen, F.-y. (2015). Optimal upstream SOE's managerial delegation and downstream industrial policy under successive duopoly. *SSRN*. https://ssrn.com/abstract=2414690 or https://doi.org/10.2139/ssrn.2414690

Chang, W. W., & Ryu, H. E. (2015). Vertically related markets, foreign competition and optimal privatisation policy. *Review of International Economics, 23*(2), 303–319.

Chen, T.-L. (2017). Privatisation and efficiency: A mixed oligopoly approach. *Journal of Economics, 120*(3), 251–268.

Chen, Y., Matzinger, S., & Woetzel, J. (2013). Chinese infrastructure: The big picture. *McKinsey Quarterly, 3*, 8–15.

Christiansen, H. (2011). *The size and composition of the SOE sector in OECD countries* (OECD Corporate Governance working papers 5).

Collier, P. (2010). The political economy of natural resources. *Social Research, 77*(4), 1105–1132.

Collier, P., & Hoeffler, A. (2009). Testing the neocon agenda: Democracy in resource-rich societies. *European Economic Review, 53*(3), 293–308.

Cook, P. (2006). Private sector development strategy in developing countries. In *Privatisation and market development: Global movements in public policy ideas* (pp. 78–93). Edward Elgar.

Cristina, A., & Marcel, F. (2012). The effectiveness of the tax incentives on foreign direct investments. *Journal of Public Administration, Finance and Law, 1*(1), 55–65.

Crivelli, E., & Gupta, S. (2014). Resource blessing, revenue curse? Domestic revenue effort in resource-rich countries. *European Journal of Political Economy, 35*, 88–101.

Dal Bó, E., & Dal Bó, P. (2011). Workers, warriors, and criminals: Social conflict in general equilibrium. *Journal of the European Economic Association, 9*(4), 646–677.

Darby, S. (2010). *The transparency and accountability initiative—Natural resource governance strategic summary* (S.E.B. Strategy Report).

Di Bella, J., Grant, A., Kindornay, S., & Tissot, S. (2013). *Mapping private sector engagements in development cooperation*. The North-South Institute.

Dieleman, M. (2011). New town development in Indonesia: Renegotiating, shaping and replacing institutions. *Bijdragen tot de taal-, land-en volkenkunde/Journal of the Humanities and Social Sciences of Southeast Asia, 167*(1), 60–85.

Dinh, H. T., Palmade, V., Chandra, V., & Cossar, F. (2012). *Light manufacturing in Africa: Targeted policies to enhance private investment and create jobs.* The World Bank.

Doh, J. P., Teegen, H., & Mudambi, R. (2004). Balancing private and state ownership in emerging markets' telecommunications infrastructure: Country, industry, and firm influences. *Journal of International Business Studies, 35*(3), 233–250.

Donaldson, D. (2018). Railroads of the Raj: Estimating the impact of transportation infrastructure. *American Economic Review, 108*(4–5), 899–934.

Ebert, L., & La Menza, T. (2015). Chile, copper and resource revenue: A holistic approach to assessing commodity dependence. *Resources Policy, 43*, 101–111.

Ekpo, A. H., Afangideh, U. J., & Udoh, E. A. (2014). *Private sector development and economic diversification: Evidence from West African states private sector development in West Africa* (pp. 97–110). Springer.

Erum, N., & Hussain, S. (2019). Corruption, natural resources and economic growth: Evidence from OIC countries. *Resources Policy, 63*, 101429.

Esteban, O.-O., & Roser, M. (2019). *Taxation.* Our World in Data. https://ourworldindata.org/taxation

Estrin, S., & Pelletier, A. (2018). Privatisation in developing countries: What are the lessons of recent experience? *The World Bank Research Observer, 33*(1), 65–102.

Eubank, N. (2012). Taxation, political accountability and foreign aid: Lessons from Somaliland. *Journal of Development Studies, 48*(4), 465–480.

Farooki, M., & Kaplinsky, R. (2013). *The impact of China on global commodity prices: The global reshaping of the resource sector.* Routledge.

Farooki, M., & Kaplinsky, R. (2014). Promoting diversification in resource-rich economies. *Mineral Economics, 27*(2–3), 103–113.

Fearon, J. D. (2004). Why do some civil wars last so much longer than others? *Journal of Peace Research, 41*(3), 275–301.

Fenochietto, M. R., & Pessino, M. C. (2013). *Understanding countries' tax effort* (IMF Working Paper. 13(244)).

Firman, T., & Fahmi, F. Z. (2017). The privatisation of metropolitan Jakarta's (Jabodetabek) urban fringes: The early stages of "post-suburbanisation" in Indonesia. *Journal of the American Planning Association, 83*(1), 68–79.

Frankel, J. A. (2012). *The natural resource curse: A survey of diagnoses and some prescriptions* (HKS Faculty Research Working Paper Series RWP12-014). John F. Kennedy School of Government, Harvard University.

Fukuyama, F. (2013). What is governance? *Governance, 26*(3), 347–368.

Fung, M. K., Ho, W.-M., & Zhu, L. (1999). Effects of government policy changes on the private sector development in a transitional economy: A long-run analysis. *Journal of Economic Development, 24*(2), 19–41.

Ghura, D., & Pattillo, C. (2012). *Macroeconomic policy frameworks for resource-rich developing countries.* https://www.imf.org/external/np/pp/eng/2012/082412.pdf

Gylfason, T., & Nganou, J.-P. N. (2016). Diversification, Dutch disease and economic growth: Options for Uganda. In S. Mahroum & Y. Al-Saleh (Eds.), *Economic diversification policies in natural resource rich economies* (1st ed., pp. 118–147). Routledge.

Haidar, J. I. (2012). The impact of business regulatory reforms on economic growth. *Journal of the Japanese and International Economies, 26*(3), 285–307.

Haouas, I., Yagoubi, M., & Heshmati, A. (2002). *Labour-use efficiency in tunisian manufacturing industries: A flexible adjustment model* (WIDER Discussion Paper).

Harding, T., & van der Ploeg, R. (2009). *Fiscal reactions to anticipated hydrocarbon windfalls and pension burden: Is Norway's stabilization fund prudent enough?* (OxCarre Working Papers).

Bibliography

Havranek, T., Horvath, R., & Zeynalov, A. (2016). Natural resources and economic growth: A meta-analysis. *World Development, 88*, 134–151.

Hayat, A., & Tahir, M. (2019). *Natural resources volatility and economic growth: Evidence from the resource-rich region* (MRPA 92293).

Hendrick, R., & Crawford, J. (2014). Municipal fiscal policy space and fiscal structure: Tools for managing spending volatility. *Public Budgeting & Finance, 34*(3), 24–50.

Henisz, W. J., Zelner, B. A., & Guillén, M. F. (2005). The worldwide diffusion of market-oriented infrastructure reform, 1977–1999. *American Sociological Review, 70*(6), 871–897.

Hickman, D. C., & Olney, W. W. (2011). Globalization and investment in human capital. *ILR Review, 64*(4), 654–672.

Hillbom, E. (2011). Botswana: A development-oriented gate-keeping state. *African Affairs, 111*(442), 67–89.

Hirschman, A. O. (1981). *Essays in trespassing: Economics to politics and beyond*. Cambridge University Press.

Hutchison, M. M. (1994). Manufacturing sector resiliency to energy booms: Empirical evidence from Norway, the Netherlands, and the United Kingdom. *Oxford Economic Papers, 46*, 311–329.

IMF. (2013). *Managing volatility: A vulnerability exercise for low-income countries*. International Monetary Fund.

Inoue, C. F., Lazzarini, S. G., & Musacchio, A. (2013). Leviathan as a minority shareholder: Firm-level implications of state equity purchases. *Academy of Management Journal, 56*(6), 1775–1801.

International Corporation and Development (ICD). (2019). *Economic growth: Private Sector development*. https://ec.europa.eu/europeaid/sectors/economic-growth/private-sector-development_en (23.01.2019).

Ismail, K. (2010). *The structural manifestation of the 'Dutch disease': The case of oil exporting countries*. International Monetary Fund.

Jalles, J. T. (2019). *On the cyclicality of social expenditure: New time-varying evidence from developing economies* (REM Working Paper Series, 082-2019).

James, A. (2015). The resource curse: A statistical mirage? *Journal of Development Economics, 114*, 55–63.

Jensen, A. D. (2011). State-building in resource-rich economies. *Atlantic Economic Journal, 39*(2), 171–193.

Jensen, N., & Wantchekon, L. (2004). Resource wealth and political regimes in Africa. *Comparative Political Studies, 37*(7), 816–841.

Jiang, X., He, X., Zhang, L., Qin, H., & Shao, F. (2017). Multimodal transportation infrastructure investment and regional economic development: A structural equation modeling empirical analysis in China from 1986 to 2011. *Transport Policy, 54*, 43–52.

Ji, K., Magnus, J. R., & Wang, W. (2014). Natural resources, institutional quality, and economic growth in China. *Environmental and Resource Economics, 57*(3), 323–343.

Kay, J. A., & Thompson, D. J. (1986). Privatisation: A policy in search of a rationale. *The Economic Journal, 96*(381), 18–32.

Keen, M. (2013). Taxation and development—Again. In *Critical Issues in taxation and development* (pp. 13–42). MIT Press.

Kirkpatrick, C. (2014). Assessing the impact of regulatory reform in developing countries. *Public Administration and Development, 34*(3), 162–168.

Klapper, L., Lewin, A., & Delgado, J. M. Q. (2011). The impact of the business environment on the business creation process. In W. Naudé (Ed.), *Entrepreneurship and economic development* (pp. 108–123). Springer.

Klemm, A., & Van Parys, S. (2012). Empirical evidence on the effects of tax incentives. *International Tax and Public Finance, 19*(3), 393–423.

Koven, S. G., & Lyons, T. S. (2003). *Economic development: Strategies for state and local practice*. International City/County Management Association (ICMA).

Kuczynski, P.-P. (1999). Privatisation and the private sector. *World Development, 27*(1), 215–224.

Kurlantzick, J. (2012, June 28). The rise of innovative state capitalism. *Bloomberg Businessweek.*

Kurtishi-Kastrati, S. (2013). The effects of foreign direct investments for host country's economy. *European Journal of Interdisciplinary Studies, 5*(1), 26.

Lardy, N. R. (2014). *Markets over Mao: The rise of private business in China.* Columbia University Press.

Leke, A., Lund, S., Roxburgh, C., & Van Wamelen, A. (2017). What's driving Africa's growth. *McKinsey Quarterly.*

Lin, C., Lin, P., Song, F. M., & Li, C. (2011). Managerial incentives, CEO characteristics and corporate innovation in China's private sector. *Journal of Comparative Economics, 39*(2), 176–190.

Lin, M. H., & Matsumura, T. (2018). Optimal privatisation and uniform subsidy policies: A note. *Journal of Public Economic Theory, 20*(3), 416–423.

Mahon, J. (2005). *Liberal states and fiscal contracts: Aspects of the political economy of public finance.* Paper presented at the Annual Meeting of the American Political Science Association, Washington, DC.

Majeed, M. T., Tauqir, A., Mazhar, M., & Samreen, I. (2021). Asymmetric effects of energy consumption and economic growth on ecological footprint: New evidence from Pakistan. *Environmental Science and Pollution Research, 28*, 32945–32961.

Mamkhezri, J., Muhamad, G. M., & Khezri, M. (2022). Assessing the spatial effects of economic freedom on forest-products, grazing-land, and cropland footprints: The case of Asia-Pacific countries. *Journal of Environmental Management, 316*, 115274.

Mankiw, N. G., Weinzierl, M., & Yagan, D. (2009). Optimal taxation in theory and practice. *Journal of Economic Perspectives, 23*(4), 147–174.

Mansour, M. (2015). *Tax policy in MENA countries: Looking back and forward.* International Monetary Fund.

Marcelin, I., & Mathur, I. (2015). Privatisation, financial development, property rights and growth. *Journal of Banking & Finance, 50*, 528–546.

McGuirk, E. F. (2013). The illusory leader: Natural resources, taxation and accountability. *Public Choice, 154*(3–4), 285–313.

Megginson, W. L., & Netter, J. M. (2001). From state to market: A survey of empirical studies on privatization. *Journal of Economic Literature, 39*(2), 321–389.

Mehlum, H., Moene, K., & Torvik, R. (2012). Mineral rents and social development in Norway. In *Mineral rents and the financing of social policy* (pp. 155–184): Springer.

Mehrotra, S., & Gandhi, A. (2012). India's human development in the 2000s: Towards social inclusion. *Economic and Political Weekly, 47*, 59–64.

Mejía Acosta, A. (2013). The impact and effectiveness of accountability and transparency initiatives: The governance of natural resources. *Development Policy Review, 31*(S1), s89–s105.

Mikesell, J. (2013). *Fiscal administration* (Nine). Wadswort Cengage Learning.

Mishrif, A., & Al Balushi, Y. (2018). *Economic diversification in the gulf region, Volume II: Comparing global challenges.* Springer.

Mohan, T. R. (2001). Privatisation: theory and evidence. *Economic and Political Weekly, 36*(52), 4865–4871.

Morris, M., Kaplinsky, R., & Kaplan, D. (2011). *Commodities and linkages: Industrialisation in sub Saharan Africa* (MMCP Discussion Paper; no. 13).

Morris, M., Kaplinsky, R., & Kaplan, D. (2012). "One thing leads to another"—Commodities, linkages and industrial development. *Resources Policy, 37*(4), 408–416.

Nabli, M. M. K., & Arezki, M. R. (2012). *Natural resources, volatility, and inclusive growth: Perspectives from the Middle East and North Africa* (Vol. 111). International Monetary Fund.

Nasser, A. (2019). *Introduction to ARAMCO initial public offering.*

Nellis, J. (1998). *Privatization in transition economies: An update* (World Bank Discussion Papers, pp. 13–22).

Newman, F. N. (2011). *Six myths that hold back America: And what America can learn from the growth of China's economy.* Diversion Books.

Nhema, A. G. (2015). Privatisation of public enterprises in developing countries: An overview. *International Journal of Humanities and Social Science, 5*(9), 247–256.

Nicholas, K. (1966). *Causes of slow rate of economic growth of the United Kingdom: An inaugural lecture*. Cambridge University Press.

Nissanke, M. (2011). *Commodity markets and excess volatility: Sources and strategies to reduce adverse development impacts*. Common Fund for Commodities. http://www.common-fund.org/data/documenten/CFC-Nissanke-CommodityMarketVolatility_Feb_2011.pdf

Nissanke, M. (2012). Commodity market linkages in the global financial crisis: Excess volatility and development impacts. *Journal of Development Studies, 48*(6), 732–750.

Norrbin, S. C., Pipatchaipoom, O., & Bors, L. (2008). How robust is the natural resource curse? *International Economic Journal, 22*(2), 187–200.

Odhiambo, O., & Olushola, O. (2018). Taxation and economic growth in a resource-rich country: The case of Nigeria. In J. Iwin-Garzynska (Ed.), *Taxes and taxation trends*. IntechOpen.

Ogwang, T., Vanclay, F., & van den Assem, A. (2019). Rent-seeking practices, local resource curse, and social conflict in Uganda's emerging oil economy. *Land, 8*(4), 53.

Pagano, M. A., & Hoene, C. (2010). States and the fiscal policy space of cities. In B. Michael, B. David, & Y. Joan (Eds.), *The property tax and local autonomy* (pp. 243–284). Puritan Press Inc.

Paler, L. (2013). Keeping the public purse: An experiment in windfalls, taxes, and the incentives to restrain government. *American Political Science Review, 107*(4), 706–725.

Parker, D., & Kirkpatrick, C. (2005). Privatisation in developing countries: A review of the evidence and the policy lessons. *Journal of Development Studies, 41*(4), 513–541.

Pelikan, P. (1993). Ownership of firms and efficiency: The competence argument. *Constitutional Political Economy, 4*(3), 349–392.

Pheko, M. M. (2013). Privatization of public enterprises in emerging economies: Organizational development (OD) perspectives. *International Journal of Business and Management, 8*(20), 25.

Popoola, O. O. (2016). Privatization of public enterprises in Nigeria: Critical success factors. *Journal of Law, Policy and Globalization, 49*, 85.

Popov, A. (2014). Credit constraints and investment in human capital: Training evidence from transition economies. *Journal of Financial Intermediation, 23*(1), 76–100.

Privatisation Barometer (PB). (2019). *Privatisation cumulative value*. Retrieved 22 January 2019, from http://www.privatizationbarometer.com/database.php

Ramamurti, R. (2000). A multilevel model of privatization in emerging economies. *Academy of Management Review, 25*(3), 525–550.

Ramamurti, R. (2003). Can governments make credible promises? Insights from infrastructure projects in emerging economies. *Journal of International Management, 9*(3), 253–269.

Reiner, C., & Staritz, C. (2013). Private sector development and industrial policy: Why, how and for whom? In v. d. Herausgegeben (Ed.), *Private sector development* (pp. 53–61). ÖFSE.

Rivera, M. A. (2017). The synergies between human development, economic growth, and tourism within a developing country: An empirical model for Ecuador. *Journal of Destination Marketing & Management, 6*(3), 221–232.

Robinson, J. (2013). Botswana as a role model for country success. In *Achieving development success: Strategies and lessons from the developing world* (pp. 187–203). Oxford University Press.

Rodriguez, F., & Sachs, J. D. (1999). Why do resource-abundant economies grow more slowly? *Journal of Economic Growth, 4*(3), 277–303.

Ross, M. (2001). Does oil hinder democracy? *World Politics, 53*(3), 325–361.

Ross, M. (2012). *The oil curse: How petroleum wealth shapes the development of nations*. Princeton University Press.

Rostow, W. (1990). *The stages of economic growth: A non-communist manifesto* (3rd ed.). Cambridge University Press.

Sachs, J. D., & Warner, A. M. (2001). The curse of natural resources. *European Economic Review, 45*(4–6), 827–838.

Schoneveld, G., & Zoomers, A. (2015). Natural resource privatisation in sub-Saharan Africa and the challenges for inclusive green growth. *International Development Planning Review, 37*(1), 95–118.

Schulpen, L., & Gibbon, P. (2002). Private sector development: Policies, practices and problems. *World Development, 30*(1), 1–15.

Sebudubudu, D. (2010). The impact of good governance on development and poverty in Africa: Botswana—A relatively successful African initiative. *African Journal of Political Science and International Relations, 4*(7), 249.

Sekwati, L. (2010). Botswana: A note on economic diversification. *Botswana Journal of Economics, 7*(11), 79–85.

Shaban, M., & James, G. A. (2018). The effects of ownership change on bank performance and risk exposure: Evidence from Indonesia. *Journal of Banking & Finance, 88*, 483–497.

Shayah, M. H. (2015). Economic diversification by boosting non-oil exports (case of UAE). *Journal of Economics, Business and Management, 3*(7), 735–738.

Shi, Y., & Tao, J. (2018). 'Faulty' fiscal illusion: Examining the relationship between revenue diversification and tax burden in major US cities across the economic cycle. *Local Government Studies, 44*(3), 416–435.

Singaravelloo, K. (2017). PPP: The right marriage between local government and the private sector in Malaysia? *International Journal of Institutions and Economies, 2*, 142–166.

Singh, D., Pattnaik, C., Gaur, A. S., & Ketencioglu, E. (2018). Corporate expansion during pro-market reforms in emerging markets: The contingent value of group affiliation and diversification. *Journal of Business Research, 82*, 220–229.

Sinha, S., Beijer, A., Hawkins, J., & Teglund, A. (2001). Approach and organization of Sida support to private sector development. *Sida Evaluation Report, 1*, 14.

Smith, B. (2015). The resource curse exorcised: Evidence from a panel of countries. *Journal of Development Economics, 116*, 57–73.

Spulber, N. (2006). *Redefining the state: Privatization and welfare reform in industrial and transitional economies.* Cambridge University Press.

Storm, S. (2017). The political economy of industrialization: Introduction to development and change virtual issue. *Development and Change*, 1–19. https://doi.org/10.1111/dech.12281

Su, D., & Yao, Y. (2017). Manufacturing as the key engine of economic growth for middle-income economies. *Journal of the Asia Pacific Economy, 22*(1), 47–70.

Suri, T., Boozer, M. A., Ranis, G., & Stewart, F. (2011). Paths to success: The relationship between human development and economic growth. *World Development, 39*(4), 506–522.

Su, Y., & Liu, Z. (2016). The impact of foreign direct investment and human capital on economic growth: Evidence from Chinese cities. *China Economic Review, 37*, 97–109.

Tanzi, V. (2011). *Government versus markets: The changing economic role of the state.* Cambridge University Press.

Toye, J. (1993). *Dilemmas of development: Reflections on the counter-revolution in development economics.* Blackwell Oxford.

Tura, H. A. (2018). Land rights and land grabbing in Oromia, Ethiopia. *Land Use Policy, 70*, 247–255.

Ulucak, R., & Khan, S. U.-D. (2020). Determinants of the ecological footprint: Role of renewable energy, natural resources, and urbanization. *Sustainable Cities and Society, 54*, 101996.

Usman, M., Makhdum, M. S. A., & Kousar, R. (2021). Does financial inclusion, renewable and non-renewable energy utilization accelerate ecological footprints and economic growth? Fresh evidence from 15 highest emitting countries. *Sustainable Cities and Society, 65*, 102590.

Vaaler, P. M., & Schrage, B. N. (2009). Residual state ownership, policy stability and financial performance following strategic decisions by privatizing telecoms. *Journal of International Business Studies, 40*(4), 621–641.

Van der Ploeg, F. (2010). Why do many resource-rich countries have negative genuine saving?: Anticipation of better times or rapacious rent seeking. *Resource and Energy Economics, 32*(1), 28–44.

Bibliography

Van der Ploeg, F. (2011). Natural resources: Curse or blessing? *Journal of Economic Literature, 49*(2), 366–420.

Venables, A. J. (2016). Using natural resources for development: Why has it proven so difficult? *Journal of Economic Perspectives, 30*(1), 161–184.

Vining, A. R., & Weimer, D. L. (2016). The challenges of fractionalized property rights in public-private hybrid organizations: The good, the bad, and the ugly. *Regulation & Governance, 10*(2), 161–178.

Von Haldenwang, C., & Ivanyna, M. (2018). Does the political resource curse affect public finance? The vulnerability of tax revenue in resource-dependent countries. *Journal of International Development, 30*(2), 323–344.

Wade, R. H. (2014). Market versus state or market with state: How to impart directional thrust. *Development and Change, 45*(4), 777–798.

Wang, L. F., & Chen, T.-L. (2010). Do cost efficiency gap and foreign competitors matter concerning optimal privatization policy at the free entry market? *Journal of Economics, 100*(1), 33–49.

Wang, L. F., & Chen, T.-L. (2011). Mixed oligopoly, optimal privatization, and foreign penetration. *Economic Modelling, 28*(4), 1465–1470.

WDI. (2018). *Natural resource contribution to GDP*. Retrieved 23 January 2019, from World Bank.

Weber, J. G. (2014). A decade of natural gas development: The makings of a resource curse? *Resource and Energy Economics, 37*, 168–183.

WGI. (2020). *World Governance Indicators*. Retrieved 15 January 2020, from World Bank.

Williams, A. (2011). Shining a light on the resource curse: An empirical analysis of the relationship between natural resources, transparency, and economic growth. *World Development, 39*(4), 490–505.

Williams, N., Jaramillo, P., Taneja, J., & Ustun, T. S. (2015). Enabling private sector investment in microgrid-based rural electrification in developing countries: A review. *Renewable and Sustainable Energy Reviews, 52*, 1268–1281.

Winiecki, J. (2013). *Resistance to change in the soviet economic system (Routledge revivals): A property rights approach*. Routledge.

Yarrow, G. (1999). A theory of privatization, or why bureaucrats are still in business. *World Development, 27*(1), 157–168.

Chapter 3
Methodology and Empirical Specifications

Abstract This chapter discusses the econometric issues with the estimation of panel data, system of equations and dynamic adjustment model. In doing so, the chapter discusses country heterogeneity and simultaneity effects related to the panel data. Then, the issues of the econometric model specification, model estimation and testing the speed of adjustment of the diversified factors towards minimum level of dependency on natural resource revenue (optimal level) are elaborated. This book establishes relationships between three diversification factors with natural resource rents to study natural resource economic dependency reduction. In examining this relationship, a number of estimation methods are used, including static linear regression model, traditional dynamic model and dynamic flexible adjustment model, which is linear neither in regressors nor in parameters. In this regard, the effectiveness of various policies has been examined in stimulating private sector and public sector development in natural resource rich countries. Indeed, estimating dynamic flexible adjustment models in investigating natural resource dependency reduction is econometrically challenging. This is because (a) the macro data on resource rich countries are typically unbalanced panel data, (b) the dynamic model is adjusting over time (i.e., a lagged dependent variable is included as a regressor), (c) the empirical model imposes no restrictions by allowing the speed of adjustment to be flexible (δ_{it}) and (d) in estimating the relationship between each diversified factor of PSD, privatisation and taxation with natural resource dependency, two-ways or multiple-ways of causality between each pair and all dependent variables are introduced. In such a relationship where the system is interdependent, therefore, (e) the dynamic flexible adjustment model is estimated as a system of equations.

Keywords Unbalanced panel data · Dynamic flexible adjustment model · Static model · Speed of adjustment · System of equations · Optimal level

3.1 Introduction

The conducted literature review suggested a positive impact of economic diversification on the degree of dependency on resource revenue in the natural resource rich countries. In examining this relationship, different econometric models were applied, such as static and dynamic regression models.

This chapter introduces the methodology of the study, and the empirical specifications, namely the dynamic adjustment model and its adjustment speed, specified in forms of system of equations to establish a relationship between natural resource rents, private sector development, privatisation of the public sector and taxation.[1] Four empirical models are specified to achieve the objectives set in Chapter 1.

The country heterogeneity issue resulting from panel data estimation with respect to relative dependency on natural resource revenue is discussed. Countries that produce the same rents often experience different levels of dependency. Thus, the differences in the degree of dependency across countries are often determined by unobserved characteristics of those countries.

3.2 Econometric of Panel Data Estimation

Baltagi and Song (2006) describe panel data in which the main focus is on individual trends, while it presents the pooling of time series observations across for example, countries, regions, states, firms or households. Macroeconomic data in estimating panel data models has been a subject of great interest for macroeconomists (See for example Fischer 1993; Judson & Owen 1997; Mankiw et al., 1992).

The macroeconomic panel data model overcomes the problem of bias deriving from sample selection. It also allows the problem of endogeneity and omitted variable bias to be relatively controlled (Baltagi, 2015). Judson and Owen (1997) confirm the importance of using panel data on a country level to estimate a relationship, as it allows for controlling country characteristic effects.

Nevertheless, the characteristics of the panel data show that the panel data set and its technique have many advantages and limitations, that can be summarised as follows (Baltagi, 2008, 2015; Baltagi & Song, 2006; Khayyat, 2013):

1. Panel datasets have more variable 'individual differences' and less collinearity among the variables than other datasets. Therefore, dynamic effects can best be captured by using panel data.
2. More informative panel data provides more reliable estimates with less restrictive assumptions. Panel data has more ability to control individual heterogeneity, in

---

[1] The data analysis in this book is more than correlational study. Correlation relationship is simple unconditional relationship between two variables. This study dealt with more than correlation and capture effects relationship conditional on several other control variables. To support the effect study specification and estimation tests are used accounting for simultaneity, endogeneity and interdependence which make the result to differ from simple correlation.

3.2 Econometric of Panel Data Estimation

which, the freedom of unobserved individual-specific effects would derive bias in the estimation results.

3. Panel datasets have a better ability to identify and estimate effects, it cannot be simply captured in cross-sectional (like heterogeneity) and time series (like dynamics) data. For example, in the case of omitted variable bias, where the missing explanatory variables that are correlated with other explanatory variables, are not reported in the regression, panel datasets may allow eliminate the effect of the omitted variable in this case.

Although there are several advantages associated with using panel data, there are also some limitations compared with other types of data sets such as the cross-sectional and time series as follows (Baltagi, 2008, 2015; Greene, 2012):

1. panel datasets suffer from the problem of nonresponse and measurement errors. Although these problems are negligible in country-level panel data cases, this problem would result in selectivity bias from non-randomness of the population sample (Greene, 2012).
2. Another limitation is that eliminating the effect of the omitted variable bias in panel data in a nonlinear regression model is complicated. Rather, fixed effect and random effect models are often used to deal with this issue.
3. A further limitation is that subjects may drop out of the sample as they are no longer available. This attrition is a common source of unbalanced data and could cause a bias in the inference drawn from the sample population (Baltagi, 2015).

It is possible for country-level panel data to be either balanced or unbalanced. Greene (2012) defines both types of datasets; a dataset is called to be a balanced panel where each individual in the dataset is observed the same number of times, if not each individual observed in every time, this is an unbalanced panel data. The unbalanced nature of country-level data is attributed to limited data availability. Unbalance occurs due to one, or a combination of the following factors existing; delayed entry, early exit and/or intermittent nonresponse (Kerstens & Van de Woestyne, 2014). Non-responses are also labelled missing data, which Baltagi and Song (2006) believe is a potential source of bias, i.e., attrition bias. However, attrition, non-response, exit and entry are attributed to micro-level panel data.

Baltagi (2015) states that the missing observation of time series data in macroeconomic panel data is due to either aggregation to a lower frequency, or differences in periodic observation of recording data which is typical in empirical analysis. For instance, in recording typical data, some countries might start recording a period later than others, or for some reason stop recording this type of data. This feature is known as unbalanced or incomplete panels (Baltagi & Song, 2006). Most statistical packages manage unbalanced panel data. However, in dynamic panel data the gap length is important. The number of time periods affects also the consistency of the estimators.

Baltagi and Song (2006) recommend using panel data sets to study complex issues of dynamic behaviour. Greene (2012) states that dynamic effects in panel data models raise complex issues in estimation. When dynamic effects and parameter heterogeneity coincide in a panel dataset, common estimation techniques such as ordinary least square (OLS) and feasible generalised least square (FGLS) are not effective. Avoiding the problem of endogeneity in using dynamic flexible model nevertheless, is presented, as one of the solutions to effectively estimate panel data models (Greene, 2012).

3.3 Empirical Specifications

Over the last decades the dynamic modelling approach has been growing, but it has been mainly at firm levels. The very first recognition of applying a dynamic flexible adjustment model for panel data in the study of capital structure is attempted by S. Banerjee et al. (2004).[2] Heshmati (2002) extended and developed the previous mostly theoretical models by simultaneously endogenising the adjustment factors and the financial target. However, as stated by Haouas et al. (2002), the method of flexible dynamic adjustment can be applied to other forms of dynamic model within a panel data framework.

3.3.1 The Speed of Adjustment

The first use of the adjustment concept was in the study of cost of production (firm productivity) in the neoclassical theory of firms by Eisner and Strotz (1963). Accordingly, two types of adjustment costs were defined. First, the external adjustment cost, such as input factors of production, was based on competitive prices of the market and additional purchase of unit inputs. The second type was internal adjustment cost, such as capital input of the firm and all firms' affairs sourced internally.

The main purpose of introducing the adjustment speed parameters to the literature was originally because there are two types of inputs in production: in the short-term firms have fixed costs inputs and variable costs inputs but in the long-term firms have variable costs inputs. While adjustment only takes place over time in which input factors of production are considered variable, immediate adjustment within a period is costly. Therefore, firms might only partially adjust in the long term; the adjustment cost through some functions of the amount of investment in quasi-fixed inputs is included in the firm's dynamic optimisation. This feature was proposed by C. Morrison (1986). Later, the concept of the quasi or partial adjustment was refined in the studies of dynamic factor demand and dynamic capital structure by Prucha and Nadiri (1986), and Vasavada and Ball (1988), and more recently by Khayyat (2017) and Heshmati (2002) respectively.

---

[2] The paper is written in 1999 and broadly cited in CiteSeer, but its publication in the cited reference was delayed to 2004.

3.3 Empirical Specifications

The adjustment parameter is specified in terms of factors affecting the speed of adjustment. The adjustment parameter plays a significant role in addressing the effectiveness of the factors; it is related to country-specific characteristics (denoted as δ_{it}). Thus the speed of adjustment can be controlled to attain the optimal level of the dependent variables (Banerjee et al., 2004; Heshmati, 2002; Kumbhakar et al., 2002). Despite a strong theoretical background of dynamic factor demand and dynamic capital structure, the adjustment speed was restricted by estimating as constant and similar for all units, i.e. $(1 - \delta)Y_{it-1}$ (Baltagi & Griffin, 1997; Bhattacharyya, 2012; Kumbhakar et al., 1997; Rajbhandary, 1997).

The flexible adjustment parameter is 'an adjustment factor representing the magnitude of desired adjustment between two subsequent periods or the rate of convergence of the observed level (Y_{it}) to its optimal value (Y_{it}^*), (Kim et al., 2006, p. 282). The adjustment parameter is represented as follows;

a. If $\delta_{it} = 0$, there is no adjustment,
b. If $\delta_{it} = 1$, there is a full adjustment towards an optimal level within one period,
c. If $\delta_{it} < 1$, there is a partial adjustment when the observed level is below the optimal level, and
d. if $\delta_{it} > 1$, the diversified factors adjust more than necessary (Heshmati, 2002; Kim et al., 2006).

The latter might only occur individually for factors such as privatisation or taxation during, for example, over and rapid privatisation, once politicians have vested interests towards economic condition. But overall, time is required to adjust. The degree of over- or under-optimal adjustment can be attributed to the planning and implementation of policies which takes time and meanwhile internal and external conditions change.

The empirical literature surrounding the speed of adjustment in dynamic models is subject to ongoing debates. A number of scholars have proposed estimator's properties for partial adjustment models to be consistent with dynamic panel data estimation. Flannery and Rangan (2006) and Huang and Ritter (2009) suggest an instrumental variable fixed effect estimator for the speed of adjustment estimator to be potentially unbiased. Flannery and Hankins (2013) and Öztekin and Flannery (2012) proposed dummy variables to correct for least squares bias. Elsas and Florysiak (2015) proposed a doubly censored Tobit estimator to account for a fractional dependent variable to yield unbiased adjustment speed estimates.

There was an issue in empirical capital structure related to estimating the speed of adjustment. Controlling unobserved factors affecting the estimation of speed of adjustment was discussed in the empirical literate. Instrumental variable fixed effect estimator, dummy variables and a doubly censored Tobit estimators have been used to account for fixed effects in estimating partial adjustment models, although there is no precise and preferable one.

3.3.2 Flexible Dynamic Adjustment Model

The static model assumes zero adjustment cost which means countries can immediately respond to changing market conditions. The assumption of zero adjustment cost in static drew attention to the adjustment cost hypothesis to explain change which is dynamic. The speed of adjustment hypothesis provides an appealing rationalisation that the change from the actual to the desired value is costly. Proponents of this hypothesis argue that countries cannot adjust rapidly but rather they have an incentive to adjust slowly to minimise the risk associated with rapid adjustment (Heshmati, 2002; Vasavada & Ball, 1988). This adjustment can be captured by using a flexible dynamic adjustment model.

The speed of adjustment which is the magnitude of desired adjustment between two subsequent periods, provides helpful information to predict the optimal level of the dependent variables. However, the optimal (desired) level which is the sum of observed adjustment, and the change in the speed of adjustment which cannot be observed, thereby it must be estimated using observable country economics and policy characteristics (Widnyana et al., 2018).

Models of this type are considered in the literature with different applications. At first, it was used in the study of firm productivity by C. Morrison (1986). Later, a number of researchers such as Bhandari and Heshmati (2005), Haouas et al. (2002), Kumbhakar et al. (2002) and Ncube and Heshmati (1998) used dynamic flexible adjustment model in the study of labour-use efficiency. Others such as S. Banerjee et al. (2004), Elsas and Florysiak (2015), Heshmati (2002), and Kim et al. (2006) used a similar model to study dynamic capital structure. Vasavada and Ball (1988) used dynamic model estimation in the study of US agriculture and Berndt et al. (1979) used a similar model to analyse aggregate investment behaviour.

The nature of the optimal decision rule is quite well known in the literature. Literature addressed change by using lag, but this change was constant for every country which means that every year has the same change for every country, i.e., δY_{it}^* (Baltagi & Griffin, 1997; Bhattacharyya, 2012; Rajbhandary, 1997). This is not accurate as countries have different initial conditions and are acting in various ways, thus the optimal level must be variable by country and time (Banerjee et al., 2004; Heshmati, 2002).

The static model which fails to integrate the lagged adjustment, can be estimated using OLS. However, using OLS to estimate regression models would be biased and inconsistent, due to the correlation between the residual and the lag-dependent variable (Y_{it-1}). Baltagi (2015) and Nickell (1981) indicated that traditional standard methods of OLS or fixed effects in dynamic panel models may lead to seriously biased coefficient estimates.

The full information maximum likelihood (FMIL) approach has been used in advanced statistical packages to efficiently estimate parameters. The process begins by treating missing data and computing steps from one iteration to the next until the estimates converge (Allison, 2010). Although FMIL is not technically an imputation method to create a new dataset, it estimates parameters (Enders & Bandalos, 2001;

3.3 Empirical Specifications

Schlomer et al., 2010). Then, FMIL has two simultaneous advantages (Schlomer et al., 2010); one, the imputation procedure runs until it converges and two it computes accurate standard errors. Hence, FMIL is superior in correctly estimating standard errors (Larsen, 2011).

3.3.3 System of Equations

The analysis in system of equations is more complicated than in a single equation model. In a static linear model, estimating the model with OLS can be sufficient. However, in dynamic flexible adjustment model which is a mixture of nonlinear in regressors and nonlinear in parameters, due to the existence of endogeneity, OLS estimate will be biased (Baltagi, 2015; Greene, 2012). Although a dynamic model would account for endogeneity, there is an issue of interdependence between the variables. Greene (2012) considers the interdependence between the variables in an equilibrium model of demand and supply equations as follows:

$$\text{Demand equation: } q_{d,t} = \alpha_1 p_t + \alpha_2 x_t + \varepsilon_{d,t}, \tag{3.1}$$

$$\text{Supply equation: } q_{s,t} = \beta_1 p_t + \varepsilon_{s,t}, \tag{3.2}$$

$$\text{Equilibrium condition: } q_{d,t} = q_{s,t} = q_t \tag{3.3}$$

When the model is one of the joint determinations of two variables such as price and quantity, they are jointly dependent or endogenous variables. As such, there is an interdependence between all three equations as together they determine the equilibrium. Greene named this process a complete system of equation where the number of equations equal the number of endogenous variables. Therefore, a system of equations is valuable for controlling both endogeneity and simultaneity effects (Greene, 2012).

Regarding the estimation process, while the least squares estimations is common and straightforward in single equation applications, theoretical literature of systems of equations emphasises inconsistency which arise with the least squares application due to the correlation between endogenous variables and the disturbances. As such, a two-step estimation procedure for a system of equations is proposed where the system of equation is estimated with seemingly unrelated regression (SUR) or three-stage least square (3SLS), generalised method of moments (GMM) and FIML (Greene, 2012). Nevertheless, Klein (1960) claims that the choice between single equation and system of equations requires a comparison to be made.

3.4 Model Specification

The traditional methodology approaches found in the literature are extended in three directions in this research. One extension is the application of a traditional static model to a large sample of countries with heterogeneous resource abundancy and resource revenue dependency. The second extension is the application of a dynamic flexible adjustment model as the variables (to reduce the degree of dependency on natural resources) including private sector development, privatisation and taxation are inherently dynamic and therefore adjust over time. The third extension is the application of a complete system of equations. While the dynamic flexible adjustment model accounts for endogeneity, the interdependence between the variables remains unsolved. Thus, a system of equations is used to control for all the endogeneity, simultaneity and interdependency effects.

3.4.1 The Static Model

The econometric specification starts with the estimation of the standard static model by using OLS estimation method expressed as follows:

$$Y_{it} = \alpha_\circ + \sum \alpha_1 X_{it} + \varepsilon_{it} \tag{3.4}$$

where $\alpha_\circ$ is an intercept and $\sum \alpha_1 X_{it}$ is the deterministic part of the model with X being a vector of the determinants of variations in Y. i and t represent country and time, respectively. The model, which is linear in regressors is estimated with OLS.

3.4.2 The Dynamic Flexible Adjustment Model

This model assumes, similarly to the assumption of this study, that natural resource-dependent countries are experiencing a lack of economic diversification due to inefficiency in private sector development, privatisation and taxation system. Under such conditions the observed rate (value) of natural resource dependency denoted by (Y_{it}) is different from the desired level (rate) of economic diversification to reduce natural resource dependency denoted by (Y_{it}^*), and this implies that $Y_{it} > Y_{it}^*$.

Since the main focus of the research is natural resource dependency reduction,[3] the desired level of dependency (Y_{it}^*), is defined in this research as the minimum level

---

[3] This paper changes the focus from dynamic factor demand and dynamic capital structure to economic diversification to reduce natural resource dependency reduction. The methodology is quite similar to these two subjects, mainly the process of dynamic capital structure and its adjustment by Heshmati (2002). However, they are not identical as the estimation technique is different to fit with the purpose of this research.

3.4 Model Specification

of resource revenue dependency. It is reasonable to assume that the country i at time t in reality may not be able to produce complex goods on a globally competitive basis to achieve economic diversification with the objective of less dependency on natural resources. This means that the country is inefficient as it is more dependent on resource revenue than the optimal amount. Therefore, it is expected that these countries will invest with the objective of reducing the degree of dependency on natural resources to produce the target level of economic diversification. In other words, these countries will try to adjust towards an optimum level. In this research the optimal (desired level) can be specified as follows;

$$Y_{it}^* = f(Y_{it}, X_{it}, Z) \qquad (3.5)$$

where Y_{it} is the observed value per country and per time, X_{it} is a vector of the determinants of optimal level that are country and time variants, and Z represents a vector of dummy variables.

This adjustment towards optimal, however, is costly and countries cannot rapidly adjust with the objective of diversifying the economy within one period. Sudden changes in generating countries' revenues can have significant political and economic instability costs (Le & Viñuela, 2012), thereby they tend to adjust partially towards their optimal or desired target level. In this case the following relationship can be specified;

$$Y_{it} = Y_{it}^* * \delta \qquad (3.6)$$

where the value of δ is assumed to be greater than 1.

The value of δ will determine whether the country is efficient or not. If $\delta > 1$, this indicates that the country is inefficient and needs adjustment towards the desired level. If $\delta = 1$, this indicates that it is on the frontier. In other words, the natural resource-dependent country is achieving economic diversification that is globally competitive, whereas if the value of $\delta < 1$, this means that the country is over optimising.

These countries cannot rapidly adjust with the objective of reducing resource revenue dependency in the economy as the process is time-consuming and regulations have adjustment costs over time. Given these costly adjustment expenses, countries cannot fully adjust within a set period of time. The process of adjustment requires access to capital, investment in human capital, production plants, actual production and marketing of products and services. Therefore, countries may make only partial adjustments by introducing an adjustment factor δ_{it}.

By taking Eq. 3.6 and adding a lag effect, the following dynamic equation can be formulated:

$$Y_{it} - Y_{it-1} = (Y_{it}^* - Y_{it-1}) * \delta_{it} \qquad (3.7)$$

This implies in a dynamic setting that the change in observed dependency from the previous to the present time should be exactly equal to the change required for the country to be at optimal at time t.

The parameter δ_{it} represents the speed of adjustment to the targeted level, where $\delta_{it} < 1$. It is the magnitude of adjustment between two subsequent periods that can be interpreted as the degree of adjustment per period. In a traditional dynamic panel data model, the speed of adjustment is a constant (δ), which is a strong assumption. In this research restrictions are not imposed by allowing the speed of adjustment to be flexible (δ_{it}).

Adjustment speed varies over countries and time, and it is a function of different determinant variables, such as policy variables, which affect the adjustment speed. The generalisation of the speed of adjustment is testable. Therefore, δ_{it} is a function of some observable variables, that affect the implementation of private sector development, privatisation or taxation policy and its adjustment capacity to reduce dependency.

$$\delta_{it} = f(L_{it}, L_i, L_t) \tag{3.8}$$

L_{it} is a vector of the determinants of speed of adjustment that is changing both over time and across countries, and L_i and L_t are vectors of observable country and time-variant variables, respectively. Dummy and proxy variables are also included to capture the unobservable country and time-specific unobserved heterogeneity effects.

Haouas et al. (2002) claim that the method of flexible dynamic adjustment can be applied to other forms of dynamic model within a panel data framework. Then, by restructuring Eq. (3.7) and appending an error term ε_{it}, the full dynamic models which integrate with the stylised feature of lagged adjustment, incorporating with the speed of adjustment (for each of the observed diversification factors) can be written as follows;

$$Y_{it} = (1 - \delta_{it})Y_{it-1} + \delta_{it}Y^*_{it} + \varepsilon_{it} \tag{3.9}$$

$$\varepsilon_{it} = \mu_i + \lambda_t + \upsilon_{it} \tag{3.10}$$

where, in the literature of panel data, the error term is consisted of three components: μ_i which represents country-specific effects, λ_t which represents time-specific effects and υ_{it} which is a random error in the dependent variables, or the effect of unspecified independent variables in the model, which are assumed to be independently and identically distributed with normal distribution of mean zero and a constant variance, i.e. $N(0, \sigma_\upsilon^2)$ distribution.

In the econometric literature the country- and time-specific effects based on the nature of the data are treated as fixed or random. Nevertheless, the estimated model of this research has accounted for heterogeneity, simultaneity, endogeneity and unobserved fixed effects, by introducing a set of proxy variables and dummy variables and their interactions.

3.4 Model Specification

Completely accounting for a fixed effect or a random effect model in the current estimated model is not possible due to the presence of flexible dynamic adjustment model and over-parametrisation of the model. The data contains all countries with revenue from natural resources and corresponds to the population of countries. Thus, there is no need to estimate the model with random effects. Beside the system of equations are interdependent and this is reflected in the variance–covariance and its handling in the estimation process. The speed of adjustment is specified in terms of policy variables to influence the speed of adjustment endogenously.

The general functional relationships for the optimal level of each of the diversification factors individually in country i in period t, denoted as Y^*_{it} is a function of a set of X_{it} explanatory variables as follows:

$$Y^*_{it} = \alpha_\circ + \sum \alpha_1 X_{1it} \qquad (3.11)$$

where $\alpha_\circ$ is an intercept, X_1 is a vector of determinants of optimal level of PSD, privatisation, taxation and dependency, as well as other indicators individually, which are varied across country and over time. The speed of adjustment specified in terms of the observable determinant variable is:

$$\delta_{it} = \beta_{0+} \sum \beta_1 L_{it} \qquad (3.12)$$

Then, the non-linear dynamic equation (Eq. 3.9), its associated speed of adjustment and the optimal level (Eqs. 3.11 and 3.12), are jointly estimated by using an iterative non-linear estimation method (SYSNLIN in SAS[4]). Finally, to ensure the economic conclusion is unblemished, unobservable country-specific effects including the effect of time, country, size of privatisation, degree of dependency and the effect of resource types (oil and gas) are controlled.

3.4.3 The System of Equations

Estimating a regression model such as in Eq. 3.9, which is non-linear in parameters, depends on the relationships between the different indicators which may require an estimation method that accounts for endogeneity and simultaneity effects. Ignoring the problem of endogeneity and simultaneity may cause biased estimation, and potentially does not assure unblemished economic analysis (Greene, 2012). Although, the flexible dynamic adjustment model would account for endogeneity by integrating with lagged adjustment value; the lag of the dependent variable is lag variable (Y_{it-1}) (Greene, 2012; Heshmati, 2002), the problem of interdependence remains.

---

[4] The detailed procedure can be found in in the link: http://support.sas.com/documentation/cdl/en/etsug/63939/HTML/default/viewer.htm#etsug_syslin_sect007.htm.

The current research aims to estimate the optimal level of the determinants that affect dependency on natural resources, by allowing levels to vary across countries and over time. A combination of the three different policy measures of private sector development, privatisation, and taxation is expected to reduce dependency on revenues from natural resources. To do so, distinction between observed and optimal levels of the three factors is needed. The model with interdependent components which is described in the section above, is specified as follows:

$$\text{PSD}_{it} = (1 - \delta 1_{it})\text{PSD}_{it-1} + \delta 1_{it}\text{PSD}^*_{it} + \varepsilon \text{PSD}_{it} \quad (3.13)$$

$$\text{PuSD}_{it} = (1 - \delta 2_{it})\text{PuSD}_{it-1} + \delta 2_{it}\text{PuSD}^*_{it} + \varepsilon \text{PuSD}_{it} \quad (3.14)$$

$$\text{Tax}_{it} = (1 - \delta 3_{it})\text{Tax}_{it-1} + \delta 3_{it}\text{Tax}^*_{it} + \varepsilon \text{Tax}_{it} \quad (3.15)$$

$$\text{Dep}_{it} = (1 - \delta 4_{it})\text{Dep}_{it-1} + \delta 4_{it}\text{Dep}^*_{it} + \varepsilon \text{Dep}_{it} \quad (3.16)$$

To examine the factors of diversification of PSD, privatisation and taxation, the requirement functions (3.13, 3.14, 3.15 and 3.16) are considered, and defined to be effective in reducing the degree of dependency on resource revenues, by contributing to the economic diversification of natural resource rich countries.

Furthermore, numerous processes are involved to reach diversification to reduce dependency on natural resources. Privatisation is a dynamic phenomenon that requires a continuity to attain a diversified economy. The positive effect of privatisation on economic performance can be achieved if the economy is accompanied by regulatory reform, governance and opening up for competition. The tax reduction effect is conditional on functions and productivity of the public and private sectors' income generation, and capacity in tax payment, as well as the public institutions tax collection.

As such, taxation, which is highly state regulated, is inherently and dynamically a fiscal service that adjusts over time. It is not fully determined by only the taxpayer's choices and policymakers mind; it also depends on several factors including country-specific effects, level of income, institutional quality and fiscal capacity of the government. Therefore, it is costly for resource revenue-dependent governments to rapidly adjust privatisation or the tax system towards diversification with the aim to stabilise the economy (Robinson, 2013). Natural resource-dependent countries have incentives to adjust slowly over time to minimise the risks of economic decline associated with an immediate adjustment.

As presented below, the variables PSD^*_{it}, $PuSD^*_{it}$, Tax^*_{it} and Dep^*_{it} are respectively optimal or desired levels of private sector development, public sector privatisation, taxation system and dependency on natural resources. The vectors X_1, X_2, X_3 and X_4 are vectors of determinants of the optimal level of the dependent variables.

$$PSD^*_{it} = \alpha 1_\circ + \sum \alpha 1 X 1_{it} \quad (3.17)$$

3.4 Model Specification

$$PuSD_{it}^* = \alpha 2_\circ + \sum \alpha 2 X 2_{it} \qquad (3.18)$$

$$Tax_{it}^* = \alpha 3_\circ + \sum \alpha 3 X 3_{it} \qquad (3.19)$$

$$Dep_{it}^* = \alpha 4_\circ + \alpha 4_1 PSD_{it}^* + \alpha 4_2 PuSD_{it}^* + \alpha 4_3 Tax_{it}^* + \sum \alpha 4 X 4_{it} \qquad (3.20)$$

Natural resource-dependent countries typically respond to relative change in the economy by developing the private sector and/or restructuring their public sector through either privatisation or taxation decision. This change inherently and dynamically adjusts over time. This feature is similar to the dynamic capital structure adjustment, which also requires a dynamic adjustment model specification determined mainly by the investment cost (Elsas & Florysiak, 2015; Heshmati, 2002; Kim et al., 2006; Vasavada & Ball, 1988). As such, the speed of adjustment itself is a function of some underlying variables affecting adjustment costs:

$$\delta 1_{it} = \beta 1_\circ + \sum \beta 1 L 1_{it} \qquad (3.21)$$

$$\delta 2_{it} = \beta 2_\circ + \sum \beta 2 L 2_{it} \qquad (3.22)$$

$$\delta 3_{it} = \beta 3_\circ + \sum \beta 3 L 3_{it} \qquad (3.23)$$

$$\delta 4_{it} = \beta 4_\circ + \sum \beta 4 L 4_{it} \qquad (3.24)$$

The vector of coefficients $\delta 1_{it}$, $\delta 2_{it}$, $\delta 3_{it}$ and $\delta 4_{it}$ are speed of adjustment over time. The vectors L_1, L_2, L_3 and L_4 are policy variables determining the speeds of adjustment. The speed of adjustment, which is a magnitude of desired adjustment between two subsequent periods, provides helpful information to predict the optimal level of dependency reduction on resource revenue. However, the optimal level of dependency reduction on natural resources cannot be observed, thereby it must be estimated using observable country economics and policy characteristics (Widnyana et al., 2018).

The estimation of the optimal level of reducing dependency and the adjustment speed towards the target or optimal level, allow for effective and flexible adjustment of the reduction of the degree of dependency on natural resources. The speed of adjustment towards the optimal level is country and time specific. While because of the unforeseeable movement of the speed of adjustment, the factors that affect the desired level of dependency on natural resources cannot be expected, the model provides helpful information in predicting the future behaviour of diversification to reduce resource dependency.

In this study, the dynamic flexible adjustment models (that are non-linear in parameters) in resource revenue-dependent countries, are estimated as a system of equations. The main objective is to estimate a complete system consisting of four interdependent equations, considering the estimation of the variables PSD, $PuSD$ and *Tax* which are structural equations driven on the purpose of reducing *Dep* on natural resources. Because there are interdependence and two-ways or multiple-ways of causality between each pair and all dependent variables, they are labelled jointly dependent or endogenous variables. The former three equations are modelled to reduce the degree of dependency on natural resources; thus, the system is interdependent. System of equations and lag values or predicted values are used to deal with the problem of endogeneity and simultaneity effects (Greene, 2012). As such, this technique ensures the avoidance of the problem of endogeneity and simultaneity effects.[5]

The models are estimated as a complete system of four interdependent equations (Eqs. (3.13) through (3.16)), accounting for endogeneity and simultaneity, as well as controlling for country characteristics, heterogeneity effects and dynamics. The model allows for flexible adjustment speeds (Eqs. (3.21) through (3.24)) and specification of the desired or target levels of each indicator (Eqs. (3.17) through (3.20)), incorporating policy variables as determinants of speed of adjustment and target levels of the dependent variables.

In this research, the econometric specification uses an iterative procedure and convergence criteria which when converged will be equivalent to the FIML (Schlomer et al., 2010), and as such, is an efficient method of estimation. As stated by Banerjee, 'Convergence is obtained when the decrease in the sum of squared errors and the maximum change among the parameters is sufficiently small' (Banerjee et al., 2004, p. 10). The specification and estimation partially account for the fixed effects of country heterogeneity in the dynamic panel data model by interactive effects and size, income class and location categories without losing many degrees of freedom.

3.5 Summary

This chapter has discussed the econometrics model and estimation procedure at a general level. The problem of endogeneity and the interdependence between some of the explanatory variables in the presence of panel data were explored. The dynamic flexible adjustment models of diversification to reduce resource revenue dependency in resource rich countries were specified and estimated as a system of equations.

The country heterogeneity and testing for heteroskedasticity are also considered. Heterogeneity with respect to reducing the degree of dependency on natural resource revenue, in which in this book, contains country-specific and time-specific effects is essential when estimating panel data set. Countries that produce the same rents often experience different level of dependency on resource revenue. This study controls for several country characteristics in which it captures all these heterogeneities that exist in the data serving as substitute for the country-specific fixed effects.

---

[5] For wider understanding of how endogeneity and simultaneity arise see (Greene, 2012).

In addition to heterogeneity, heteroskedasticity is a further essential issue in estimating panel data model. The heteroskedasticity in the estimated models will be presented in the error term, although existing heteroskedasticity is reasonable in the model due to differences between groups of variables. In panel data model the variances are related to time, individuals and the variance that relates to random error combining them. Nevertheless, one of the advantages of using panel data sets is that it enables the econometric models to account for this heterogeneity and heteroskedasticity.

In examining this relationship, a number of estimation methods are used, including static linear regression model, traditional dynamic model and dynamic flexible adjustment model, which is linear neither in regressors nor in parameters and then, to test for the interdependence between the four models of PSD, privatisation, taxation and dependency, a complete system of equations with interdependence is specified and estimated.

Bibliography

Allison, P. D. (2010). *Missing data*. Sage.
Baltagi, B. H. (2008). *Econometric analysis of panel data* (4th ed.). Wiley.
Baltagi, B. H. (2015). *The Oxford handbook of panel data*. Oxford Handbooks.
Baltagi, B. H., & Griffin, J. M. (1997). Pooled estimators vs. their heterogeneous counterparts in the context of dynamic demand for gasoline. *Journal of Econometrics, 77*(2), 303–327.
Baltagi, B. H., & Song, S. H. (2006). Unbalanced panel data: A survey. *Statistical Papers, 47*(4), 493–523.
Banerjee, S., Heshmati, A., & Wihlborg, C. (2004). The dynamics of capital structure. *Research in Banking and Finance, 4*(1), 275–297.
Berndt, E., Fuss, M., & Waverman, L. (1979). *A dynamic model of cost of adjustment and interrelated factor demands* (Institute for Policy Analysis Working Paper, 7925).
Bhandari, A. K., & Heshmati, A. (2005). Labour use and its adjustment in Indian manufacturing industries. *Global Economic Review, 34*(3), 261–290.
Bhattacharyya, A. (2012). Adjustment of inputs and measurement of technical efficiency: A dynamic panel data analysis of the Egyptian manufacturing sectors. *Empirical Economics, 42*(3), 863–880.
Eisner, R., & Strotz, R. H. (1963). *Determinants of business investment*. Prentice-Hall.
Elsas, R., & Florysiak, D. (2015). Dynamic capital structure adjustment and the impact of fractional dependent variables. *Journal of Financial and Quantitative Analysis, 50*(5), 1105–1133.
Enders, C. K., & Bandalos, D. L. (2001). The relative performance of full information maximum likelihood estimation for missing data in structural equation models. *Structural Equation Modeling, 8*(3), 430–457.
Fischer, S. (1993). The role of macroeconomic factors in growth. *Journal of Monetary Economics, 32*(3), 485–512.
Flannery, M. J., & Hankins, K. W. (2013). Estimating dynamic panel models in corporate finance. *Journal of Corporate Finance, 19*, 1–19.
Flannery, M. J., & Rangan, K. P. (2006). Partial adjustment toward target capital structures. *Journal of Financial Economics, 79*(3), 469–506.

Greene, W. H. (2012). *Econometric analysis.* Pearson Education.
Haouas, I., Yagoubi, M., & Heshmati, A. (2002). *Labour-use efficiency in Tunisian manufacturing industries: A flexible adjustment model* (WIDER Discussion Paper).
Heshmati, A. (2002). The dynamics of capital structure: Evidence from Swedish micro and small firms. *Research in Banking and Finance, 2*(1), 199–241.
Huang, R., & Ritter, J. R. (2009). Testing theories of capital structure and estimating the speed of adjustment. *Journal of Financial and Quantitative Analysis, 44*(2), 237–271.
Judson, R. A., & Owen, A. L. (1997). *Estimating dynamic panel data models: A practical guide for macroeconomists.* Federal Reserve Board of Governors. Finance and Economics Discussion Series, 3.
Kerstens, K., & Van de Woestyne, I. (2014). Comparing Malmquist and Hicks–Moorsteen productivity indices: Exploring the impact of unbalanced vs. balanced panel data. *European Journal of Operational Research, 233*(3), 749–758.
Khayyat, N. T. (2013). *Exploring demand for energy in the South Korean industries.* Doctoral dissertation, SMC University, Zurich, Switzerland.
Khayyat, N. T. (2017). *ICT investment for energy use in the industrial sectors.* Springer.
Kim, H., Heshmati, A., & Aoun, D. (2006). Dynamics of capital structure: The Case of Korean listed manufacturing companies. *Asian Economic Journal, 20*(3), 275–302.
Klein, L. R. (1960). Single equation vs. equation system methods of estimation in econometrics. *Econometrica: Journal of the Econometric Society,* 866–871.
Kumbhakar, S. C., Heshmati, A., & Hjalmarsson, L. (1997). Temporal patterns of technical efficiency: Results from competing models. *International Journal of Industrial Organization, 15*(5), 597–616.
Kumbhakar, S. C., Heshmati, A., & Hjalmarsson, L. (2002). How fast do banks adjust? A dynamic model of labor-use with an application to Swedish banks. *Journal of Productivity Analysis, 18*(1), 79–102.
Larsen, R. (2011). Missing data imputation versus full information maximum likelihood with second-level dependencies. *Structural Equation Modeling: A Multidisciplinary Journal, 18*(4), 649–662.
Le, T. M., & Viñuela, L. (2012). *The political economy of natural resource taxation: Building credibility and investing in tax administration capacity.* Retrieved from Washington, DC. http://documents.worldbank.org/curated/en/888451468167353276/The-political-economy-of-nat ural-resource-taxation-building-credibility-and-investing-in-tax-administration-capacity
Mankiw, N. G., Romer, D., & Weil, D. N. (1992). A contribution to the empirics of economic growth. *The Quarterly Journal of Economics, 107*(2), 407–437.
Morrison, C. (1986). The impact of Quasi-fixed inputs in US and Japanese manufacturing: A development and application of the generalized Leontief restricted cost function. *Review of Economics and Statistics, 70*(2), 275–287.
Ncube, M., & Heshmati, A. (1998). A flexible adjustment model of employment with application to Zimbabwe's manufacturing industries. *Journal of Productivity Analysis, 18*(1), 79–102.
Nickell, S. (1981). Biases in dynamic models with fixed effects. *Econometrica: Journal of the Econometric Society,* 1417–1426.
Öztekin, Ö., & Flannery, M. J. (2012). Institutional determinants of capital structure adjustment speeds. *Journal of Financial Economics, 103*(1), 88–112.
Prucha, I. R., & Nadiri, M. I. (1986). A comparison of alternative methods for the estimation of dynamic factor demand models under non-static expectations. *Journal of Econometrics, 33*(1–2), 187–211.
Rajbhandary, A. (1997). *Capital structure of firms in developing countries: Results for India* (Unpublished Manuscript).
Robinson, J. (2013). Botswana as a role model for country success. In *Achieving development success: Strategies and lessons from the developing world* (pp. 187–203).

Schlomer, G. L., Bauman, S., & Card, N. A. (2010). Best practices for missing data management in counseling psychology. *Journal of Counseling Psychology, 57*(1), 1.

Vasavada, U., & Ball, V. E. (1988). A dynamic adjustment model for US agriculture: 1948–79. *Agricultural Economics, 2*(2), 123–137.

Widnyana, I. W., Warmana, G. O., & Suarjana, I. W. (2018). The determinantand speed adjustment of bank capital structure in Indonesia. *Academy of Social Science Journal, 3*(7), 1222–1225.

Chapter 4
Data Presentation and Analysis

Abstract This chapter covers a variety of variables so as to identify the most important factors influencing private sector development, privatisation and taxation in the context of natural resource rich countries. It continues to introduce the description of data. In the elaboration of the data source, types and collection procedure, attention has been paid to the complementary role of non-economic factors, including governance, political instability and institutional quality, along with traditional factors, in determining diversified factors of private and public sector development. The chapter discusses the sampling strategy and its selection from a population of countries. It also explains how the data go through various stages. The method is parametric and estimated the aggregation weights. It reduces the dimension of the data and minimises the problems of collinearity and subsequent confounded effects. Then, the full list of variables related to dependent and independent variables is reported based on the literature, their relevance and data availability. The chapter further discusses the classification of the selected sample of 110 countries of different sizes and of different political systems. It accounts for country-specific and time-specific effects, by introducing two groups of dummy variables to capture country and time differences. Thus, attention is being paid to the multicollinearity issues and countries heterogeneity and variance heteroskedasticity. Then, summary statistic of the data is presented and explained how missing data is managed. The chapter, then provides the model specification and the estimation results of the traditional static model, the dynamic model, the dynamic flexible adjustment model, and the system of equations.

Keywords Non-economic factors · Sampling strategy · Multicollinearity issues · Heterogeneity · Heteroskedasticity · Principle component analysis

4.1 Introduction

This chapter continues to then describe the data for estimation. The data used in this study is aggregate country level. It constitutes an unbalanced panel for 28 years (1990–2017) comprises of information on a large sample of 110 countries that have heterogeneous natural resources revenue in developed, developing and emerging countries of different sizes and following different political systems. The total number of observations ranges from 937 to 1373 based on the estimation model used.[1] It is obtained from the World Bank's World Development Indicators (WDI), World Governance Indicators (WGI) and the United Nations Development Program (UNDP).

Several variables related to the dependent and independent are selected due to their relevance based on literature and data availability. Several new variables are computed for the analysis of the study using various method of computations. Some of the independent variables were constructed as composite indices using the principle component analysis (PCA). Further, dummy variables are also included as independent variables to capture country- and time-specific heterogeneity effects.

Over the sample period, many politically and economically significant developments took place which had a devastating effect on the sampled countries' economic diversification processes. As such, the period 1990–2017 was split into three time periods (decenniums) to better capture the flexible adjustment in the sampling countries towards their dependency reduction.

4.2 Data Presentation

4.2.1 Data Sources

The data used in this research is an unbalanced panel dataset, which includes a large sample of 110 natural resource rich countries of different sizes and political systems. The data consists of 1207 observations[2] observed from 1990 to 2017. It is obtained from the World Bank World Development Indicators (WDI), World Governance Indicators (WGI) and United Nations Development Programme (UNDP).

The WDI is a database which includes the World Bank's premier compilation of high quality cross-country, comparable data on various areas of development. The 2019 WDI database contains a 1,600 time-series cross-section of observations from as far back as 1960 for 217 world economies organised in various tables, sections and more than 40 country groups. The five data themes include poverty and inequality, environment, economy, states and markets and global links (WDI, 2018). In addition to the data source, the UNDP database provides the important human development statistics on a country level in collaboration with several organisations (UNDP, 2019).

The data is in percentage, mainly as shares of GDP reported in Table 4.1. Percentage data is widely used to describe different results in economics and other

---

[1] The number of observations is changed according to the models' due to missing unit values, use of lagged values, and different information.

[2] The number of observations is changed according to the models due to missing unit values, use of lagged variables and different set of information.

4.2 Data Presentation

sciences. This type of data is preferable because percentage is a simple and convenient way to present binomial data (Zhao et al., 2001). The main advantage of using percentages is that it addresses the need for no fixed value transformations and the elimination of inflation effects which vary greatly among the sample countries and over time.

The data collected was subjected to missing unit observations. In order to fully use the data and its potential, a series of imputations have been conducted.[3] The imputations were based on the countries own mean values in three rounds, if there are any missing data, (1) by mean obtained from a combination of countries and periods, in which three periods had already been created, (2) by mean of countries and (3) by mean of the year. The advantage of this data set is that it provides data series for almost all natural resource rich countries. Since the imputed values are generated from countries' own mean, it will not influence the estimation result to deviate from the average. The main benefit is that full information can be used in the estimation, generating correct and stable parameter estimates.

4.2.2 Sampling Strategy

As the dataset is an unbalanced panel dataset, the sample size is determined by data availability and selected from a population of countries. The provision of the data came in different stages. In the first stage, most of the measurements were taken from the database used either as regressors or response variables. The second stage was to reduce the dimension of several indicators substituted using composite indices. Key indicators of the measurements were subjected to a principal component analysis (PCA) to make composite indices for credit to the private sector, institutional quality and infrastructure as indicated in Tables 3.2, 3.3 and 3.4. PCA provides mathematical transformation for a number of correlated variables into fewer uncorrelated variables (Khayyat & Lee, 2015; Tausch et al., 2007). The method is parametric and estimated the aggregation weights. It reduces the dimension of the data and minimises the problems of collinearity and subsequent confounded effects. PCA enabled use of variables in multidimensional form.

Tables 4.2, 4.3 and 4.4 show the high correlations among several variables. The cumulative weights for the principle component 1 (PC1) for both institutional quality and credit to the private sector respectively forms 0.855 and 0.834 which indicate that around 85% and 83% of the variations in the data can be explained by the combination of determinants of these principle components. Most importantly, PC1 Eigenvalues in all three are greater than unity (2.5). For the infrastructure, although the cumulative weights for the principle component 1 (PC1) is 0.62, the PC1 Eigenvalues are greater than unity.

$p \leq 0.10 = {}^c, p \leq 0.05 = {}^b, p \leq 0.001 = {}^a$

---

[3] In statistics, imputation is the process of replacing missing data with substituted values (Van Buuren, 2018).

Table 4.1 Definition of variables (WBD: World Bank Database, UNDP; United Nations Development Programme)

Variables	Caption	Description	Source
Country	Code	110 natural resources countries are selected	WBD
Year	Period	1990–2017	WBD
Private sector Development	PSD3	Gross fixed capital formation, private sector (% of GDP)	WBD
Privatisation	Pusd2	Expense (% of GDP)	WBD
Taxation	Tax	Tax revenue (% of GDP)	WBD
Natural resource dependence	Dep1	Total natural resources rents (% of GDP)	WBD
Oil and gas	Dep2	The sum of oil and gas rent (% of GDP)	WBD
Diversification	Pusd1	Economic Fitness Ranking (1 = high, 149 = low)	WBD
Credit to the private sector	A01	Domestic credit provided by financial sector (% of GDP)	WBD
Credit to the private sector	A02	Domestic credit to private sector (% of GDP)	WBD
Credit to the private sector	A03	Domestic credit to private sector by banks (% of GDP)	WBD
FDI inward	A04	Foreign direct investment, net inflows (% of GDP)	WBD
Economic growth	A10	GDP growth (annual %)	WBD
Governance	A15	Governance effectiveness: Percentile Rank	WBD
Political stability	A16	Political Stability and Absence of Violence/Terrorism: Percentile Rank	WBD
Regulation quality	A17	Regulation Quality: Regulatory Quality: Percentile Rank	WBD
Rule of law	A18	Rule of Law: Percentile Rank	WBD
Accountability	A19	Voice and Accountability: Percentile Rank	WBD

(continued)

4.2 Data Presentation

Table 4.1 (continued)

Variables	Caption	Description	Source
Human capital development	A20	Human Development Index (HDI)	UNDP
Fiscal factors	A21	Real Interest rate (%)	WBD
Trade openness	A25	Trade (% of GDP)	WBD
Public investment	C13	Gross capital formation (% of GDP)	WBD
Export	C01	Export: Exports of goods and services (% of GDP)	WBD
Import	C02	Import: Imports of goods and services (% of GDP)	WBD
Agricultural production	C19	Agriculture, forestry, and fishing, value added (% of GDP)	WBD
Manufacturing production	C20	Manufacturing, value added (% of GDP)	WBD
Tax capacity	D01	Taxes on income, profits and capital gains (% of revenue)	WBD
Unemployment	C05	Unemployment: Unemployment, total (% of total labour force)	WBD
Wage and salary	C08	Compensation of employees (% of expense)	WBD
Subsidy	C17	Subsidies and other transfers (% of expense)	WBD
Total GDP	GDPtot	GDP (constant 2010 US$)	WBD
GDP per capita	GDPpc	GDP per capita (constant 2010 US$)	WBD
Population	Pop	Population, total	WBD

Table 4.2 Correlation coefficient of PCA for institutional quality

	A1	A2	A3
A1 Regulatory Quality: Percentile Rank	1		
A2 Rule of Law: Percentile Rank	0.854^a	1	
A3 Voice and accountability: Percentile Rank	0.742^a	0.750^a	1

	Eigenvalue	Difference	Proportion	Cumulative
1	2.566	2.277	0.855	0.855
2	0.288	0.145	0.096	0.951
3	0.145		0.049	1

$p \leq 0.10 = {}^c, p \leq 0.05 = {}^b, p \leq 0.001 = {}^a$

Table 4.3 Correlation coefficient of PCA for credit to the private sector

	A1	A2	A3
A1 Domestic credit by financial sector	1		
A2 Domestic credit to private sector	0.692^a	1	
A3 Domestic credit by banks	0.622^a	0.937^a	1

	Eigenvalue	Difference	Proportion	Cumulative
1	2.503	2.073	0.834	0.834
2	0.430	0.362	0.143	0.977
3	0.068		0.023	1

$p \leq 0.10 = {}^c, p \leq 0.05 = {}^b, p \leq 0.001 = {}^a$

Table 4.4 Correlation coefficient for PCA for infrastructure

	F1	F2	F3	F4	F5
Transport services for export	1				
Transport services for import	0.645^c	1			
Fixed broadband subscription	-0.041^a	-0.124^a	1		
People using basic drinking water	0.219^a	-0.219^a	0.113^a	1	
Access to electricity	0.269^a	-0.283^a	0.914^b	0.866^b	1

	Eigenvalue	Difference	Proportion	Cumulative
F1	2.107	0.966	0.621	0.621
F2	1.141	0.245	0.428	0.650
F3	0.897	0.171	0.479	0.829
F4	0.726	0.597	0.145	0.974
F5	0.129		0.026	1

$p \leq 0.10 = {}^c, p \leq 0.05 = {}^b, p \leq 0.001 = {}^a$

4.2 Data Presentation

The main variables used in this study, in addition to the abovementioned composite indices, include but are not limited to, private investment, government expenses, tax revenue and natural resource rents. Almost all the variables are in percentage which makes fixed price transformation of monetarily measured variables unnecessary. Descriptions of the computed variables used are presented in Table 4.1.

4.2.3 The Dependent and Independent Variables

This research and its quality of the econometric models depend on both the dependent and independent variables. The full list of variables related to dependent and independent variables reported in Table 4.1 were selected by their relevance based on the literature and data availability. Some variables such as credit to the private sector, institutional quality, infrastructure, total investment, income groups, private sector size, degree of dependency group countries and several new variables were computed and reported in Table 4.5.

The dependent variable 'private sector development' is correlated to a set of explanatory variables that affect the private sector in the context of natural resource countries. To measure the private sector development in this research, this study followed Ben Hammouda et al. (2006), and Cammett et al. (2019), in which, private investment is used, and captured by its share in the Gross fixed capital formation.

There have been some arguments in the privatisation literature considering a precise measurement for capturing the effect of country level of privatisation. The country-level determinant of the private sector is believed to be the most significant variable, because privatisation decision is political rather than economic, and it does not occur until the country ruling parties are motivated (Bortolotti & Pinotti, 2008; Ramamurti, 2000).

Furthermore, the macroeconomic effects of privatisation have not been broadly discussed in the theoretical literature (Sheshinski & López-Calva, 2003). This reflects the macro empirical investigation of measuring privatisation. Some of the literature has made indices to measure privatisation, or made a comparison between the pre- and post-privatisation efficiency, or analysed the impact of privatisation on firms performance (See for instance: Arocena & Oliveros, 2012; Hagemejer et al., 2014; Németh & Schmidt, 2011).

Therefore, there is no precise measurement of privatisation at the macroeconomic level. Accordingly, this study used expense as a share of GDP to measure privatisation effect based on the third abovementioned objectives of privatisation addressed in the literature review chapter.

The dependent variable 'taxation' is affected by a set of explanatory variables that affect taxation system structure and its capability, including previous and upcoming dependent variables and time trend. Accordingly, two methods of measuring taxation effect on natural resource dependency have enriched the related literature. The first has used non-resource taxes as a dependent variable to measure taxation such as Crivelli and Gupta (2014), Knebelmann (2017) and Prichard et al. (2014). This

Table 4.5 List of computed variables

Variables	Formula	Caption
Credit to the private sector	PCA	Domestic credit provided by financial sector (% of GDP)
		Domestic credit to private sector (% of GDP)
		Domestic credit to private sector by banks (% of GDP)
Total investment	The sum of private and public investment	Gross fixed capital formation, private sector (% of GDP)
		Gross capital formation (% of GDP)
Institutional quality	PCA	Regulation Quality: Regulatory Quality: Percentile Rank
		Rule of Law: Percentile Rank
		Voice and Accountability: Percentile Rank
Infrastructure	PCA	Transport Services (% of service exports, BoP)
		Transport Service (% of service imports, BoP)
		Fixed Broadband Subscription
		People using at least basic drinking water services (% of population)
		Access to electricity (% of population)
OG dummy variable	if oil and gas = 2, then ogdumy = 1	The sum of oil and gas rent (% of GDP)

(continued)

4.2 Data Presentation

Table 4.5 (continued)

Variables	Formula	Caption
Time trend	trend = year-1989	Year
Period	if year < 2000, then period = 1; if 1999 < year < 2010, then period = 2; if year > 2009, then period = 3;	Year
Lower income	if gdppc < 725 then incgr = 1;	GDP per capita (constant 2010 US$)
Low middle income	if 725 < = gdppc < 1630 then incgr = 2;	
Middle income	if 1630 < = gdppc < 3500 then incgr = 3;	
Upper middle income	if 3500 < = gdppc < 7000 then incgr = 4;	
Higher income	if gdppc = > 7000 then incgr = 5;	
Private Sector Size	if PSD < 5.1, then PSgr = 1; if 9.1 < = PSD < 10.2, then PSgr = 2; if 10.2 < = PSD < 15.3, then PSgr = 3; if 15.3 < = PSD < 20.4, then PSgr = 4; if PSD = > 20.4, then PSDgr = 5;	Gross fixed capital formation, private sector (% of GDP)
Degree of dependency on natural resources	if NR < 10.01, then Depgr = 1; if 10.01 < = NR < 18.02, then Depgr = 2; if 18.02 < = NR < 24.03, then Depgr = 3; if 24.03 < = NR < 32.04, then Depgr = 4; if NR = > 32.04, then Depgr = 5;	Total natural resources rents (% of GDP)

research follows the second method, which measures traditional taxation by using tax revenue as a share of GDP, as a dependent variable, due to the unavailability of reliable data to some extent on non-resource taxes revenue, and its components, especially for resource rich countries (See for example: Ajaz & Ahmad, 2010; McGuirk, 2013; Von Haldenwang & Ivanyna, 2018). Another reason is that extracting the share of tax revenue that comes from resource activities is relatively difficult to achieve (Morrison, 2015; Prichard, 2016).

Dependency on natural resources is the main dependent variable that is correlated to a set of explanatory variables, including the abovementioned dependent variables and time trend. There are discussions around measuring economic dependence on natural resources. In this study, to measure economic dependency on natural resources, the measure of resource rents as a share of GDP was used, following the method of a number of scholars as presented in Table 4.6. This measure was initially developed by Richard Auty (2007). Total natural resource rents are the sum of oil rents, natural gas rents, coal rents (hard and soft), mineral rents and forest rents (WDI, 2018).

Regarding the independent variables, different determinants based on theory and data availability have been included. The independent variables are factors that affect the dependent variables. Investigation is made to assess correlations among them. Some variables were subjected to the principle component analysis to composite indices and they are included as independent variables. Furthermore, dummy variables are also included as independent variables to capture the country and time-specific effects.

Table 4.6 Common indicators to measure natural resource dependency

Indicator	Proxy	Authors
Natural Resource Dependence	Primary exports over GDP	Arezki and Van der Ploeg (2011), Beck (2011), Boschini et al. (2013), Neumayer (2004) and Sachs and Warner (1995)
	Natural resource share of GDP	Richard Auty (2007), S. Bhattacharyya and Collier (2013), S. Bhattacharyya and Hodler (2014), Boos and Holm-Müller (2013), Collier and Hoeffler (2009) and Hayat and Tahir (2019)
	Share of natural capital in national wealth	Gylfason (2001) and Gylfason and Zoega (2006)
	Share of mineral exports in total exports	Dietz et al. (2007)

Source Author's own construction, 2020

One of the independent variables is 'human capital development'. This variable is a geometric mean of the composite index of Human Development Index (HDI). The index is made from reducing the dimension of country level of human development, including health such as life expectancy index, knowledge such as education index and Gross National Income (GNI) index for the standard of living (UNDP, 2019a). Further independent variables are worldwide governance indicators. As presented in Table 4.5, each of these indicators captures the quality of governance. It is annual percentile rank indicators that have been adjusted to correct for changes over time. Countries are ranked from 0–100 corresponding to the lowest and the highest rank, respectively (WGI, 2020).

To capture the economic diversification effect, economic fitness measure is used as an independent variable. This is a measure of both a country's economic diversification and competitiveness in producing complex goods worldwide (W. B. World Bank, 2019). Accordingly, countries with low levels of economic fitness compared to other countries, which have less predictable growth and suffer from low capability, tend to diversify faster. Furthermore, the macroeconomic variables of monetarily measures for example total GDP and GDP per capita are all given in constant 2010 US dollar.

4.2 Data Presentation

4.2.4 County Classification

The selected sample of 110 countries is further classified into developed, developing and emerging countries of different sizes and of different political systems, that have some degree of dependency on natural resources. These countries derive relatively different shares of fiscal revenues from the natural resource sector including oil, natural gas, minerals and other natural resources. The sample countries are classified into income groups and degree of dependency on natural resources, as reported in Appendix Table A.1.

All the sampling countries are to some extent, blessed with natural resources which can generate crucial revenue for their governments. However, the degree and the composition of natural resource rents in the GDP of the countries are varied. The country's GDP composition of rents is accounted for in this research from 0.01% as one of the sampling countries. The degree of dependence on natural resources refers to the share of the sum of oil rents, natural gas rents, coal rents, mineral rents and forest rents to the national outcome (WDI, 2018).

4.2.5 Validation and Multicollinearity Results

The problem of multicollinearity arises because of a shortage of information (Hill & Adkins, 2001). Cortina (1993) argues that when parameters are added to an equation, some degree of power of a given predictor is lost, due to the corresponding loss in the degrees of freedom. Multicollinearity issues, consequently, have multiple impacts on estimation results, as it may lead to a change in the size and the sign of the coefficients. According to Greene (2012), in most common cases, the variables are highly correlated, but not perfectly. This leads to some statistical problems such as small changes in the data reflecting largely in the parameter estimates, the coefficient of the two correlated variables is significant with a high enough coefficient of variation (R^2), and then the coefficient may have a misleading sign. High correlation coefficient is an indication of confounded effects of the two variables. The confounded effect can be avoided by transforming one of the two variables into a different form, leading to no correlation (Khayyat, 2013).

Based on the Spearman's rank order, the correlation within the interval 0–0.3 is considered weak, between 0.3 and 0.7 is viewed moderate and between 0.7–1.0 is ranked as highly correlated (Wooldridge, 2016). Nevertheless, Wheeler and Tiefelsdorf (2005) accept below 0.59 for the value of correlation coefficients, otherwise the two variables are perfectly correlated and thereby the variance is infinite (Greene, 2012). However, in treating this issue, Green suggests having either more data, or dropping the suspected unimportant variables which are causing the problem from the equations.

For the specification of the estimation in this study, there is a desire to select regressor variables that show higher correlation with the dependent variables. Some of the regressor variables that are highly correlated with each other either dropped out from the model or were subjected to a principal component analysis to make composite indices such as PCA credit to the private sector and PCA institutional quality reported in Tables 4.2, 4.3 and 4.4. PCA is a way to reduce the dimensionality of the data and avoid collinearity problems and confounded effects.

To avoid omitting important variables, the remaining regressors are treated in the model by correcting for heteroskedasticity in all the models underestimation as recommended by Greene (2012). In addition to the treatment, the estimation models of the book have a number of interactions in all models, which provides larger information in the estimation, and thereby the variables are statistically independent of each other (Cortina, 1993). Thus, resolving a severe problem of multicollinearity in estimating the models.

The Pearson product moment is applied to compute the values of correlation coefficients. While the correlation between two predictors, X and Y arises when it is nonzero, the two are highly correlated when the value of correlation coefficients is between 0.7 and 1.0. In this book, all the model's correlation coefficients of the explanatory variables are reported in Appendix Tables A.2–A.4.

Table 4.7 shows the natural resource dependence model, in which, all the coefficient correlations are less than 0.59, and almost statistically significant at 90% level of significance, except for PSD (private investment), which is highly correlated with public investment (0.717). While some of the explanatory variables are positively correlated with each other, the remaining have negative correlation relationships. Hence, multicollinearity is not a serious problem in this study.

4.2.6 Countries Heterogeneity and Variance Heteroskedasticity

The most widely stated advantage of panel data is that it permits the introduction of heterogeneity in intercepts. This study accounts for country-specific and time-specific effects, by introducing two groups of dummy variables to capture country and time differences. Kumbhakar (1997) and Wager and Athey (2018), argue about the importance of existing heterogeneity to provide an unbiased estimate, otherwise ignoring such heterogeneity will lead to incorrect inference.

This issue requires attention in such that the econometrics of the panel data used in this study is heterogenous by country with respect to relative dependency on natural resource revenue. Countries that produce the same rents often experience different levels of dependency on resource revenue. Thus, differences in the degree of dependency across countries are often determined by unobserved country characteristics. The error components in the panel data which are often assumed to be homoscedastic, consist of two parts in the estimated models. The error term here is deconstructed into individual-specific, time-specific and random error components.

4.2 Data Presentation

Table 4.7 Pearson correlation coefficient of dependency model

	Dep	PSD	PRV	Tax	IQ	A16	A20	C13	C20	E13	trn
Dep	1										
PSD	−0.044	1									
PRV	−0.050	0.105	1								
Tax	−0.220	0.127	0.436	1							
IQ	−0.340	0.142	0.341	0.276	1						
A16	−0.186	0.173	0.317	0.261	0.688	1					
A20	−0.087	0.294	0.465	0.251	0.599	0.463	1				
C13	0.036	0.717	−0.058	0.159	0.044	0.160	0.180	1			
C20	−0.235	0.064	−0.165	−0.008	0.223	0.075	0.212	0.082	1		
E13	−0.079	−0.077	−0.128	−0.114	−0.102	−0.050	−0.067	−0.052	−0.025	1	
trn	0.045	0.187	−0.022	0.052	−0.009	−0.063	0.256	0.095	−0.083	0.024	1

Natural Resource Dependence (Dep), Private sector development (PSD), Privatisation (PRV), Taxation (Tax), PCA Institutional Quality (IQ), Political stability (A16), Human development (A20), Public Investment (C13), Manufacturing Production (C20), Real exchange rate (E13) and Time Trend (trn)

They can be assumed as fixed parameters or random with zero mean and constant variances (Khayyat, 2013).

This research controls for several country characteristics to capture all heterogeneities that exist in fixed effects. Furthermore, fixed effects are controlled through the estimated parameters and their functional forms in terms of interactions presented in the estimation model, as well as grouping the country's sample. Another way of dealing with the fixed effect is by capturing the variation of the time effect. Then, the more parameters that are added, the smaller the variation in its residual becomes. Therefore, when residual becomes smaller through capturing countries' specific and time effects, very little variation in errors remains unexplained.

The data used in this research comprises of information on a large number of countries that have heterogeneity of natural resources revenue. The data which constitutes an unbalanced panel during a period of 28 years (1990–2017), consists of different ranges of observations from 1373 to 937 based on model estimations. The number of observations varies as different set of information is used in each model.

The results reported in Table 4.8 include figures for the sample mean of country groups in every estimated model with its standard deviation. The F-test statistic is conducted for the comparison between the two variation parts of mean squares for natural resource dependence model, for example, it is equal to 28.68, and is statically significant at a 99% level of significance reported in Table 3.8. This result indicates that the output means of the different groups of countries in the model are different, thereby concluding the presence of heterogeneity.

In addition to heterogeneity, heteroskedasticity is a further issue when estimating a panel data model. It is necessary to test for the presence of heteroskedasticity in the data. Existing heteroskedasticity is reasonable as it allows for differences between groups of variables in the model. In a panel data model, the variance relates to time, individuals and the variance that relates to the random error combining them.

Studies which have performed quantitative analysis have proposed different tests for heteroskedasticity, including the White test, White (1980), and the Breusch-Pagan test, Breusch and Pagan (1979). These tests provide separate testing for each variable

Table 4.8 Heterogeneity among the country groups—analysis of variance

Country group	Mean	Std. Dev		
Lower income	0.195	0.397		
Lower middle income	0.211	0.408		
Middle-income	0.176	0.381		
Upper middle income	0.165	0.372		
Higher income	0.252	0.434		
Source DF	Sum of Squares	Mean Square	F Value	Pr > F
Model 10	53,596	5359.62		
Error 1256	234,733	186.89	28.68	<0.0001

Source Author's own construction, 2020

4.2.7 Summary Statistics

The data set for the final model estimation is comprised of 937 observations from 110 natural resource wealthy countries, observed for the period of 1990–2017. The data includes a number of variables on the country level of private sector development, privatisation, taxation and natural resource dependence. The data contains all countries with revenue from natural resources and corresponds to the population of the countries. Definitions of variables and their raw data are presented in Table 4.1.

Prior to the estimation, the dataset was subjected to missing unit observations. The missing observation was managed with the SAS statistical package through imputation. The imputation was based on countries' own mean values in three rounds of combination of countries and periods mean, mean of countries and mean of the years. The imputed values are generated from countries own mean and as such will not cause the estimation result to deviate from the average.

In addition to the imputation of the raw data, different variables were created from the existing variables which are presented in Table 4.5. Accordingly, a variable period is created with three time periods to capture the data within different economic periods as follows: Period 1 is for the time period of 1990–1999, period 2 is for the period of 2000–2008 and period 3 is for 2009–2017. These correspond to the liberalisation of the economy, the Asian financial crises, the Global economic crisis and the late oil crisis.

Table 4.9 shows that the average measure of natural resource dependency was 6% indicating that the sampling resource-dependent countries on average have 6% natural resource rent share of GDP.

The sampling period average annual growth rate was nearly 4% with substantial differences across countries associated with the economic and non-economic factors the research has accounted for. The Table also shows that privatisation of state-own enterprises among the sampling countries was 22%, while the level of taxes collected on average as a percentage of GDP was 15%.

Table 4.9 shows that the average measure of governance for the study period was 41% implying that resource rich countries had poor quality state governance. One can also see that there was a huge difference between the sampling countries. For example, regarding rule of law the minimum figure is 0.5% while the maximum is around 100% which shows that there was a clear difference among countries concerning rule of law; this was also true for the other two variables of regulation quality, voice and accountability.

Table 4.9 Summary statistics of the variables

Variable	Mean	Std Dev	Minimum	Maximum
Country	54.795	31.91	1	110
Year	2003.5	8.079	1990	2017
Period	1.929	0.799	1	3
Tax	15.168	6.675	0	45.253
Private sector development	15.685	8.156	0	50
Natural resource dependence	5.906	11.928	0	64.106
Diversification	83.599	40.272	1	152
Privatisation	22.056	9.254	1.878	50
Credit to private sector (PCA)	1.231	1	0	11.402
Institutional quality (PCA)	1.72	1	0	4.387
Infrastructure (PCA)	0	1	−2.473	3.864
Time trend	14.5	8.079	1	28
Oil and gas dummy variable	0.625	0.484	0	1
FDI inward	3.855	8.558	−82.892	161.824
FDI outwards	0.915	7.614	−202.824	167.329
Economic growth	3.946	7.477	−64.047	149.973
Saving	18.264	18.211	−141.974	95.807
Governance	41.301	24.388	0.51	99.039
Human development	0.604	0.157	0.199	0.953
Fiscal factor	8.838	24.616	−97.616	572.936
Trade openness	75.901	42.002	0.021	531.737
Total investment	39.712	21.091	−21.124	344.283
Export	34.461	20.105	−7.469	127.555
Import	41.67	25.048	0.016	424.817
Unemployment	7.658	5.726	−2.545	31.84
Wages and salary	31.192	20.871	2.142	250.601
Public investment	24.117	11.921	−2.424	219.069
Subsidy	33.771	16.506	0	90.652
Agricultural production	16.843	13.545	0	93.977
Manufacturing production	14.352	11.502	0	123.96
Tax capacity	23.118	12.332	−1.348	79.539
Real exchange rate	101.83	47.93	2.96	2321.549
Credit provided by financial sector	50.765	62.16	−114.694	2066.185

(continued)

Table 4.9 (continued)

Variable	Mean	Std Dev	Minimum	Maximum
Domestic credit to private sector	36.319	36.884	0.001	221.289
Domestic credit to private sector by banks	32.903	30.36	0.001	194.387
Political stability	38.971	24.586	0	99.468
Regulation quality	41.509	23.807	0.481	99.51
Rule of law	38.553	24.509	0.47	100
Voice and accountability	38.477	23.432	0	100
Transport Services of export	23.915	15.76	−3.213	144.811
Transport Service of import	38.606	14.967	3.035	106.069
Fixed Broadband Subscription	2,253,449.43	14,131,177.4	0	378,540,000
People use basic drinking water	80.444	18.755	22.213	101.299
Access to electricity	68.003	35.182	0.01	100.13
GDP per capita	7550.712	13,999.226	67.39	91,617.28
GDP total	363,961.722	1,468,498.43	214.577	17,304,984.28
Population	49.847	162.874	0.07	1386.395
Low income	0.195	0.397	0	1
Lower middle income	0.211	0.408	0	1
Middle income	0.176	0.381	0	1
Upper middle income	0.165	0.372	0	1
Higher income	0.252	0.434	0	1

4.3 Data Analysis, Model Specification, Estimation and Testing

This section introduces the model specification and the estimation results of the traditional static model, the dynamic model, the dynamic flexible adjustment model and the system of equations.

There is a dynamic pattern of private sector development, privatisation and taxation to reduce natural resource dependency. Thus, while at first a static model is applied for comparative purposes, it did not provide a result that correctly addressed the research questions. This model does not control for issues such as endogeneity and simultaneity effects. To avoid such problems, two more specifications are provided, namely dynamic flexible adjustment model and system of equations. Dynamic flexible adjustment model is applied to control for endogeneity,[4] as one of the solutions to estimate effectively in the case of panel data models. Nevertheless, an interdependence between some of the explanatory variables was kept to study. A system of equations to overcome the problem of endogeneity and simultaneity effects was applied.

The specification of the model as discussed in chapter three, started with the estimation of the standard static model for comparative purpose, which is linear in parameter (Eq. 3.4), by using the OLS estimation method.

Then, the dynamic Eq. 3.9 which is non-linear in parameter was estimated for each of the observed diversification factors to capture the effect of their dependency reduction. This model included speed of adjustment and the optimal levels of PSD_{it}^*, $PuSD_{it}^*$, Tax_{it}^* and Dep_{it}^* were jointly estimated by using an iterative non-linear estimation method (SYSNLIN in SAS). Dummy and proxy variables such as the effect of time, country, size of privatisation, degree of dependency and the effect of resource types (oil and gas) were included, to capture the unobservable country and, time specific heterogeneity effects, this ensuring greater reliability of the results.

4.3.1 Static vs Dynamic Models

To estimate the effects of determinants of the diversified factors to reduce resource revenue dependency in resource rich countries, the traditional static and dynamic models were used for the purpose of comparison.

Table 4.10 presents a comparison of the different values between the static and dynamic models, including RMSE and coefficient of determination (R^2) values of both models. RMSE is the square root of mean square error (MSE) which is the variance of the error term. It can be calculated as the proportion of the residual sum of squares (SSE) to the degrees of freedom (DF) SSE/($n-k$); the latter is the difference between the number of observations (n) and the number of parameters (k) (Hahs-Vaughn & Lomax, 2013). Although RMSE has been widely used for forecasting in times series data analysis, it is also proposed for assessing the predictive accuracy of models in panel data analysis (Greene, 2012). The lower the RMSE value is, the less scattering of the data around the mean.

Table 4.10 shows the value advantage of the flexible dynamic model over the restricted adjustment dynamic model and static model by confirming lower RMSE (2.877 vs. 3.176 and 6.633) and higher (R^2) (0.847 vs 0.814 and 0.188) for private sector development model. The lower RMSE of the model value 2.877 indicates that the flexible adjustment estimation model is more accurate than the others and the value of (R^2) implies that 85% of the variability of the dependent variable has been accounted for. For the privatisation model, the RMSE and coefficient of determination (R^2) values of the flexible dynamic model is much better compared to the other

---

[4] This means a dependent variable is treated as an independent variable in another equation.

4.3 Data Analysis, Model Specification, Estimation and Testing

Table 4.10 Static vs. dynamic models

	Static	Restricted dynamic	Unrestricted dynamic
M1 Private Sector Development			
Adjusted R^2	0.188	0.814	0.847
RMSE	6.633	3.176	2.877
M2 Privatisation			
Adjusted R^2	0.546	0.924	0.950
RMSE	5.112	2.099	1.703
M3 Taxation			
Adjusted R^2	0.496	0.900	0.938
RMSE	3.471	1.542	1.215
M4 Natural Resource Dependence			
Adjusted R^2	0.258	0.949	0.965
RMSE	13.436	3.535	2.900

models with; lower RMSE (1.703 vs. 2.099 and 5.112) and higher (R^2) (0.950 vs. 0.924 and 0.546).

Regarding the taxation model, the RMSE and coefficient of determination (R^2) values of the dynamic model compared to the static model is much better with; lower RMSE (1.215 vs.1.542 and 3.471) and higher (R^2) (0.938 vs. 0.900 and 0.496). Similar to the other models, the explanatory power of the flexible adjustment dynamic model of the natural resource dependence reduction model has a value advantage over both the static and the traditional dynamic models. Accordingly, the values of the flexible dynamic model; the root mean squares error (RMSE) and coefficient of determination (R^2), are better compared to the other models with; lower RMSE (2.900 vs. 3.535 and 13.436) and higher (R^2) (0.965 vs. 0.949 and 0.258).

In addition to adding extra explanatory variables into the flexible dynamic model the statistical F-test can be used to evaluate the model's performance. F-test is used to test whether adding more variables into the model contributes to the model's explanation of the dependent variable. It can be also used to compare two models when one model is a special case (nested model) of the other model (Hahs-Vaughn & Lomax, 2013). The F-test can be calculated as follows;

$$F - \text{test} = \frac{Rss_r - Rss_u/(DF_r - DF_u)}{Rss_u/DF_u} \quad (4.1)$$

where Rss_r is residual sum of square for the static model and Rss_u is the residual sum of square for the flexible dynamic model. DF_r is degrees of freedom for the static model and DF_u is the degree of freedom in the flexible dynamic model.

The result shows that the F-test value for comparing the static with dynamic flexible adjustment model is equal to 34.3, with a critical value of 4.944 at 95% significance. The value of the F-test is larger than the critical value, and as such it is large enough to reject the null hypothesis that all explanatory (slope) variables are zero. This indicates that the model as a whole accounts for a significant portion of the variability in the dependent variable (Hrong-Tai Fai & Cornelius, 1996; Khayyat, 2013). This implies the superiority of the dynamic adjustment model over the static one.

When, batteries of the explanatory power of the two models are compared, the results indicate that the flexible dynamic model has a better fit to model the private sector development, privatisation, taxation and natural resource dependency reduction. The estimation results suggest that the traditional static and dynamic models are not always satisfactory in studying resource dependency reduction due to their failure to capture possible nonlinear influences of private and public sector development. The dynamic model which included flexible adjustment speed made a key difference compared with the static model. The sign and significance of some of the exogenous variables were slightly changed and improved. The flexible dynamic model has more explanatory power than the traditional static model.

4.3.2 Single Equation vs. System of Equations Estimations[5]

A system of equations was used to account for endogeneity and interdependence between some of the explanatory variables, while single equation estimation only accounts for endogeneity. Table 4.11 shows the overall performance of the two estimation methods. The model's coefficient of determination (R^2) in every single model in the system of equations indicates the better fit of the system of equations of flexible dynamic estimation over the single equation. This implies that the variation in the data can be explained more by system of equations.

Another measure of goodness of fit is the MSE. The value of MSE reported in Table 4.11 in system of equations compared to the single equation shows that observations on average are closer to the mean. In other words, there is a relatively low rate of scattering of the data around the mean.

The econometric results herewith suggest that the traditional static model is not always satisfactory, due to the failure to capture possible nonlinear influences of the effects of privatisation, taxation and some non-economic factors such as institutional quality in reducing natural resource dependency. Furthermore, the value of the F-test statistics between both the static and flexible dynamic models confirms the superior performance of flexible dynamic model estimation over the static model estimation results. In addition to the value advantage of the dynamic model over the static model, the values of the different goodness of fits presented in Table 4.11 indicate better performance of the system of equations over single equation. Thus, the analysis of data is based on the unrestricted dynamic adjustment model of system of equations estimation.

---

[5] The result based on single equation estimation for all the four models is presented in Appendix 2.

Table 4.11 Different values between single and system of equations estimations

		Single	System
MSE			
	PSD	9.962	8.521
	PRV	4.770	2.874
	Tax	2.188	1.476
	Dep	10.683	8.429
Adjusted R^2			
	PSD	0.820	0.843
	PRV	0.929	0.950
	Tax	0.908	0.938
	Dep	0.953	0.965
DF			
	PSD	33	33
	PRV	31	31
	Tax	26	26
	Dep	29	29
Observations			
	PSD	1191	937
	PRV	1188	937
	Tax	950	937
	Dep	1207	937

4.4 Summary

This chapter presented the estimation-related issues in the presence of unbalanced panel data sets. The statistical package of SAS managed unbalanced panel data through several imputations. However, in dynamic panel data, the length of the gap and the number of time periods which affect the consistency property of the estimators are important. Panel data sets used in this study enabled better identification and estimation effects in which it cannot be simply captured in cross-sectional and time series data such as heterogeneity and dynamics, respectively.

The sample size choice depends on the data availability and is selected from a population of countries. The provision of the data came into different stages to deal with either the issue of unbalanced panel data or the measurement of the indicators. However, the model choice also depends on data availability, it relies on the complexity of the issues that the researcher studies. The model choice relies on the focus of the study, either measuring the relationship between some interdependent factors or a main focus on reducing the degree of dependency on natural resources in resource rich countries.

Bibliography

Ajaz, T., & Ahmad, E. (2010). The effect of corruption and governance on tax revenues. *The Pakistan Development Review, 49*(2), 405–417.

Arezki, R., & Van der Ploeg, F. (2011). Do natural resources depress income per capita? *Review of Development Economics, 15*(3), 504–521.

Arocena, P., & Oliveros, D. (2012). The efficiency of state-owned and privatised firms: Does ownership make a difference? *International Journal of Production Economics, 140*(1), 457–465.

Auty, R. (2007). Natural resources, capital accumulation and the resource curse. *Ecological Economics, 61*(4), 627–634.

Beck, T. (2011). *Finance and oil: Is there a resource curse in financial development?* (European Banking Center Discussion Paper 004).

Ben Hammouda, H., Karingi, S., Njuguna, A., & Sadni Jallab, M. (2006). *Diversification: Towards a new paradigm for Africa's development* (MPRA paper, No: 35). United Nations Economic Commission for Africa.

Bhattacharyya, S., & Collier, P. (2013). Public capital in resource rich economies: Is there a curse? *Oxford Economic Papers, 66*(1), 1–24.

Bhattacharyya, S., & Hodler, R. (2014). Do natural resource revenues hinder financial development? The role of political institutions. *World Development, 57*, 101–113.

Boos, A., & Holm-Müller, K. (2013). The relationship between the resource curse and genuine savings: Empirical evidence. *Journal of Sustainable Development, 6*(6), 59.

Bortolotti, B., & Pinotti, P. (2008). Delayed PRIVATISATION. *Public Choice, 136*(3–4), 331–351.

Boschini, A., Pettersson, J., & Roine, J. (2013). The resource curse and its potential reversal. *World Development, 43*, 19–41.

Breusch, T. S., & Pagan, A. R. (1979). A simple test for heteroscedasticity and random coefficient variation. *Econometrica: Journal of the Econometric Society, 47*(5), 1287–1294.

Cammett, M., Diwan, I., & Leber, A. (2019). *Is oil wealth good for private sector development?* (Economic Research Forum Working Paper 1299).

Collier, P., & Hoeffler, A. (2009). Testing the neocon agenda: Democracy in resource-rich societies. *European Economic Review, 53*(3), 293–308.

Cortina, J. M. (1993). Interaction, nonlinearity, and multicollinearity: Implications for multiple regression. *Journal of Management, 19*(4), 915–922.

Crivelli, E., & Gupta, S. (2014). Resource blessing, revenue curse? Domestic revenue effort in resource-rich countries. *European Journal of Political Economy, 35*, 88–101.

Dietz, S., Neumayer, E., & De Soysa, I. (2007). Corruption, the resource curse and genuine saving. *Environment and Development Economics, 12*(1), 33–53.

Greene, W. H. (2012). *Econometric analysis*. Pearson Education

Gylfason, T. (2001). Natural resources, education, and economic development. *European Economic Review, 45*(4–6), 847–859.

Gylfason, T., & Zoega, G. (2006). Natural resources and economic growth: The role of investment. *World Economy, 29*(8), 1091–1115.

Hagemejer, J., Tyrowicz, J., & Svejnar, J. (2014). *Measuring the Causal effect of privatisation on firm performance* (University of Warsaw, Faculty of Economic, Sciences Working Paper 14), 131.

Hahs-Vaughn, D. L., & Lomax, R. G. (2013). *Statistical concepts—A second course*. Routledge.

Hayat, A., & Tahir, M. (2019). Natural resources volatility and economic growth: Evidence from the resource-rich region. *MRPA*(92293).

Hill, C., & Adkins, L. (Eds.). (2001). *Collinearity*. Blackwell.

Hrong-Tai Fai, A., & Cornelius, P. L. (1996). Approximate F-tests of multiple degree of freedom hypotheses in generalized least squares analyses of unbalanced split-plot experiments. *Journal of statistical computation and simulation, 54*(4), 363–378.

Khayyat, N. T. (2013). *Exploring demand for energy in the South Korean Industries*. Doctoral dissertation, SMC University, Zurich, Switzerland.

Bibliography

Khayyat, N. T., & Lee, J.-D. (2015). A measure of technological capabilities for developing countries. *Technological Forecasting and Social Change, 92*, 210–223.

Knebelmann, J. (2017). *Natural resources' impact on government revenues* (WIDER Working Paper 10).

Kumbhakar, S. C. (1997). Efficiency estimation with heteroscedasticity in a panel data model. *Applied Economics, 29*(3), 379–386.

McGuirk, E. F. (2013). The illusory leader: Natural resources, taxation and accountability. *Public Choice, 154*(3–4), 285–313.

Morrison, K. (2015). *Nontaxation and representation*. Cambridge University Press.

Németh, J., & Schmidt, S. (2011). The privatization of public space: Modeling and measuring publicness. *Environment and Planning b: Planning and Design, 38*(1), 5–23.

Neumayer, E. (2004). Does the "resource curse" hold for growth in genuine income as well? *World Development, 32*(10), 1627–1640.

Prichard, W. (2016). Reassessing tax and development research: A new dataset, new findings, and lessons for research. *World Development, 80*, 48–60.

Prichard, W., Salardi, P., & Segal, P. (2014). Taxation, non-tax revenue and democracy: New evidence using new cross-country data. *World Development, 109*, 295–312

Ramamurti, R. (2000). A multilevel model of privatization in emerging economies. *Academy of Management Review, 25*(3), 525–550.

Sachs, J. D., & Warner, A. M. (1995). *Natural resource abundance and economic growth* (National Bureau of Economic Research (No. w 5395)).

Sheshinski, E., & López-Calva, L. F. (2003). Privatization and its benefits: Theory and evidence. *CESifo Economic Studies, 49*(3), 429–459.

Tausch, A., Heshmati, A., & Bajalan, C. S. (2007). *On the multivariate analysis of the lisbon process* (IZA Discussion Papers, Institute for the Study of Labor (IZA) 3198).

UNDP. (2019). *Human Development Index (HDI)*. Retrieved 03.01.2019, from United Nations Development Programm.

Van Buuren, S. (2018). *Flexible imputation of missing data*. CRC Press.

Von Haldenwang, C., & Ivanyna, M. (2018). Does the political resource curse affect public finance? The vulnerability of tax revenue in resource-dependent countries. *Journal of International Development, 30*(2), 323–344.

Wager, S., & Athey, S. (2018). Estimation and inference of heterogeneous treatment effects using random forests. *Journal of the American Statistical Association, 113*(523), 1228–1242.

WDI. (2018). *Natural resource contribution to GDP*. Retrieved 23 January 2019, from World Bank.

WGI. (2020). *World Governance Indicators*. Retrieved 15 January 2020, from World Bank.

Wheeler, D., & Tiefelsdorf, M. (2005). Multicollinearity and correlation among local regression coefficients in geographically weighted regression. *Journal of Geographical Systems, 7*(2), 161–187.

White, H. (1980). A heteroskedasticity-consistent covariance matrix estimator and a direct test for heteroskedasticity. *Econometrica, 48*(4), 817–838.

Wooldridge, J. M. (2016). *Introductory econometrics: A modern approach* (4th ed.). Nelson Education.

World Bank. (2019). *Economic fitness*. In W. Bank (Ed.). https://databank.worldbank.org/source/economic-fitness-2

Zhao, L., Chen, Y., & Schaffner, D. W. (2001). Comparison of logistic regression and linear regression in modeling percentage data. *Applied and Environmental Microbiology, 67*(5), 2129–2135.

Chapter 5
Presentation of Results

Abstract This chapter presents the empirical analysis of the results. By examining the effects of the diversification factors of private sector development, privatisation and taxation to reduce the degree of dependency on revenue from natural resources, several estimation methods are applied including static linear regression model, traditional dynamic model and dynamic flexible adjustment model in a single equation and system of equations. The determinants of reaching an optimal level of reduction of dependency on natural resources with its adjustment speed will be investigated. The analysis includes the investigation of the relationship between the dynamic of private sector development in natural resource rich countries to answer the RQ_1. Further result of measuring the relationship between privatisation and resource revenue dependency to answer RQ_{2_1} is presented. To answer RQ_{2_2}, the outcome of the effect of taxation on natural resource revenue dependency is provided. Finally, the analysis of private and public sector development and diversification of income to reduce dependency on natural resources to answer RQ_4 is offered. The results suggest that public sector reforms can have better performance in reducing natural resource dependency than private sector development. Nevertheless, there are other factors that contribute to effective reduction of the relative dependency on natural resource revenue namely human development and institutional quality.

Keywords Private sector development · Taxation · Natural resource dependency reduction · Static linear regression model · Traditional dynamic model · Dynamic flexible adjustment model · A single equation · System of equations

5.1 Introduction

As discussed in Chapter 2, the factors of private sector development, privatisation and taxation have been attributed to economic diversification. The diversification process tends to change the economic structure of the natural resource rich countries from a single commodity to more diverse streams of income; as such, the relative dependency on natural resource revenue diminishes.

This chapter presents the results according to the procedure stated in Chapter 3. It includes the presentation of the results organised by the research questions set out in Chapter 1. In doing so, results of static model without adjustment, a restricted dynamic model with constant adjustment and an unrestricted dynamic model with flexible adjustment are presented. Then, after accounting for the interdependence between the four models of PSD, privatisation, taxation and dependency, results of a complete system of equations with interdependence are discussed.

There are variations in the level of significance for the coefficients of the determinants between static and dynamic models. The dynamic model performs reasonably well in terms of bias, root mean squared error (RMSE) and power compared to the static one. Therefore, the results based on all three models are expected to be varied. The justification for these differences in the results is that they use different sets of information as they are different model specifications. While a single model accounts only for endogeneity, the system of equations accounts for endogeneity, simultaneity and interdependence. In such a complicated system of equations, more estimation steps are involved that cannot be seen, and thereby the significance level can change. There is no restriction on the coefficients across equations, which lead to changes in sign, size and significance.

The mean indicators (observed, optimal and adjustment speed) are computed based on the estimation result, by different country characteristics and time period. The mean of the variables is computed with lag dependent variable that excludes one year of observation.

In this chapter the determinants of the optimal level of diversified factors and their speed of adjustment towards the desired level are presented to address the third objective of the study set out in Chapter 1. Then, the determinants of the desired level of the degree of dependency on natural resources (dependency reduction), alongside its adjustment speed are presented to answer the research questions. In doing so, a number of tables, charts and analysis of results in accordance with the research questions are presented, providing evidence for either the acceptance or rejection of each hypothesis as stated in Chapter 1.

5.2 Results of Private Sector Development

5.2.1 Determinants of Optimal Private Sector Development (PSD)

Table 5.1 reports the results of the estimated parameters of the Private Sector Development. In the business environment, a tax regime significantly affects the operational decisions of the private sector. Even though taxes have implications for government revenue, tax incentives directly affect the development of the private sector (Bruhn, 2011). The coefficient of *Taxation* is negative and statistically significant at the level of 95%. This implies that the optimal level of the private sector is associated with

5.2 Results of Private Sector Development

decreased taxes in natural resource rich countries. This is consistent with the finding of a previous study by Klemm and Van Parys (2012) who found a negative relationship between tax rate and private investment. Accordingly, a decrease of 10% in corporate tax is associated with an increase in FDI between 0.33 and 4.5% of GDP.

Workforce skills and capabilities matter for economic development. Drucker (2012) points out that knowledge-based development is much more critical than traditional economic factors such as monetary factors, physical labour and raw materials in organisational development. However, the large positive coefficient of *Human Development* indicates that it is not only organisational success that largely depends on the quality of human capacity, but also the country level of the PSD, which affects the strategic development of the private sector on a country level. This result is in line with the findings of Akinyemi (2011) who noted that due to human development policy, the business landscape in Rwanda has become one of the most suitable places in the world to start a business.

Table 5.1 Static and dynamic model parameters estimates (PSD)

Model	Static model		Restricted dynamic		Unrestricted dynamic	
Variables	Estimate	Std error	Estimate	Std error	Estimate	Std error
Intercept	20.278[a]	2.889	9.825	11.044	7.187	5.742
Taxation	−0.137[b]	0.047	−0.298[c]	0.168	−0.297[b]	0.079
Natural resource rents	−0.035[c]	0.016	−0.049	0.058	0.114[b]	0.032
Credit to private sector	−0.677[c]	0.287	−1.923[c]	0.993	−2.552[a]	0.631
Infrastructure quality	4.298[a]	0.587	3.334	2.139	2.263[c]	1.128
FDI inward	0.017	0.024	0.054	0.081	0.046	0.033
Economic growth	0.238[a]	0.058	1.158[a]	0.235	0.354[a]	0.078
Governance	0.030[c]	0.017	0.083	0.059	0.083[c]	0.036
Political stability	0.045[b]	0.012	0.054	0.042	0.076[b]	0.027
Human development	−14.582[b]	4.814	8.802[b]	17.999	36.033[a]	9.517
Interest rate policy	−0.008	0.009	−0.025	0.030	−0.119[a]	0.029
Trade openness	0.025[a]	0.006	0.016	0.022	0.012	0.013
Agricultural production	−0.012	0.031	−0.033	0.122	−0.118[c]	0.053
Manufacturing production	−0.066[b]	0.045	0.009	0.059	−0.068	0.041
Trend	0.143[b]	0.038	0.181	0.131	−0.067[b]	0.064
Low middle income			−1.812	3.448	−5.305[b]	1.814
Middle income			−7.405[c]	4.395	−12.889[a]	2.275
Upper middle income			−5.610	5.081	−12.137[a]	2.513
Higher income			−9.473[c]	5.459	−24.512[a]	2.797
Observations	937		937		937	
Adjusted *R*-squared	0.188		0.814		0.847	
RMSE	6.633		3.176		2.877	

Note The dependent variable is PSD and the *p* value is: [a]$p \leq 0.001$, [b]$p \leq 0.05$, [c]$p \leq 0.10$

The parameter estimate of *Economic Growth* is positive and highly statistically significant, indicating that the more the economy grows, the faster the private sector develops towards the optimal level. Economic growth in natural resource rich countries is typically a result of resource booms, mostly oil booms. As such, rents generated from natural resources can indirectly foster the development of the private sector in some instances.

Manufacturing leads the economic transformation of many successful developing countries such as China, Vietnam and Ukraine. This transformation increases the productivity of private firms by providing quality products to the domestic market (Brown et al., 2019; Dinh et al., 2012). The coefficient of *Manufacturing Production* is negative and non-significant. The development of manufacturing in natural resource revenue countries is stagnated because of commodity price volatility. The 'resource movement effect' leads to increased movement of manpower from the traded goods sector into the non-traded sector meaning that it becomes increasingly better to work in the latter sector (Schoneveld & Zoomers, 2015; Weber, 2014). As such, it is inversely affecting the development of other sectors.

The coefficient of *Agricultural Production* is negative and weakly significant, indicating that an agricultural production extension system does not support the development of the private sector in resource-based economies. Agricultural productivity extension has the potential to improve income diversification through transfer and facilitation of knowledge, skills and technologies (Feder et al., 2010; Swanson & Rajalahti, 2010). The results however, show the opposite of this in terms of the impact of agricultural production extension systems on private sector development. This result can be explained in two ways; first, it relates to the contribution of the agricultural program in these countries that have a different rate of return (Ragasa et al., 2016). Second, it may be related to, for example, a decline in the quality of mineral reserves which has increased pressure for exploitation (Mason et al., 2011). Then, competition among alternative uses of lands increased, and thus conflicts and social vulnerabilities in such areas emerged (Muradian et al., 2012).

Time Trend is included to capture the variation in the development of the private sector across countries. Normally, the amount of private investment either increases or decreases over time. However, the time trend analysis for PSD in resource rich countries indicates that the level of economic diversification is significantly lowered over time. The reported result shows that *Time Trend* is negative and significant, meaning that the variation of PSD over time is decreased. PSD faces challenges in natural resource rich countries. When addressing challenges to PSD in natural resource rich countries, Mazaheri (2016) states that, greater rents from natural resources translate into a larger resource curse, and as such private sector development is less effective.

Natural resource-dependent countries receive most of their revenue from resource commodities. Therefore, variability in resources is expected to be negatively related to the development of the private sector. The resource curse undermines the competitiveness of the private sector, the investment climate and manufacturing production through increased costs for private agents and unbroken threats on a country's macroeconomic stability. Nonetheless, once natural resources derive economic growth, resource rents might be positively related to the optimal PSD. The coefficient of *Natural Resource Rents* is positive and significant at the level of 95%, indicating that the more revenues from resources there are, the faster private sector development is. This finding of positive relationship is consistent with a study by Ji et al. (2014) who found positive effects of resource abundance on the economic growth of China.

Furthermore, access to financial resources such as direct loans, purchase of non-equity securities, trade credits and other accounts receivable are key drivers of PSD. Beck et al. (2010) indicate that financial resources foster the development of industries that are dependent on external finance. While the coefficient of *Credit to the Private Sector* is highly significant, it is surprisingly negative with the value of 2.552. The negative coefficient has two justifications; first it may relate to a natural resource curse in financial development. The curse, according to Abor and Quartey (2010), caused banks to provide fewer loans to the private sector, while the banks were better capitalised and more profitable. The second is possibly associated with the risk to financial agencies. Direct lending in the form of loans and equity to private agencies increases the risk to banks and financial agencies (Hodge, 2006). However, the impact of such credit in poorly institutionalised resource countries makes this debate controversial. Thus, it is recommended that further research is conducted to investigate this issue.

Unlike Thompson (2007) who found a negative relationship between FDI and an embryonic private sector in the economic development of Ghana, the present research finds that FDI has no statistically significant impact on PSD in resource rich countries.[1]

Infrastructure, which is a key factor for economic growth is one of the determinants that shape the development of the private sector. The significance and advantages of infrastructure to economic growth have been acknowledged for a while (Castells-Quintana, 2017; Deng, 2013; Lewis, 2014). The coefficient of *Infrastructure Quality* is positive and weakly significant, meaning that it is one of the determinants of optimal PSD. Investment in infrastructure is not only fundamental in the process of economic growth per se, but also in improving the whole economy. A study on the effect of infrastructure on economic growth in India finds two-way relationships between road transportation and infrastructure investment, and bidirectional causality between infrastructure investment and economic growth (Pradhan & Bagchi, 2013).

Interest rate is one of the macroeconomic determinants that shape the development of the private sector. It is a deliverable channel of funds from savers to borrowers, which determines the financial decisions of private firms (Aftab et al., 2016). According to monetary views, there is an inverse relationship between interest rate and private investment; any increase in interest rate causes private investment to decrease. This study indicates that a reduction in interest rate has a positive impact on

---

[1] The non-significant of FDI effect on PSD might be related to the following: The resource curse logic suggests that there is an inverse relationship between PSD and natural resource dependency. However, the results contradict the resource curse logic by finding a positive relationship between those two in line with Cammett et al. (2019), and thereby the positive relationship between those two might affect the relationship between FDI and PSD.

PSD in resource-wealthy countries, similar to a study by Malawi and Bader (2010) on the effect of interest rate on private investment in Jordan. The authors found a significant negative coefficient indicating that a one per cent increase in interest rate reduces private investment value by 44%.

The coefficient of *Interest Rate Policy* is negative and highly statistically significant, confirming that interest rate reduction policy has a positive effect on the development of the private sector. Unlike a study by Beck and Hesse (2006) who found no robust and economically significant relationship between interest spread of foreign bank and the private sector, the results of this study are similar to C. Jiang et al. (2013) who found that a reduction in central bank interest rates significantly helped real economic sector reforms. However, resource-dependent countries have procyclical government spending that leads to larger volatility in public spending (Frankel, 2012). This produces inflation especially in the time of a resource boom. Consequently, the depreciation of the real exchange rate alongside a relative increase in inflation may not allow the interest rate to effectively impact the development of the private sector.

Alongside economic determinates, non-economic determinates are also important for the development of the private sector. For an economy to operate effectively, it requires an environment with a high degree of political stability. International Finance Institutions (2011) has reported that when the government enables a stronger private sector through the provision of security and stability, the private sector is effective. The coefficient of *Political Stability* is positively significant at the level of 95% indicating that it is a significant determinant of the private sector in natural resource rich countries. Political stability has implications for transparency and corruption within countries. During political turmoil, governments might apply inefficient regulatory policy to redistribute incomes through resource rents. This offers rent seeking and corruption opportunities to the government of resource-dependent countries (Auzer, 2017).

The role of governance is of paramount importance in private sector development in resource rich countries. A positive and significant coefficient for the *Governance* variable at the level of 90% is found in this study, which is in line with the analysis of International Finance Institutions (2011) and S. Sinha et al. (2001). Accordingly, the best interest for private sector companies to invest is enhanced environmental with governance standards, which encourage private companies to improve their standards.

When the sample is split into different groups of incomes, the coefficients of all income country groups are negative and highly statistically significant. The negative coefficients show that PSD is more restricted and has less scope in such countries confirming the challenges facing PSD. Generally, in lower income countries wages, energy prices and access to raw materials are in favour of the private firms. Since the market is highly competitive in higher income countries, the private sector has more scope to develop in lower income natural resource rich countries.

5.2 Results of Private Sector Development

5.2.2 The Speed of Adjustment Values

The speed of adjustment is formed as a function of a number of policy variables (see, Appendix Table A.9), some of which are partially overlapping with the determinants of optimal PSD level and affect the adjustment of the private sector.

The effect of oil and gas resources on the speed of adjustment was controlled for in this research. The coefficient of the *Oil and Gas* dummy variable is positive and highly statistically significant. While a negative coefficient may be expected, the positive coefficient indicates that the private sector can adjust more efficiently towards an optimal level in countries with oil and gas, compared to those without oil and gas. Although, in the literature, the resource curse effect is demonstrated in other types of resources, the curse is most observable in oil and gas exporting countries (Ross, 2012, 2015). The interpretation for this result is that oil and gas rents are much larger than other resource rents, thereby they affect PSD relatively more than other forms of rent. This finding is in line with a recent study by Cammett et al. (2019) who contradicts some of the key claims in the resource curse literature by finding that the size of oil rents per capita has a significant effect on private sector development.

The variation of the speed of adjustment over time was expected to be in either direction, considering the impact of several crises which occurred during the sample periods. Some indicators are computed based on the estimation result, including observed, optimal and adjustment speed, which are all time and country specific. The mean of each indicator by different country characteristics was computed such as time period, income groups, private sector size, degree of dependency, year and country, and their interpretations will now be presented.

Mean by Time Period

The mean adjustment parameter δ in Table 5.2 shows the size of the gap between the actual PSD and its long-run optimal value. The adjustment moved over three sub-periods; 1990–1999, 2000–2009 and 2010–2017 from 13 to 4% and −4% respectively, showing that the speed of adjustment in all three periods decreases over time. The first period shows the highest adjustment towards optimal PSD which is consistent with the introduction of the economic liberalisation policy in the 1980s, which aimed to develop the private sector (Cook, 2006). However, the continues downward trend is possibly due to less opportunities in the private sector of these countries to promote economic growth. Natural resource rents undermine the competitiveness of the private sector, and thereby PSD faces challenges in natural resource rich countries. As explained in the previous section PSD may be ineffective in such countries due to poor institutional quality and the structure of the economy which require improvement. This result implies that the greater the resource rents, the less effect the private sector development.

There are two possible explanations for the downgrade in adjustment during the sample period. First, the global financial crisis effect in 2007–2008 affected the

Table 5.2 Mean of speed of adjustment by time period

Period	Observed	Optimal	Delta
1990–1999	14.210	20.567	0.127
2000–2009	15.886	20.867	0.037
2010–2017	17.431	20.204	−0.039

development of the private sector and caused a larger downgrading adjustment speed towards optimal PSD by reducing the mean adjustment parameter to −4% (reported in Table 5.6). Second, the sharp and long-lasting drop in oil prices in 2014–2016 increased and decreased the macroeconomic fortunes of many countries (Grigoli et al., 2019). The oil shock caused a decline in the adjustment towards optimal level of PSD to the second lowest adjustment parameter value during the sample, to −6% in 2014. The effect of rapid decline in oil prices on the adjustment speed of the PSD confirms the significance of oil and gas in developing the private sector in natural resource rich countries.

Means by Income Group

The private sectors speed of adjustment towards optimal both increases and decreases over time, based on income level. The adjustment seems more flexible between two groups of income, lower and lower-middle income than other groups. However, the adjustment speed in upper-middle and higher-income countries changes downward indicating that the private sector in these countries needs to be promoted. These results are consistent with the estimation of the coefficient in Table 5.1.

This finding implies that in low-income resource rich countries, the adjustment speed is approximately 36% closer to the desired level of PSD within a year, which means that adjustment develops each year by 36% and the full development of the private sector takes almost three years (Table 5.3).

This rapid acceleration in the speed of adjustment may be mainly attributed to radical changes in general economic policy, ranging from import substitution to liberalisation, which resulted in increased capital mobilisation. In addition to that, the privatisation of many economy sectors such as information and communication technology (ICT), health, education and infrastructure, and the rapid growth of emerging and transition economies may have contributed to rapid speed of adjustment. Finally,

Table 5.3 Mean of speed of adjustment by income group

Income group	Observed	Optimal	Delta
Low income	11.602	20.157	0.365
Lower middle-income	16.611	22.751	0.141
Middle-income	17.205	20.385	0.052
Upper middle-income	17.926	23.134	−0.072
Higher income	16.798	18.228	−0.150

5.2 Results of Private Sector Development

Table 5.4 Mean of speed of adjustment by private sector size

Size	Observed	Optimal	Delta
Smaller size	2.380	21.755	0.214
Lower middle-size	7.901	18.509	0.193
Middle-size	12.965	19.105	0.033
Upper middle-size	17.787	19.694	−0.033
Larger size	26.990	22.349	−0.009

China's aggressive investment in resource rich countries, and the achievement of five-year economic plans around the world, have made the speed of adjustment relatively fast.

Means by Size of Private Sector

As indicated in Table 5.4, the speed of adjustment varies with the size of the private sector. There is a large gap from observed to optimal in countries that have smaller levels of privatisation. This means there is a large amount of adjustment which is hard to gain.

By contrast, the private sector can adjust more effectively in middle and upper middle-sized private sectors towards optimal level due to less space between the observed and optimal level.

Means by Degree of Dependency

The level of dependency on natural resources affects the speed of adjustment. The results presented in Table 5.5 show that the adjustment speed towards optimal PSD is faster in lower-middle dependency than other groups as the gap between observed to optimal is less observable in this dependency level than others.

This faster adjustment implies that resource rich countries that have lower-middle dependency adjust towards optimal PSD each year by 19% and the full development of PSD would take place during a period of five years. This is due to the scope of

Table 5.5 Mean of speed of adjustment by degree of dependency

Degree of dependency	Observed	Optimal	Delta
Higher dependency	16.388	20.108	−0.018
Upper middle-dependency	13.129	18.863	0.164
Middle dependency	15.690	22.087	0.159
Lower middle-dependency	15.990	22.667	0.186
Less dependency	16.365	24.488	0.162

the private sector to invest in other sectors rather than natural resource sectors. The lower the degree of dependency, the faster the speed of adjustment is.

Means by Year

Table 5.6 and Fig. 5.1 show the movement of the observed, optimal and speed of adjustment of PSD. According to the reported figures, the mean adjustment parameter (δ) in 1991 starts with the highest value within the sample accounting for 16%. This is consistent with the introduction of the economic liberalisation policy in the 1980s which aimed to develop the private sector. Surprisingly, the effect of the Asian financial crisis in 1997 and its consequences did not affect the development of the private sector in natural resource rich countries. The trend of the adjustment during the first period fluctuated between 16 and 10%. However, there is a sudden drop in the adjustment parameter in the first year of period two 2000–2009. The mean adjustment parameter in 1999 was 12.3% and decreased to 8.9% in 2000. This is possibly due to the consequences of a decline in economic activity in 2000 mainly in developed countries.

The global financial crisis in 2007–2008 affected the development of the private sector and caused expansion in the gap between actual and optimal PSD by declining the mean adjustment parameter to -2%; early impact appeared in 2006 with -0.5%, then in 2007 and 2008 the effect was more impactful by enlarging the size of the downgrading respectively to -4% and -2%. The relative global economic recovery increased the adjustment parameter to 6% in 2009.

Later, due to the sharp decline in oil prices in 2014, the private sector's adjustment towards the optimal level declined to the lowest -6% in 2014. Again, the impact of sharp drop in oil prices confirms the positive impact of oil on private sector development.

Means by Country[2]

The mean of the speed of adjustment by country is shown in Table 5.7. The gap between actual and optimal PSD varies across countries within a year. The larger the speed of adjustment, the closer the observed PSD is towards its optimal. Countries such as the Democratic Republic of the Congo, Burundi, Madagascar and Azerbaijan have had the quickest speeds of adjustment of 66, 47, 45 and 40% respectively. In contrast, countries such as Kyrgyz republic, Albania, Congo Republic and Georgia have had the slowest adjustment with 9, 8, 7, and 7% respectively. There are other countries that have normally adjusted towards optimal PSD such as Equatorial Guinea, Iran, Kazakhstan and Algeria.

Regarding the most rapidly adjusting countries, the first three countries are an indication of the faster growth of African economies. The Democratic Republic

---

[2] The whole country mean of PSD is reported in Appendix Table A.13.

5.2 Results of Private Sector Development

Table 5.6 Development of mean indicators of PSD by year

Year	Observed	Optimal	Delta
1991	12.734	20.609	0.162
1992	12.764	20.249	0.154
1993	13.211	19.949	0.117
1994	14.983	21.123	0.139
1995	14.447	20.736	0.150
1996	15.186	20.991	0.100
1997	15.146	20.736	0.111
1998	15.090	20.148	0.101
1999	14.267	20.497	0.123
2000	14.375	21.452	0.089
2001	15.104	20.889	0.101
2002	14.813	21.064	0.072
2003	15.602	21.251	0.070
2004	15.751	21.485	0.040
2005	16.390	21.316	0.032
2006	16.084	21.578	−0.005
2007	16.818	20.899	−0.040
2008	17.364	20.681	−0.015
2009	16.546	18.431	0.063
2010	16.966	20.224	−0.021
2011	16.945	20.726	−0.006
2012	17.491	20.491	−0.027
2013	17.112	20.540	−0.043
2014	17.597	20.593	−0.059
2015	17.521	19.637	−0.036
2016	17.851	19.548	−0.049
2017	17.991	19.877	−0.072

of the Congo has the fastest adjustment speed towards PSD. Its economy largely depends on natural resource wealth mainly copper, gold, diamonds and oil. While agriculture is intended to provide subsistence, it has a potential to be an African food basket. This sector provided employment for 20 million people in 2010, despite low productivity (Otchia, 2014). The political instability and conflict until the early 1990s, have lowered national output. The relative stability of recovering from years of internal conflict and lack of infrastructure and institutions provides opportunities for policy and institutional reforms (Ragasa et al., 2016).

After a structural change with cooperation of international financial institutions and international donors in 2002, beginning with the adoption of a new mining law with the objective to encourage foreign direct investment, the Congo's economic

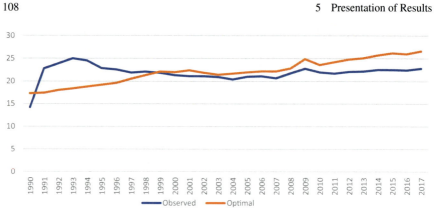

Fig. 5.1 Mean of observed and optimal of PSD by year

Table 5.7 Country mean value of PSD

Level	Country	Observed	Optimal	Delta
Faster Adjustment ≥ 0.2	Congo, Dem. Rep	10.077	15.821	0.664
	Burundi	5.450	11.431	0.467
	Madagascar	11.798	20.805	0.454
	Azerbaijan	27.060	27.949	0.349
	Botswana	18.328	22.828	0.310
0.1 ≥ Medium Adjustment < 0.2	Equatorial Guinea	28.630	9.241	0.188
	Iran, Islamic Rep	20.525	28.336	0.148
	Kazakhstan	20.849	25.293	0.147
	Algeria	18.378	18.578	0.110
0.1 < Slow Adjustment > 0	Kyrgyz Republic	15.631	26.202	0.099
	Albania	20.895	23.755	0.087
	Congo, Rep	17.342	20.125	0.074
	Georgia	17.086	26.816	0.074

conditions slowly began to improve. The economic activity in the resource sector was renewed and the country experienced relative economic growth (Mazalto, 2009).

Azerbaijan is another country that has a faster speed of adjustment towards PSD. Its economic growth is mainly attributed to an expanding oil and gas sector. However, the improvement in non-oil sectors resulted from improvement in most economic sectors which expanded the non-energy economies, namely infrastructure and social projects, which are useful for socio-economic development (Hasanov, 2013; Kardaş & Macit, 2015).

As for the countries that have a middle adjustment parameter, Equatorial Guinea as one of the African upper middle-income countries grew faster to become a high-income country. It has large diverse commodities such as cocoa, coffee, uranium,

5.2 Results of Private Sector Development

gold and diamond, even though it is largely dependent on oil. Since the discovery of petroleum in 1990, Equatorial Guinea became the third-largest producer of oil in Sub-Saharan Africa, after Nigeria and Angola. Alongside Botswana, Equatorial Guinea managed to graduate from the least developed countries in 2017. It has the highest GDP per capita among the African countries which amounts to more than 38,699 US dollars.

The government of Equatorial Guinea concluded the first phase of the National economic Plan Horizon 2020 towards development in 2012 focusing on infrastructure development. The ongoing second phase has been emphasising economic diversification through public investment towards the development of new strategic economic sectors such as agriculture, tourism and finance (Appel, 2017).

The figure reported in Table 5.7 shows that Algeria is among the middle fastest adjustment towards optimal PSD. Algeria's economy is highly dependent on hydrocarbons. The World Bank reports the advantage of the oil boom in Algeria which enabled the country to clear external debt, invest in infrastructure projects, and improve the country's Human Development Index (Bakari, 2018; World Bank, 2020).

The shift towards a more diversified economy has helped Algeria move slightly towards generating extra non-hydrocarbon revenues. For example, Algeria has significantly improved its human capital development, quality of education, budget deficit, subsidies, spending on goods and tightening of import policies. Its overall economic freedom score has increased due to improvements in property rights, monetary freedom and investment freedom (Economic Freedom, 2019a, 2019b).

In addition to these diversified actions, commercial services, industrial, construction and public works continue to drive non-hydrocarbon growth. Consequently, there has been a slight increase in non-hydrocarbon revenues (Bakari, 2018). The advantage of oil and gas rents in accelerating adjustment towards optimal PSD confirms the finding that on average the private sector can adjust better in oil and gas countries than other resource-type rich countries.

Congo Republic, with the value of 7.4% is one of the slowest countries to move towards PSD. It is one of the African countries that have been in chaos for many years. In fact, Congo's relative dependency on natural resources has been the same since 1990. Its relative dependency on natural resources has slightly increased from 42.5% of GDP in 1990 to 42.7% in 2017 (WDI, 2018). However, relatively unstable political conditions and less optimism of the private sector about business conditions due to the smaller size of the private business may justify the slowest adjustment parameter (Sinha & Kalayakgosi, 2018). The private sector activities have been limited due to high dependency on public expenditure, and as such its economic sectors experienced weak inter-sectorial diversity connections (Sekwati, 2010).

5.3 Privatisation Effect Results

5.3.1 Determinant of Optimal Privatisation

The relationships between explanatory variables with the optimal level of privatisation are presented in Table 5.8. The correlation between the optimal privatisation and the explanatory variables in resource revenue countries depends on political preferences, governance indicators and economic factors (Bortolotti & Pinotti, 2008; Jiang et al., 2015; Kay & Thompson, 1986).

One objective of privatisation is to provide fiscal capacity for the government by creating scope for tax collection (Estrin & Pelletier, 2018). Before privatisation, taxes imposed on state-owned enterprises were the main sources of tax revenue. However, in the early stages of implementation of the economic liberalisation, tax revenue

Table 5.8 Static and dynamic model parameter estimates (privatisation)

Model	Static model		Restricted dynamic		Unrestricted dynamic	
Variables	Estimate	Std error	Estimate	Std error	Estimate	Std error
Intercept	14.246[a]	1.135	7.856	6.401	5.942[c]	3.224
Taxation	0.634[a]	0.041	0.418[c]	0.197	0.146[c]	0.068
Natural resource rents	−0.037[b]	0.012	−0.034	0.058	−0.012[a]	0.034
Institutional quality	0.799[b]	0.271	2.447[c]	1.394	2.343[b]	0.621
Credit to private sector	−0.907[a]	0.213	−0.691	1.001	0.385	0.482
Unemployment	0.176[a]	0.034	0.183	0.162	0.209[c]	0.084
Salary & wages	−0.013[c]	0.007	−0.019	0.034	−0.108[b]	0.028
Subsidies	0.051[a]	0.012	0.088	0.057	0.006	0.025
Agricultural Productions	−0.197[a]	0.018	−0.077	0.125	0.099[c]	0.053
Manufacturing Productions	−0.066[a]	0.015	−0.102	0.072	−0.144[c]	0.059
Economic Growth	−0.164[b]	0.045	−0.376[c]	0.215	−0.253[a]	0.056
Trade openness	0.014[b]	0.005	0.042[c]	0.024	0.049[a]	0.012
Total Investment	−0.035[b]	0.012	−0.066	0.056	−0.087[b]	0.023
Trend	0.011	0.028	0.215	0.135	0.375[a]	0.071
Lower middle income			1.831	3.371	7.761[a]	1.943
Middle income			1.932	3.878	9.368[a]	2.237
Upper middle income			3.310	4.406	8.007[b]	2.284
Higher income			1.532	4.686	11.446[a]	2.477
Observation	937		937		937	
Adjusted R-squared	0.5461		0.9235		0.9496	
RMSE	5.1121		2.099		1.7034	

Note The dependent variable is Privatisation and the p value is: [a]$p \leq 0.001$, [b]$p \leq 0.05$, [c]$p \leq 0.10$

5.3 Privatisation Effect Results

was particularly affected (Crivelli, 2013; Martinez-Vazquez & McNab, 2000). As such, the privatisation process has widened the tax system in many transition- and industrialisation-based economies (Kuczynski, 1999).

Table 5.8 reports positive and significant coefficient of *Taxation* at the level of 90% highlighting the link between taxation and privatisation in natural resource-dependent countries. The structure of the tax system affects the privatisation process and its objectives. Crivelli (2013) explains how poorly structured taxation, including the traditional tax bases, the capacity of the tax administration and tax incentives to attract investments in the pre-transition period of privatisation, resulted in a significant decline in tax revenue collections. Generally, natural resource rich countries do not have tax administration capacity and have less tax incentives to attract investors.

Dependency on natural resources has been viewed with some scepticism. The most sceptical views include the resource curse argument either from a political economy (Auty, 1993, 2001) or an economic perspective (Sachs & Warner, 1995, 1997, 2001). Both perspectives identified natural resource dependency as a critical factor to reduce economic growth; however, the coefficient of *Dependency*, which is negative, it is non-significant, highlights no role of natural resources in compromising privatisation. Previous studies conducted by for example Van der Ploeg (2011); Venables (2016) and Von Haldenwang and Ivanyna (2018) have found that natural resource rents undermine the competitiveness of other sectors in the economy.

Some natural resource rich countries found difficulties in funding government enterprises during the oil shocks, and as such a number of enterprises were privatised. For instance, Saudi Arabia, in order to finance budget deficits, increased the degree of privatisation. It was ranked seventh in non-European countries by total privatisation revenues and in 2014 had a value of 6125 million dollar projects (Estrin & Pelletier, 2018). Furthermore, in sub-Saharan Africa, increasing privatisation causes a rise in shares of primary goods from 72% in 2000 to 78% in 2011 in total African exports.

An important finding from the literature relates to the natural resource dependency analysis highlighting the role of institutions in explaining negative economic growth. The role of institution and regulatory conditions has been promoted since the liberalisation reforms in the 1980s that enables competitors to consider investment in the economy. For example, African governments which are rich in natural resources, have introduced different incentive policies to enhance private investment and competitiveness resulting from the influential international private pro-investment (Zoomers, 2013). Similarly, privatisation as a productive activity requires effective institutional quality, otherwise it may not be productive or may lead to corruption scandals, such as those in Russia (Estrin & Pelletier, 2018).

Credit is essential for every single economy, especially for the resource rich countries that have experienced insecurity in income resulting from resource revenue volatility. As such, credit would boost economic development in those countries. Credit to the private sector refers to financial resources provided to the private sector through loans, purchases of nonequity securities and trade credits and other accounts receivable (WDI, 2019). The coefficient of *Credit to the Private Sector* is positive and non-significant.

In addition to credit to the private sector, governments may intervene to support either public or private enterprises. Typically, they apply a subsidy policy to mitigate the problem of inefficient allocation of resources. As a result, the implication of privatisation may change (Lin & Matsumura, 2018). The coefficient of *Subsidy* is positive and non-significant.

Theories on privatisation affirm that if institution capacity is weak, governments are better off delaying privatisation (Mohan, 2001; Nellis, 1998). A composite index, including different measures of institutional quality to identify the overall impact of institutional quality on privatisation has been used in this study. The coefficient of *Institutional Quality* is positive and statistically significant at the level of 95% indicating the importance of good governance and institutions on the development of privatisation. This means that privatisation progress in natural resource rich countries is associated with higher quality institutions. This finding supports the key elements of the regulatory framework listed in the OECD privatisation report (OECD, 2009), and is consistent with the finding of a number of studies that indicate the association of privatisation with the improvement of institutional quality.

Balza et al. (2013) found that privatisation is robustly associated with improvements in quality of institutions in the Latin American electric sector. Percoco (2014) in a study of private participation in transport infrastructure investment in developing countries, found that private participation in public–private partnership contracts is associated with better institutions. Marcelin and Mathur (2015) analysed how existing institutional arrangements affected privatised firms' performance, capital markets development and economic growth. They found that privatised firms performed better in countries with better regulatory and legal frameworks.

The negative and statistically significant coefficient of *Salary and Wages* indicates the discouragement of the direct impact of this variable on the privatisation process in natural resource rich countries. In most resource rich countries, the public sector is large (Ali et al., 2016; Estrin & Pelletier, 2018). It is not necessary for people to be skilled when they work in the government sector (Busse & Gröning, 2013). As such, it might be true that at the very stage of privatisation, a number of people lose their jobs due to disqualification.

Employee's salary and wages can affect macroeconomic performance including the privatisation process through the power of unions or labour regulations. Studies such as Agrawal and Matsa (2013) and Alimov (2015) reported that such labour regulations, including employment protection laws and the power of unions in the economy, significantly affect firm-level costs and labour market values. A more recent study by Subramanian and Megginson (2018) documented the large economic effect of labour regulations on privatisation by showing that strengthening employment protection discourages privatisation in subsequent periods and vice versa.

The coefficient of *Manufacturing Production* is negative and weakly significant. This means that privatisation progress in natural resource rich countries is associated with lower level of manufacturing. This explains the crowding out effect of natural resource rents. The resource curse undermines the competitiveness of the private sector, the investment climate and manufacturing production through increasing costs for private agents and unbroken threats on a country's macroeconomic stability. As such, this would derive de-industrialisation in the non-resource traded goods sector and thereby discourage privatisation activity.

The abundance of natural resources as stated by Frankel (2012) and Weber (2014) leads to crowding out manufacturing. The lure of revenue from natural resource rents reduces the impact of the manufacturing sector on privatisation. Manufacturing production is low and slow in natural resource-dependent countries due to the resource curse effects (Frankel, 2012; Weber, 2014). Such a slow growth of manufacturing does not support structural transformation and a sustained growth rate (McMillan & Rodrik, 2011; Rodrik, 2016).

Various studies have investigated the relationship between privatisation and economic growth; studies such as Yuyu Chen, Igami, Sawada, and Xiao (2018) and S. Zhao (2013) found a positive correlation between the two, while Bennett et al. (2007) did not identify a statistically significant relationship between the share of private sector and growth in 26 transition economies.

The coefficient of *Economic Growth* is negative and highly statistically significant in line with Nikolić and Kovačević (2014) and Zinnes et al. (2001) who found negative relationships between economic growth and privatisation. This indicates that once natural resources derive economic growth, economic growth might be negatively related to the optimal privatisation. Nevertheless, if privatisation was in line with in-depth institutional reforms in these countries, visible positive effects of economic growth might be noted.

The relationship between privatisation and trade policies has been investigated. The positive and highly significant coefficient of *Trade Openness* suggests that privatisation strategy in natural resource revenue countries is affected by trade openness. This finding is consistent with Han (2012) and Yu and Lee (2011) who found that privatisation strategy is strongly affected by trade policies, but this strategy is varied in the difference of trade instruments.

Investment is seen as an essential factor for development, in particular, to bring technology spill overs and stimulate competitiveness. Generally, there is a causal relationship between investment and privatisation. Kurtishi-Kastrati (2013) confirm this relationship by reporting the annual trend of foreign direct investment inflow and privatisation revenues that have moved in the same direction in South East Europe. Accordingly, privatisation has been a major channel for FDI, which in turn is a significant source of revenue for the privatised company.

The coefficient of *Total Investment* shows that progress in privatisation to some extent does not depend on the amount of investment in natural resource rich countries. This is consistent with studies such as those by Atkinson and Hamilton (2003); Frankel (2012); Gylfason and Zoega (2006) and Van der Ploeg (2011) who confirm the crowding out of physical capital effect of natural resources.

The trend of a volatile economy in natural resource-dependent countries during the past few decades has given reason for these countries to search for new sources of revenue. Some natural resource economies opened investment opportunities in the source of privatisation. This presented new opportunities to private investors and caused a growing trend of privatisation over the period of the study. The coefficient of *Time Trend* is positive and highly statistically significant indicating the ambitious efforts of these countries to diversify the economy, despite the occurrence of several economic crises during the sample periods.

The reference (intercept) which captures the effect of low-income countries is positive and statistically significant at the level of 90% indicating the opportunities these countries have to privatise. These countries in the sample include, but are not limited to, Mauritania, the Republic of Guinea, Ghana, Peru, the Democratic Republic of Congo, Mongolia, Kenya, Madagascar, Mozambique, Lao PDR and Timor-least. These countries generally have a larger state sector than other countries, and which is better for privatisation (Estrin & Pelletier, 2018).

The country group income coefficients show that the coefficient of all income groups compared to the reference is positive and highly significant. This means that regardless of income level, natural resource-based economies can adjust towards privatisation. This finding confirms critical facts that resource wealth countries tend to focus on diversifying their economies. However, literature has suggested that privatisation is better in countries that have larger state sector and better administration capabilities (Estrin & Pelletier, 2018).

5.3.2 The Speed of Adjustment Values

To estimate the adjustment speed of optimal privatisation, an empirical framework was constructed to identify the factors that affect the speed of adjustment in the context of natural resource dependency. Several policy variables, in which some are partially overlapping with the determinants of privatisation, have been used to estimate the speed of adjustment (see, Appendix Table A.10).

When the effect of resource types is estimated, the result shows that there are no statistically significant relationships between the speed of adjustment towards optimal privatisation and *Oil & Gas* rents. This means that resource type may not impact the adjustment speed of privatisation in natural resource rich countries.

The mean values from the unrestricted dynamic model report some of the key variables of privatisation by period, income group, degree of dependency on natural resources, year of observation and mean adjustment of privatisation by country. The mean adjustment parameter δ explains the size of the gap between the actual privatisation and its long-term optimal value. All computed indicators (observed, optimal, and speed of adjustment) are time and country specific.

Mean Indicator Values by Time Period

The mean value of adjustment speed of privatisation reports by Delta is positive in all three sub-periods (1990–1999, 2000–2009, 2010–2017), meaning that there is an improvement in the economy of the natural resource rich countries towards diversifying the economy by promoting privatisation policy. Although the mean adjustment parameter is positive in all three periods, it slowed down over the three

5.3 Privatisation Effect Results

Table 5.9 Mean adjustment speed of privatisation by time period

Period	Observed	Optimal	Delta
1990–1999	22.918	19.636	0.117
2000–2009	21.239	23.064	0.093
2010–2017	22.273	26.432	0.082

sub-periods from 12% (1990–1999), to 9% (2000–2009) and finally to 8% (2010–2017). However, the first period is higher as a response to the fast wave of privatisation that started in the early 1980s. This change is presented in Table 5.9.

The mean of *Delta* reported in the table shows that there is a fast improvement in adjustment speed towards optimal privatisation starting from 12% in the first period of 1990–1999, and decreasing to 8% in the third period. However, the change from the first to the second period (25%) is larger than the change from the second to the third period (13%). The econometric interpretation for this decrease in the size of change is that during the second period of 2000–2009 a series of crises such as the 2000 technology bubble as a result of the internet-driven economy, the September 11th terrorist attacks, the war on terror and Iraq war in 2003, the global recession from 2007–2008 and the energy crises throughout this period, all weakened global economic competitiveness (Ghosh et al., 2017; Gonza & Burger, 2017).

Mean Indicator Values by Income Group

The sampled countries were divided into groups based on their level of income. Table 5.10 shows that the privatisation adjustment speed mean is improving in all income groups. While the mean adjustment parameter is fastest in higher income countries, it is the slowest in lower income resource rich countries.

The mean adjustment seems more flexible between Upper middle-and higher-income countries. The mean value of upper middle-income groups implies that the adjustment speed is approximately 10% closer to the desired level of privatisation within a year. This implies that each year the adjustment towards privatisation develops by 10% and the full development of privatisation takes almost 10 years to reach the optimal level.

As for the higher income countries, the mean value implies that the adjustment speed is approximately 11% closer to the optimal level of privatisation within a

Table 5.10 Mean adjustment speed of privatisation by income group

Income Group	Observed	Optimal	Delta
Lower income	14.547	15.447	0.057
Lower middle-income	17.576	22.529	0.091
Middle-income	20.683	24.471	0.086
Upper middle-income	22.900	23.983	0.099
Higher income	26.651	27.559	0.110

Table 5.11 Mean adjustment speed of privatisation by private sector size

Size	Observed	Optimal	Delta
Smaller size	25.574	21.145	0.130
Lower middle size	17.978	21.807	0.063
Middle size	19.570	24.091	0.101
Upper middle size	21.377	23.502	0.074
Larger size	21.880	23.890	0.076

year. The adjustment towards privatisation each year develops by 11% and the full development of privatisation takes almost 9 years to reach the optimal level.

While immediate adjustment is costly and might not take place, this adjustment is possible. Generally, government sectors in these two groups of income are larger (Estrin & Pelletier, 2018). This provides wider opportunities for privatisation within these periods, and thus the lure of revenue received from selling the SOEs speeds the privatisation process as well as widens privatisation policy. The flexibility of the adjustment speed towards optimal privatisation in all the income groups resulted in increasing capital mobilisation, rapid growth of transition economies and the achievement of the development plan globally which have made this adjustment relatively fast. Furthermore, this positive adjustment, although mainly attributed to radical changes in general economic policy, has shown a greater incentive of these countries to diversify their economies as they have insufficient resources to generate revenues.

Mean Indicator Values by Private Sector Size

The results reported in Table 5.11 indicate that adjustment is varied with the variation in the size of the private sector. The result shows that privatisation in countries with middle- and smaller-sized private sectors have faster adjustment towards the optimal privatisation.

By contrast, the gap from observed to optimal in countries that have upper middle and larger size of privatisation left a large space for adjustment which is hard to regain. For instance, in recent years, due to a sharp drop in oil prices, Russia's economy has struggled. Despite extremely large privatisation, there is limited scope for new developments.

Mean Indicator Values by Degree of Dependency

Table 5.12 shows the mean adjustment speed of privatisation by degree of dependency on natural resources. The mean value indicates that regardless of the level of dependency on natural resources the speed of privatisation is adjusting towards an optimal level. However, the figure depicts that countries with less dependency on natural resources adjust faster than those with other degrees of dependency. For

5.3 Privatisation Effect Results

Table 5.12 Mean adjustment speed of privatisation by degree of dependency on natural resources

Degree of dependency	Observed	Optimal	Delta
Higher dependency	22.566	24.208	0.079
Upper middle-dependency	19.573	21.815	0.103
Middle-dependency	18.508	19.080	0.090
Lower middle-dependency	20.558	20.048	0.110
Lower dependency	22.587	21.901	0.196

example, different countries from developed, developing and transition economies such as Norway, Turkey, Panama, Tunisia, Vietnam, Mexico and Chile are a number of sampled countries that have a relatively lower degree of dependency on natural resources.

Some specific characteristics of these countries can explain the relative faster adjustment towards optimal privatisation. For example, Norway provides resources for long-term investment through a large sovereign wealth fund from oil revenue instead of depositing the surplus wealth (Bernstein et al., 2013), despite enjoying strong institutions. Meanwhile, Turkey has been following liberal economic policy for decades and has recently encouraged foreign investment to upgrade infrastructure development and other services. However, the recent acceleration of privatisation is due to two factors (Zaifer, 2015). First, greater integration with foreign investors that accumulate domestic production and second, a new reproduction strategy and profit imperatives which achieve economic expansion and produce relative internal political stability. Vietnam, which has been restructuring their economy including privatisation of SOEs, spends money on infrastructure projects, thereby foreign investment accelerates the relative adjustment speed of privatisation (Tran et al., 2015).

Mean Indicator Values by Year

Table 5.13 presents the development of mean indicator of privatisation by year. The adjustment parameter shows the movement of privatisation during the sampled periods. As it is shown in Fig. 5.2, the mean adjustment parameter (δ) has a slow movement (up and down) reflecting the global economy as well as country-specific characteristics.

The Asian financial crises in 1997 slightly affected the adjustment towards privatisation. The mean adjustment parameter in 1997 was 12.5% and decreased to 10.7% until 1999. Surprisingly, a decline in economic activity in the 2000s, mainly in developed countries, did not affect privatisation and its adjustment process. In fact, it started to progress in 2000 from 10.8%.

However, the global economic recovery in 2009 downsized the gap between actual and optimal privatisation by improving (δ) from 6% in 2007 to a peak of 15% in 2009. This relative larger adjustment towards optimal privatisation was possibly due to a global increase in investment. While private domestic investment has grown since 2000 reaching 2.6 trillion US dollars in 2009, public investment even during the

Table 5.13 Development of mean indicator of privatisation by year

Year	Observed	Optimal	Delta
1991	22.783	17.141	0.116
1992	23.884	17.595	0.103
1993	25.005	18.338	0.122
1994	24.525	18.732	0.109
1995	22.867	19.619	0.130
1996	22.571	19.989	0.122
1997	21.891	20.983	0.125
1998	22.111	21.248	0.125
1999	21.833	21.990	0.107
2000	21.326	22.136	0.108
2001	21.112	22.618	0.109
2002	21.100	22.281	0.064
2003	20.927	22.057	0.073
2004	20.405	22.112	0.083
2005	21.004	22.778	0.075
2006	21.103	22.772	0.069
2007	20.682	23.239	0.063
2008	21.769	24.007	0.135
2009	22.778	25.844	0.147
2010	21.983	24.670	0.119
2011	21.715	25.037	0.088
2012	22.098	25.650	0.061
2013	22.169	26.251	0.068
2014	22.532	26.699	0.061
2015	22.512	27.450	0.100
2016	22.434	27.553	0.088
2017	22.810	28.171	0.076

global financial crisis in 2008, continued to increase as a countercyclical tool against the economic slowdown (United Nations, 2011). This is reflected in the economic growth of many countries and the private sector is the centre of attention.

Later, the sharp decline in oil prices in 2014 further stimulated adjustment towards an optimal level of privatisation, the adjustment parameter grew from 6% in 2014 to 10%, 8% and 7.6% in 2015, 2016 and 2017 respectively. For example, during the oil shock of 2014, countries such as Saudi Arabia found difficulties in funding government enterprises. As such, as indicated by privatised projects in 2014 to the value of 6125 million US dollars, this increased the degree of privatisation (Ait-Laoussine & Gault, 2017; Estrin & Pelletier, 2018).

5.3 Privatisation Effect Results

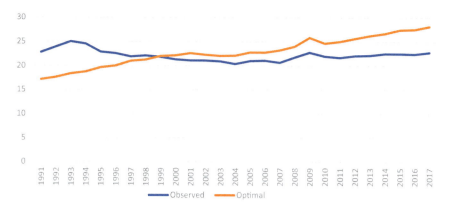

Fig. 5.2 Mean of observed and optimal of privatisation by year

Mean Indicator Values by Country[3]

Table 5.14 presents the adjustment parameter mean indicator values related to speed of adjustment by country. The six countries that have the fastest adjustments towards optimal level of privatisation are Zambia, Angola, the Republic of Congo, Russia, Botswana and Azerbaijan in which four of them are from Africa. This is an indication of faster-growing African economies. In contrast, countries such as Uzbekistan, Benin, the Philippines and Indonesia have the lowest value of mean of adjustment speed. Interestingly, the results show that Mali has no adjustment at all towards optimal privatisation.

Zambia, which has the fastest adjustment mean of privatisation among the studied countries, had been listed in the six leaders of privatised firms in Africa (Nellis, 2003). This faster adjustment is possibly due to a number of factors. First, the comparative advantage in some products made Zambia a positive trade balance in 2017 (Mzumara et al., 2012). Second, Zambia's human development index has improved over the sample period from 0.401 in 1990 to 0.588 in 2017 (UNDP, 2019). Third, the establishment of a number of multi-facility economic zones is a consequence of the promotion of privatisation policy (Fessehaie et al., 2016).

Poland is among the fastest groups of middle adjustment countries with the value of 19%. It is a high-income country that enjoys relatively high economic growth. The major components of its economy are the sectors of services, industry, agriculture and natural resources including natural gas, copper, coal and silver. Poland's economy is ranked 24 in the Ease of Doing Business in 2017. Since pursuing economic liberalisation policy in 1990, the economic fitness of the country (a measure of a country's diversification and ability to produce complex goods) improved dramatically. As such, its dependency on natural resources reduced from 3.4% of GDP in 1990 to only 1% by 2017 (WDI, 2020a).

---

[3] The full list of country mean values are presented in Appendix Table A.14.

Table 5.14 Country mean value of privatisation

Level	Country	Observed	Optimal	Delta
Faster Adjustment ≥ 0.2	Zambia	19.069	18.902	0.620
	Angola	25.352	26.654	0.366
	Congo, Republic	22.962	25.224	0.274
	Russian Federation	23.648	26.115	0.242
	Botswana	30.109	30.289	0.232
	Azerbaijan	21.414	20.828	0.226
0.1 ≥ Medium Adjustment < 0.2	Poland	32.898	35.880	0.190
	Moldova	31.254	27.654	0.180
	Ukraine	35.540	26.141	0.179
	Algeria	22.982	22.617	0.144
0.1 < Slow Adjustment > 0	Uzbekistan	18.935	25.676	0.004
	Benin	12.600	20.470	0.005
	Philippines	15.158	22.599	0.005
	Indonesia	15.683	19.366	0.008
No Adjustment = 0	Mali	12.434	21.199	0

With regard to the level of adjustment towards optimal privatisation, Uzbekistan, with a closed and state-dominated economy is the slowest. After 25 years of independence, the economy still maintained a soviet-style command economy. Uzbekistan's government subsidies every economic activity related to production, prices and foreign currencies. State-led investments and the export of cotton, natural gas and gold are major foreign exchange earner and a significant deriver of economic growth (Trushin, 2017).

When the speed of adjustment, which is a magnitude of desired adjustment between two subsequent periods, is equal to zero ($\delta_{it} = 0$), there is no adjustment. The country mean value of privatisation indicates that Mali does not have any interest to adjust towards privatisation.

5.4 The Result of Taxation Effects

5.4.1 Determinant of Optimal Taxation

The expected relationships between explanatory variables with the optimal level of taxation in resource rich revenue countries depend on the degree of dependency on natural resources for generation of revenue and countries' institutional quality (Arezki & Van der Ploeg, 2011; Ji et al., 2014; Odhiambo & Olushola, 2018).

5.4 The Result of Taxation Effects

Table 5.15 presents the estimated coefficients of the explanatory variables. Natural resource-dependent countries suffer from revenue instability due to high international market price volatility, thereby they are highly vulnerable to external shocks. While economic diversification of resource rich countries is exceedingly important, it is rather difficult to achieve the stability objectives. Hendrick and Crawford (2014); Pagano and Hoene (2010) and Shi and Tao (2018) claim that revenue diversification helps countries to reduce revenue volatility; the most sufficiently diversified economy is one which is least vulnerable to specific shocks (Afonso, 2013; Odhiambo & Olushola, 2018).

The coefficient of *Diversification* is positive and statistically significant at the level of 90%. It shows that the optimal level of taxation in resource-dependent countries is associated with a more diversified economy. This result is in line with a study by Shi and Tao (2018) who found that revenue diversification leads to effective taxation in countries with poor fiscal conditions.

Privatisation, which provides large government revenue, also allows consumers to pay for services, and reduces the government's role in the economy (Mikesell, 2013; Tanzi, 2011). Yet, the relationship between privatisation and optimal taxation in natural resource rich countries is equivocal. Natural resource rich countries receive most of their revenue from resource rents which are highly volatile. Then, the

Table 5.15 Static and dynamic model parameter estimate (taxation)

Model	Static model		Restricted dynamic		Unrestricted dynamic	
Variables	Estimate	Std error	Estimate	Std error	Estimate	Std error
Intercept	−1.359[c]	0.746	−0.607	4.182	1.523	2.012
Privatisation	0.423[a]	0.016	0.207[c]	0.103	0.264[a]	0.050
Natural resource rents	−0.032[b]	0.009	−0.071	0.047	−0.147[a]	0.025
Diversification	0.025[a]	0.004	0.030	0.024	0.010[c]	0.012
Economic growth	0.108[b]	0.030	0.780[a]	0.197	0.296[a]	0.045
Governance	−0.003	0.007	−0.018	0.038	−0.015	0.017
Export	−0.039[a]	0.008	−0.088[c]	0.048	0.058[b]	0.019
Import	0.061[a]	0.008	0.130[b]	0.049	0.019	0.012
Tax capacity	0.150[a]	0.009	0.188[a]	0.048	0.274[a]	0.018
Trend	0.026	0.019	0.028	0.095	0.158[b]	0.050
Lower middle income			0.004	2.210	−2.704[c]	1.137
Middle Income			1.292	2.246	−0.941	1.294
Upper middle income			3.079	2.624	−2.098	1.362
Higher Income			0.666	2.962	−4.865[b]	1.539
Observation	937		937		937	
Adjusted *R*-Squared	0.4955		0.9004		0.9382	
RMSE	3.4706		1.5417		1.2149	

Note The dependent variable is Taxation and the *p* value is: [a]$p \leq 0.001$, [b]$p \leq 0.05$, [c]$p \leq 0.10$

resource curse which is a long-lasting threat on a country's macroeconomic stability, undermines the competitiveness of the private sector and the investment climate through increasing costs for private agents with negative growth effect.

Thus, the expected effect of privatisation could be either positive or negative on taxes in resource-dependent countries. The coefficient of *Privatisation* is positive and highly statistically significant, indicating that the higher the pressure to privatise the economy, the higher the marginal return of the taxes received.

The correlation between natural resource rents and taxation was expected to be negative, as natural resource revenue-dependent countries have no concern with taxing their citizens (Besley & Persson, 2011; Jensen, 2011). The more resource revenue, the lower the level of taxation. As expected, the *Natural Resource Rents* coefficient is negative and highly statistically significant, indicating that countries which generate revenue from natural resource rents are unlikely to rely on taxes. This result is consistent with A. D. Jensen (2011) who found that an increase in the share of natural resource rents is associated with lower revenue from taxes. Crivelli and Gupta (2014) found a sizable impact of natural resource rent not only on total taxes but also on different tax sources. Taxes increase access to other forms of revenue which in turn expand revenue diversification, thereby overcoming the problem of resource dependency.

While the coefficient of *Economic Growth* was expected to have a positive relationship with taxation, it may also have been negative as economic growth does not mechanically translate into a higher tax (Besley & Persson, 2014; Piketty & Qian, 2009). The coefficient is positive and highly significant in relation to taxation similar to studies by Crivelli and Gupta (2014), and Fenochietto and Pessino (2013). These findings are unlike those of Besley and Persson (2014) who found a negative correlation between tax and the growth of income of some oil states. It is important to note however that economic growth does not translate into higher taxes (Besley & Persson, 2011).

Previous studies have shown that growth from resource rents leads to lower taxation as it reduces incentives to generate revenue from local non-resource production sources (see for example: Besley & Persson, 2011; Jensen & Johnston, 2011). Nevertheless, the income generated from resource rents, which foster the decline in tax rate, causes citizen's wealth to grow faster than the economy.[4] Natural resource revenue-dependent governments find it difficult to achieve a stable economy due to the volatility of resource revenue. However, the problem of weak governance has often led to an excessive reliance on regressive taxation (Deacon, 2011). While the reported results in Table 5.15 found a negative and non-significant relationship between governance and taxation, previous studies suggested a causal relationship between the two. Le and Viñuela (2012) claim that taxation is an important aspect of governance. Countries with a stronger governance structure tend to benefit from a taxation system more than those with weaker ones, thus, countries may strengthen

---

[4] For a broader picture on how increased dependency on natural resources fosters less economic growth and greater inequality in income distribution across countries, see Gylfason and Zoega (2003).

5.4 The Result of Taxation Effects

their tax system through improvement of their governance structure (Ajaz & Ahmad, 2010).

The reported results show that the coefficient of *Tax Capacity* is positive and highly statistically significant. This indicates that taxation is proportional to tax capacity when other factors are held constant. It is generally challenging for resource rich countries to generate non-resource revenue from taxation due to poor tax capacity in the process of revenue generation. Natural resource wealthy economies often have poorly developed tax structures (Fenochietto & Pessino, 2013), and rents lower domestic tax efforts (Le & Viñuela, 2012). Interestingly, tax capacity and its administration primarily depend on political will (Kidd & Crandall, 2006; Osmundsen, 2009), but this will is unsustainable in resource rich countries (Le & Viñuela, 2012). Resource-dependent countries experience deteriorated tax administration capacity due to discretionary power over taxes (Knack, 2009).

Trade measures such as export and import duties are adopted internationally. Economic analysis provides rational justifications for imposing barriers in terms of changes in international trade terms, thus the economic consequence of various trade policies is to pursue domestic price stability (Bouët & Debucquet, 2012). The coefficient of export is positive and significant at the level of 90%, meaning that the more products countries export, the higher taxes received. The economic interpretation for this relationship is that a number of natural resource countries may still be reliant on trade tax revenue. This indicates that there is a trade-off for the resource revenue-dependent government either to go for trade liberalisation or stay behind export taxes. Baunsgaard and Keen (2010) claim that trade liberalisation could be impeded unless countries are enabled to develop alternative sources of revenue. The coefficient of *Import* is positive, but non-significant. Import tariffs are associated with increasing higher taxes. Although higher taxes on import protect domestic good prices, it affects the national welfare[5] (Bouët & Debucquet, 2012).

Time trend is included in the model specification to capture the variation in countries tax systems over time. The share of tax changes over time by either increasing or decreasing. The positive significant *Time Trend* coefficient presents development of taxation over time during the sampled period to finance growing service provision and government intervention in the market.

Country-specific factors such as level of income play a major role in explaining the emergence of taxes in resource-wealthy countries. Contrary to the prior expectation, the share of taxes does not seem to increase with the level of income in natural resource rich countries; the coefficients of lower middle income and higher income are significant at the level of 90 and 95% respectively. Although tax theory suggests that high-income countries raise more taxes than low-income countries, the coefficients of all *Income Groups* reported in Table 5.15 are negative relative to that of low-income countries (reference).

The economic interpretation for this result is that revenue driven from resource rents reduces the incentives to generate revenue from taxes (Jensen, 2011). This

---

[5] For further understanding of the mechanism of export and import barriers see Bouët and Debucquet (2012)

result is consistent with natural resource curse literature arguing that resource rents reduce the government's need to tax its citizens (Cabrales & Hauk, 2011; Jensen & Wantchekon, 2004; Ross, 2001). This finding is consistent with Besley and Persson (2014) who found a negative correlation between tax share and level of income in several oil states. However, the intercept which captures the effect of low-income group is positive, but non-significant, indicating that countries with a low level of income have a relatively greater incentive to generate taxes.

5.4.2 The Speed of Adjustment Values

The speed of adjustment parameters is specified as the function of several policy variables (see, Appendix Table A.11) that affect the adjustment of taxation at the country level. Some of the variables partially overlap with the determinants of optimal taxation without influencing the consistency of the estimates. Variability of the flexible speed of adjustment and its explanation through observable and commonly practiced policy variables is the distinguishing feature of this study compared with the traditional dynamic models where the speed of adjustment is of unknown form and remains constant across countries and over time.

The *Oil & Gas* dummy variable is included as a policy variable to capture the unobserved effects of adjustment speed of resource types on taxation. The lure of revenue from oil and gas derives a negative relationship between the oil and gas dummy variable and taxation. Similar to the impact of natural resource rents, oil and gas resource types negatively affect the adjustment towards optimal taxation. The negative and statistically significant coefficient of *Oil & Gas* explains the key role of existing rents in ignoring the importance of generating domestic non-resource sources of revenue.

In other words, the negative coefficient indicates that there is no adjustment towards optimal level of taxation in oil and gas countries unless their governments limit their fiscal dependence on oil and gas rents. This finding is consistent with previous studies by Crivelli and Gupta (2014); Ossowski and Gonzáles (2012), and Thomas and Trevino (2013) who found a negative relationship between tax revenue and oil and gas resource revenues for a number of oil and gas producers in Latin American, the Caribbean and Sub-Saharan African resource rich countries.

The mean values of some of the key variables of optimal taxation by time period, income group, degree of dependency on natural resources, year of observation and country are reported. The mean adjustment parameter δ explains the size of the gap between the actual taxation and its long-term optimal value.

Mean Indicator Values by Time Period

The adjustment speed reported in Table 5.16 is positive in all three periods. It moved positively over the three sub-periods from 9.6% (1990–1999), to 8% (2000–2009)

5.4 The Result of Taxation Effects

Table 5.16 Mean adjustment speed of taxation by time period

Period	Observed	Optimal	Delta
1990–1999	6.99	3.054	0.096
2000–2009	9.342	8.323	0.082
2010–2017	11.243	11.051	0.041

and finally to 4% (2010–2017). The positive adjustment towards optimal taxation in all three periods suggests that resource rich countries have a desire to move towards diversified resources that provide greater economic stability.

The table shows that there is a slow downward trend in adjustment speed of taxation starting at 9.6% in the first period of 1990–1999 to 4.1% in the third period of 2010–2017. The change in the adjustment parameter from the second period to the last period (100%) is faster than the change from the first to the second period (17%). But the overall trend decreased by 134% during the sample period. The economic interpretation for this decrease in adjustment speed is that countries generate lower levels of taxation, while having access to other forms of revenue (Besley & Persson, 2014; Odhiambo & Olushola, 2018).

A second interpretation is that since the global economy has placed great importance on natural resources, especially oil and gas, the prices of these resources as a response to the market will be higher. Hence, the higher prices of natural resources provide larger revenue for the resource rich countries. As there is a negative relationship between taxation and natural resource rents, this explains the downward trend of adjustment speed towards taxation. Accordingly, the size of the natural resource rents (% of GDP) on average during the three periods was 1.5, 2.9 and 3.3 respectively (WDI, 2018).

Since several shocks and economic crises occurred over the sample period,[6] the positive trend of the adjustment speed addresses the need for adjustment towards taxation. This is critical given that the resource rich countries tend to focus on avoiding the resource curse.

Mean Indicator Values by Income Group

The adjustment speeds of taxation in the middle and lower-income resource rich countries are faster than the other income groups reported in Table 5.17. The mean value of income groups implies that the adjustment speed is approximately nine per cent closer to the desired level of taxation within a year in middle-income natural resource revenue countries. This means that adjustment develops each year by nine per cent and the full development of the tax system takes almost 11 years to reach the optimal level. This long period of development of national taxation is possibly

---

[6] Crises include; the 1990 oil price shock in response to the Iraqi invasion of Kuwait, the Asian financial crises in 1997, the global financial crisis in 2008, and the sharp decline in oil prices in 2014.

Table 5.17 Mean adjustment speed of taxation by income group

Income group	Observed	Optimal	Delta
Lower income	4.780	4.357	0.078
Lower middle-income	5.502	4.493	0.057
Middle-income	10.466	10.132	0.090
Upper middle-income	13.281	7.627	0.056
Higher-income	11.805	9.964	0.070

Table 5.18 Mean value of taxation by private sector size

Size	Observed	Optimal	Delta
Smaller size	9.480	7.345	0.141
Lower middle-size	5.909	5.056	0.081
Middle-size	8.669	7.377	0.070
Upper middle-size	9.952	7.939	0.046
Larger size	10.168	8.345	0.089

due to weak governance, weak tax capacity, and political, economic distributional and industry competitiveness considerations in resource rich countries.

Furthermore, the desire to adjust in these countries is probably due to a shortage or inefficiency of resource activity that is not sufficient to generate revenues. This finding is consistent with the result for lower-income country determinates of optimal taxation reported in Table 5.15, which confirms that countries with a low level of income have a greater incentive to generate taxes in natural resource rich countries. This analysis suggests, in turn, that low- and middle-income resource rich countries tend to reduce their revenue vulnerability through diversifying their revenue sources.

Mean Values of Taxation by Private Sector Size

The activity of the private sector, and a firm's size, affect the rate of taxes. As indicated in Table 5.18, the mean indicator value of adjustment speed is flexible enough to adjust as the firms develop. However, the flexibility of the adjustment speed is faster in smaller sized private sectors. As such, natural resource rich countries adjust at every size of the private sector, but private sectors' smaller sized countries may adjust towards optimal taxation faster than other private sector sized countries. This result relates to the capacity of the resource-dependent government in taxing economic activities which is relatively weak.

Mean Indicator Values by Degree of Dependency

The differences in the economic structure of natural resource rich countries affect the common features among them. Table 5.19 reports mean taxation values from

5.4 The Result of Taxation Effects

Table 5.19 Mean value of taxation by degree of dependency

Degree of dependency	Observed	Optimal	Delta
Higher dependency	10.546	8.092	0.059
Upper middle dependency	6.549	5.663	0.087
Middle dependency	7.435	6.293	0.102
Lower middle dependency	4.940	5.023	0.117
Lower dependency	6.143	6.822	0.128

the unrestricted dynamic model based on degree of dependency. The mean value by degree of dependency shows that taxation adjustment speed in countries with less dependency on natural resources is faster than those with other degrees of dependency. Although the adjustment speed is much lower in higher and upper middle dependency, the flexibility of the adjustment in all groups suggests that regardless of the degree of dependency, natural resource rich countries would have a greater incentive to avoid resource volatility by relying on taxes and developing their tax bases accordingly.

This is an indication that governments of resource rich economies tend to limit their fiscal dependency on natural resources. Since revenues derived from resource rents are vulnerable to external shocks, these countries tend to diversify revenue sources to stabilise macroeconomic conditions and thus, reduce dependency on natural resources. This finding aligns with Crivelli and Gupta (2014, p. 17) who stated that 'countries with a lower dependency on natural resources would have a greater incentive to preserve their non-resource revenue base'.

Mean Indicator Values by Year

Table 5.20 and Fig. 5.3 show the movement of the observed, optimal and delta of taxation. According to the figure, during the first four years there was a large gap between observed and optimal which is hard to regain.

Generally, during economic crises and recessions, buying and selling fall. As such, the growth of tax revenue decreases. The Asian financial crises in 1997 affected the development of taxation. The mean adjustment parameter in 1996 was 9.4% and decreased to 6.9% until 1999.

Surprisingly, a decline in economic activity in 2000s mainly in developed countries did not affect the development of a taxation system in the sampled countries, but rather, it reached a peak by having a faster adjustment of 14.6%. This might be the case as while the decline in manufacturing employment caused a drop in employment rate especially among less educated workers, employees worked more hours on average compared to previous years (Charles et al., 2019).

The global financial crisis between 2007 and 2008 affected the development of taxation and caused an expansion in the gap between actual and optimal PSD by declining the mean adjustment parameter from 9% in 2006, to 5.5% in 2008. The

Table 5.20 Development of mean indicator of taxation by year

Year	Observed	Optimal	Delta
1991	6.660	0.100	0.096
1992	6.726	0.100	0.092
1993	6.665	0.100	0.097
1994	6.598	0.100	0.061
1995	6.965	4.853	0.136
1996	7.079	5.088	0.094
1997	7.256	5.294	0.084
1998	7.342	5.623	0.137
1999	7.678	6.284	0.069
2000	7.697	6.886	0.146
2001	8.015	6.505	0.067
2002	7.915	7.218	0.099
2003	8.279	7.695	0.050
2004	9.109	8.628	0.046
2005	9.649	9.410	0.073
2006	10.502	9.387	0.091
2007	10.527	9.462	0.089
2008	10.986	9.263	0.055
2009	10.738	8.777	0.105
2010	10.889	10.635	0.085
2011	11.224	11.094	0.037
2012	11.516	11.098	0.046
2013	11.159	10.794	0.022
2014	11.439	10.697	0.014
2015	11.394	11.077	0.036
2016	11.412	11.523	0.045
2017	10.910	11.489	0.047

relative global economic recovery increased the adjustment parameter to 10% in 2009.

However, the adjustment towards an optimal level of taxation declined to its lowest (1.4%) because of the sharp decline in oil prices in 2014. An opposite impact was expected, whereby a fall in oil prices impacted taxation. Nevertheless, the stability in oil prices affected the adjustment speed of taxation.

5.4 The Result of Taxation Effects

Fig. 5.3 Mean of observed and optimal of taxation by year

Table 5.21 Mean indicator of taxation by country

Level	Country	Observed	Optimal	Delta
Faster Adjustment ≥ 0.2	Azerbaijan	8.484	7.521	0.430
	Angola	13.672	15.37	0.315
	Algeria	33.498	16.369	0.295
	Zambia	2.802	3.33	0.288
	Mozambique	6.362	2.699	0.284
0.1 ≥ Medium Adjustment < 0.2	Suriname	8.809	7.622	0.198
	Gambia, The	4.117	5.963	0.175
	Botswana	15.938	14.989	0.173
	Belarus	18.32	15.08	0.171
0.1 < Slow Adjustment > 0	Tunisia	19.76	17.421	0.003
	Benin	9.470	8.128	0.006
	Rwanda	2.875	2.022	0.014
	Indonesia	9.946	16.181	0.032

Mean Indicator Values by Country[7]

The mean indicator values related to speed of adjustment by country are presented in Table 5.21. The adjustment mean parameter resulted from the variation in the gap between actual and optimal taxation across countries within a given year. The larger the speed of adjustment, the closer the observed taxation is towards its desired level.

Countries such as Azerbaijan, Angola, Algeria, Zambia and Mozambique have had the quickest speed of adjustment of 43%, 31%, 29.5%, 29% and 28% respectively.

---

[7] The complete list of country mean value is presented in Appendix Table A.15.

Countries such as Suriname, Gambia, Botswana and Belarus have recorded middle adjustment speeds of 19.8%, 17.5%, 17.3% and 17.1% respectively. Nevertheless, a number of countries from all the three models overlapped in recording relatively good adjustment, for example, Zambia, Azerbaijan, Botswana and Algeria (see Tables 5.7 and 5.14).

The figure reported shows that Algeria has the third fastest adjustment towards optimal taxation, although Algeria's economy is highly dependent on hydrocarbons.

Algeria improved domestic investment as one of the necessary solutions to promote economic growth of the country (Bakari, 2018). The shift towards a more diversified economy has helped Algeria move slightly towards generating extra non-hydrocarbon revenues. For example, Algeria has significantly improved its human capital development, quality of education, budget deficit, subsidies, spending on goods and tightening of import policies. Its overall economic freedom score has increased due to improvements in property rights, monetary freedom and investment freedom (Bakari, 2018; Economic Freedom, 2019a, 2019b).

Gambia is an African country that has a middle adjustment level towards taxation. This country, unlike many African countries, has been politically stabilised since its independence. Gambia relies less on natural resources; mining, which is the main industry, is underdeveloped, and thereby plays no significant role in the economy. The main sectors of the economy are tourism, agriculture and remittances. Gambia applies a liberal policy to privatise a number of SOEs in which it was the first of the six leaders in terms of number of firms privatised (Nellis, 2003). This policy boosted credit to the private sector from 3% in 2017 to 32% in 2018. As a result, the main sectors grew strongly; there was a 26% increase in number of tourists recorded compared to the previous year, and agriculture growth witnessed a 0.9% increase compared to the previous year. As such, the more sectors that are privatised, the faster adjustment is towards taxation. Consequently, the country's GDP was recorded as 1.7% higher than the previous year of 2017 (World Bank, 2019).

In contrast, countries such as Tunisia, Benin, Rwanda and Indonesia had the poorest adjustment of 0.3%, 0.6%, 1.4% and 3.2% respectively. Benin and Indonesia are two countries that previously recorded the poorest adjustment speed towards privatisation. Thus, the figures reported in the table above are consistent with the result for the relationship between privatisation and taxation reported in Table 5.15. Hence, a more privatised economy has a better chance of better taxation performance.

5.5 Results of Natural Resource Dependency Reduction

It was discussed in the literature review that natural resource dependence can be reduced through the promotion of economic diversification. This diversification would reduce revenue volatility, and hence less vulnerable economies become those

5.5 Results of Natural Resource Dependency Reduction

which are the most sufficiently diversified. In this regard, the private sector development and reforms in the public sector, including privatisation of state-owned enterprises and the development of national taxation system, would raise the diversification of the economy.

However, there are some factors such as quality of institutions, political stability and the structure of the economy which affect this diversification. As such, countries typically restructure their diversification decisions in response to relative temporal changes in the economy. Thus, diversification to reduce resource revenue dependency is a dynamic process that adjusts over time. Therefore, it is costly for resource rich countries to rapidly adjust privatisation or the tax system towards diversification with the aim to reduce resource revenue dependency. Therefore, natural resource-dependent countries have incentives to adjust slowly over time to minimise the risks of economic decline associated with an immediate adjustment.

5.5.1 Factors Affecting the Reduction of Dependency

While the effects of natural resource rents on institutional quality, economic structure and well-being of the people are noted, the effects of the private sector and taxation on diversification to reduce this dependency are subjected to ongoing debate, especially in natural resource rich countries. Table 5.22 presents a number of factors that have been related to natural resource dependency reduction.

Private sector development is a critical factor in shaping economic growth, job creation and revenue diversification. In natural resource rich countries, nevertheless, PSD faces challenges. The coefficient of *PSD*, which is statistically significant at 90% level of significance, is positive. This indicates a positive relationship between natural resource dependence and PSD. While in the result of the first model estimation (see Sect. 5.2) the coefficient of *Natural Resource Rents* was significant and positive, indicating that the more revenues from resources, the faster private sector development is. It is not expected for PSD to have a resource dependency reduction effect.

The interpretation of this result is that PSD might be not effective in natural resource rich countries, due to the structure of the economy that translated rents form natural resources to further resource curse (Mazaheri, 2016). This result then implies that the greater the resource rents, the less effect the private sector is.

Public sector reforms across the privatisation process raises substantial cash for governments (see Fig. 1.1) and develop the remaining public enterprises. This effect has been found in the estimation results. The coefficient of *Privatisation* reported in Table 5.22 is negative and statistically significant at a 95% level of significance indicating its effect in reducing relative dependency on resource revenue. This feature can be seen in the Saudi Arabian oil company's recent initial public offering to generate revenue to diversify its heavily oil-dependent economy (Nasser, 2019).

Saudi Arabia found difficulties in funding government services during the oil shocks from 2014, thus a number of enterprises were privatised. Saudi Arabia

Table 5.22 Static and dynamic model parameter estimate (dependency)[8]

Model	Static		Dynamic restricted		Dynamic unrestricted	
Variables	Estimate	Std error	Estimate	Std error	Estimate	Std error
Intercept	48.424[a]	3.379	137.737[a]	29.372	116.083[a]	8.388
PSD	−0.394[a]	0.092	1.024	0.640	0.331[c]	0.143
Privatisation	−0.095	0.085	0.003	0.535	−0.218[b]	0.124
Taxation	−0.105	0.117	−0.518	0.734	−0.468[b]	0.132
Institutional quality	−5.948[a]	0.730	−4.174	4.748	−2.755[c]	2.348
Political stability	−0.017	0.025	0.096	0.157	0.259[a]	0.064
Human development	0.095[c]	4.891	−73.528	47.537	−133.817[a]	15.771
Public Investment	0.137[b]	0.081	−0.845	0.538	0.141	0.122
Manufacturing production	−0.086	0.035	0.009	0.218	−0.389[b]	0.103
Exchange rate	−0.178[b]	0.016	−0.444[a]	0.112	−0.102[a]	0.012
Trend	−0.053	0.072	−0.817[c]	0.494	−0.699[a]	0.158
Low middle income			−19.886[c]	11.303	−15.264[a]	5.202
Middle income			−10.183	13.288	17.127[a]	3.480
Upper middle income			−4.008	16.188	21.572[a]	4.465
Higher income			−0.053	17.567	26.101[a]	5.033
Observations	937		937		937	
Adjusted R-squared	0.2579		0.9486		0.9654	
RMSE	13.4364		3.5352		2.9003	

Note The dependent variable is Dependency and the p value is: [a]$p \leq 0.001$, [b]$p \leq 0.05$, [c]$p \leq 0.10$

increased the size of privatisation, and as such it was ranked seventh in non-European countries by total privatisation revenues in 2014 with projects valued at 6125 million US dollars (Estrin & Pelletier, 2018). Another example includes Zambia in which the provision of privatisation with a number of liberalised polices is promoted to develop industrialisation (Fessehaie et al., 2016).

When the private sector engages in the economic activity, it may provide a normal rate of return to the resource rich countries in the form of taxes. Taxation is a significant government instrument of fiscal policy to mobilise revenue and promote economic growth (Odhiambo & Olushola, 2018). The coefficient of *Taxation* is negative and statistically significant at the level of 95% indicating the impact of taxation to reduce long-term resource revenue dependence. This finding is in line with a study by Okafor (2012) who found a positive impact of improving taxation in the growth of the economy of rich resources of Nigeria. Previously, Kuczynski (1999) concluded that the privatisation process has widened the tax system in many transition and industrialised economies.

---

[8] To estimate the minimum level of dependency (optimal), the following explanatory variables are optimal value, PSD, Privatisation and Taxation.

5.5 Results of Natural Resource Dependency Reduction

Literature has described two ways in which taxation can effectively enhance economic growth including reducing resource volatility and strengthening accountability (McGuirk, 2013; Von Haldenwang & Ivanyna, 2018). As such, improving a tax base and its collection would correspondingly strengthen public demand for democratic accountability. However, introducing taxes should not distort economic incentives or adversely affect investment and growth.

The relationship between institutional quality and natural resources has been confirmed in the literature. A large body of the literature argues that the negative growth of natural resource rents or the so-called 'the resource curse' is associated with the quality of institutions (Bhattacharyya & Hodler, 2014; Ji et al., 2014; Venables, 2016). The finding of the current research suggests that natural resource dependence can be relatively reduced through institutional quality. The results show the coefficient of *Institutional Quality* is negative and statistically significant at the level of 90%, indicating that the more institutionalisation of governments in natural resource rich countries, the lesser the degree of natural resource dependence.

Ait-Laoussine and Gault (2017) confirm the significance of institutional quality in the diversification process by stating that weak governance could halt it. For example, Norway, which is richly endowed with natural resources, has been able to avoid the financial crisis and subsequent economic turmoil that has affected most of the European and oil exporter countries. Although the oil-price drop in 2014 has significantly impacted Norway's economy, there has been no economic policy towards austerity (Sverdrup et al., 2016). One reason for this is that the country has benefited from having reasonably well-performing institutions over the last 20 years with an average rank of 96.4 (which in recent years has improved to 98[9]; [WDI, 2020b]). As such, the finding confirms that institutional quality of natural resource rich countries contributes to economic diversification.

The results reported in Table 5.22 indicate that there is no statistically significant relationship between public investment and natural resource dependence. Nevertheless, if revenue generation grew with different sources rather than resource rents, visible positive effects might be noted.

With reference to stability, political stability is of vital importance in either developing natural resources or economic diversification. The coefficient of political stability was positive and highly statistically significant, indicating that in the absence of political instability, in particular conflict and civil war, natural resource rich countries may develop the extractive sector much faster. Jensen and Johnston (2011) tested the connection between political risk and the resource curse in natural resource-dependent countries and found a high connection between political risk and a country's reliance on a natural resource.

That the political stability coefficient is positive, indicates that natural resource dependency reduction is not affected by such stability. This might be true at the initial stage, but it certainly requires continuity in the other stages of diversification. One aspect of economic diversification is stability that requires continuity. Ait-Laoussine

---

[9] The data sources estimation is based on percentile rank among all countries ranging from 0 (lowest) to 100 (highest).

and Gault (2017) confirm the connections between stability and economic diversification, in particular noting a causal relationship between political stability and economic diversification.

With regard to manufacturing production and industrialisation, in a modern economy, industrialisation has been identified as an engine of sustainable economic growth (Cantore et al., 2017; Su & Yao, 2017). Manufacturing increases the productivity of private firms by providing quality products to the domestic market, raising the share of industry in regional markets and accumulating experiences with technology, management and marketing (Dinh et al., 2012). One of the main aims of the liberalisation programme started in the 1980s was to encourage growth and the manufacturing sector (Haouas et al., 2002). The coefficient of *Manufacturing Production* is negative and highly statistically significant at a level of 99%. This result implies that the greater the manufacturing production, the smaller the resource dependency. This result is in line with a study by Van der Ploeg (2011), who exemplifies four out of 65 resource rich developing countries (Botswana, Indonesia, Malaysia and Thailand) that successfully managed to overcome the problem of resource dependency through economic diversification and industrialisation policies.

The Indonesian national government's pro-growth economic policies that changed the public and private sector's role, contributed to diversification of exports. The private sector has contributed to a visible development through investments in industrialisation, banks and real estate developments (Firman & Fahmi, 2017; Shaban & James, 2018). This contributed to the diversification of the Indonesian economy by reducing the degree of dependency on petroleum export from 40.1% in 1977 to 7.4% by 2014 and expanding the share of manufactured goods from 2.3% to 40.2% (Ait-Laoussine & Gault, 2017). Indonesia has a value advantage among the OPEC members with the lowest petroleum export and highest manufactured export.

Human development has been identified as the core objective of development (Mehrotra & Gandhi, 2012; Suri et al., 2011). Popov (2014) emphasises the importance of the availability of finance to invest in human capital. Therefore, natural resource rich countries have opportunities to use resource rents to improve the country level of human development. However, Carmignani (2013) finds evidence of a strong, direct negative effect of resource abundance on human development.

Human development has also been identified as a factor of economic diversification of natural resource rich countries. Suslova and Volchkova (2012) investigated industry-level growth of natural resource endowment countries and found that human development is a transmission mechanism to affect the industrial growth of resource-abundant countries. Similar to this finding, the present research found a highly significant, large and negative coefficient of human development (-133.817) indicating that human capital has a direct diversification effect of resource dependency reduction.

Most importantly, there is evidence of a direct positive effect of human development on economic growth. A study of the determinants of growth in China between 1991 and 2010 found that the growth rate positively correlated with investment rate in physical capital and human capital (Su & Liu, 2016). China is one of the fastest-growing economies with an average growth rate of 10% since the end of the 1970s.

5.5 Results of Natural Resource Dependency Reduction

Human capital accumulation has been marked as one of the most crucial factors in the growth of the Chinese economy.

Frankel (2012) reviewed the most relevant studies on natural resource curse and argued that commodity prices have a long-term impact on the real exchange rate, where the real exchange rate is depreciated. However, in general the impact of real exchange rate on natural resource dependence is not clearly measured in previous studies.

Real exchange rate is an important macroeconomic factors for an open economy and can be affected by country-specific effects including interest rate, purchasing power parity conditions or trends in productivity (Bodart et al., 2012; Lee & Chinn, 2006). Variation in real exchange rate within a country is attributed to an imbalanced current account, procyclical government spending, sectoral productivity shocks and new discovery of natural resources (Bodart et al., 2012).

In this research the coefficient of exchange rate is negative and highly statistically significant pointing to the role of the exchange rate in reducing the effect of natural resource dependency by providing fiscal space through increased revenue in terms of domestic currency (Grigoli et al., 2019). Exchange rate would lead to a relatively strong economy if it is flexible, and as such would increase the economic opportunities of income diversification to reduce natural resource dependency. In studying the impact of the sharp, long-lasting drop in oil prices between 2014 and 2016 a recent study by Grigoli et al. (2019) found that countries with a flexible exchange rate regime were less impacted than those with a fixed regime.

Time trend is included in this research to capture the variation of resource dependency reduction as a response to the diversified factors and other explanatory variables across countries. To summarise, the degree of dependency on natural resource revenue changes over time either. Nonetheless, the coefficient of *Time Trend* shows that the trend is negative and highly statistically significant meaning that the degree of dependency reduces over time during the selected period. This result is consistent with the attempts of several resource rich countries to diversify, such as Saudi Arabia, Russia and other aforementioned successful countries.

The country sample is split into different income groups. The coefficients of all income groups are highly statistically significant, with only low middle-income being negative. Compared to the reference (intercept), which captures the effect of *lower-income* countries (which are highly statistically significant and positive) these groups show that countries with these levels of income tend to greatly rely on natural resource rents except for low middle-income countries. However, there is the biggest reduction in resource dependency for low middle-income countries compared to the reference. The coefficient of *Low Middle-Income* countries is negative and highly statistically significant, indicating that these countries move towards diversifying their sources of revenues.

5.5.2 The Speed of Adjustment Values

The speed of adjustment is estimated as a function of several policy variables (see, Appendix Table A.12). Some of them overlap with the determinants of optimal dependency reduction and affect the adjustment towards less dependency on natural resource revenue.

The mean values from the unrestricted dynamic model of system of equations report the key relationships between the variables of dependency and diversified factors by period, income group, private sector size, degree of dependency on natural resources, year of observation and country. The mean adjustment parameter δ explains the size of the gap between the actual dependency and its long-term optimal value to reduce the degree of dependency on natural resource revenues. All computed indicators, similar to the previous models, are time and country specific.

Mean Indicator Values by Time Period

The mean values of adjustment speed towards dependency reduction by *Delta* are presented in Table 5.23 and are positive in all the three sub-periods. This indicates improvement in the economy of the natural resource rich countries towards diversifying the economy and in line with the result of the *Time Trend* coefficient result reported in Table 5.22 which indicated improvements in the economy of natural resources towards less dependency over the sampled period. Although the adjustment speed is positive in all three periods, it fluctuated slightly over the three sub-periods from 5.1% (1990–1999) to 6% (2000–2009) and 4.7% (2010–2017).

The adjustment towards dependency reduction means increasing opportunities to generate non-resource revenue in natural resource rich countries, which is time and resource consuming. Therefore, the slow movement of the adjustment parameter towards diversification to reduce natural resource dependency is reasonable as such change requires technological improvement, infrastructure development and institutional empowerment. This positive movement is consistent with the finding reported for the coefficient of *Time Trend* presented in Table 5.22.

The economic interpretation for this improvement is that in the 1990s the second wave of privatisation relatively improved the economy of some resource rich countries. Although during 2000 to 2009 a series of crises weakened global economic competitiveness, resource rich countries adjusted towards a better economy with an advantage of higher price of resources. However, the sharp drop in oil prices

Table 5.23 Mean value of resource dependency reduction by time period

Period	Observed	Optimal	Delta
1990–1999	9.429	8.118	0.051
2000–2009	11.709	10.424	0.060
2010–2017	11.264	7.327	0.047

5.5 Results of Natural Resource Dependency Reduction

in 2014 might explain this small change in the rate of improvement of speed of adjustment towards dependency reduction over the period of 2010 to 2017 as this time period is not enough to develop. Hence, it might be true that the volatility in natural resource revenue causes these countries to implement a development plan of economic diversification.

Mean Indicator Values by Income Group

The sampled countries are divided into groups based on their level of income. Table 5.24 shows that improvement in adjustment speed varies based on the income of the countries. Countries with lower and lower middle-income have slower adjustment towards dependency reduction. In contrast, countries with middle and higher income have incentives to quickly adjust towards more diversified economies.

The mean value of middle-income groups, indicating the fastest adjustment towards dependency reduction, shows that the adjustment speed is approximately 6.8% closer to the desired level of dependency within a year. This figure indicates that adjustment towards dependency reduction develops each year by 6.8% and the full diversification would take almost fourteen years and seven months to reach the optimal level.

These findings are consistent with the mean adjustment parameters of privatisation and taxation developed in previous subsections of 5.3.2 and 5.4.2. The economic interpretation for this faster adjustment towards optimal dependency reduction is based on three main points. First, middle and higher income groups have a relatively larger sized government (Estrin & Pelletier, 2018); thus privatisation effects will be large enough to generate non-resource revenue. Saudi Arabia, Botswana and Indonesia are examples, and through this have expanded their tax revenue. Second, there is a consistency in the development of the adjustment speed towards dependency reduction. For example, the full development of privatisation (Table 5.10) and taxation (Table 5.17) in middle-income countries took place in periods of 11 and 12 years respectively, and then the full development of economic diversification to reduce natural resource dependency took place in almost 15 years. Third, the full development of both privatisation and taxation with relative improvement in human development, manufacturing production and institutional quality (Table 5.22) explains the positive adjustment speed towards dependency reduction.

Table 5.24 Mean value of dependency reduction by income group

Income group	Observed	Optimal	Delta
Lower income	12.507	10.450	0.045
Lower middle-income	8.695	2.659	0.034
Middle-income	10.128	14.538	0.068
Upper middle-income	11.081	10.368	0.060
Higher income	11.590	7.375	0.065

Table 5.25 Mean value of dependency reduction by private sector size

Size	Observed	Optimal	Delta
Smaller size	12.461	2.832	0.068
Lower middle-size	11.689	10.795	0.056
Middle-size	10.620	11.801	0.045
Upper middle-size	9.545	10.219	0.039
Larger size	9.056	12.833	0.091

Mean Indicator Values by Private Sector Size

As presented in Table 5.25, the mean value of the size of the private sector indicates that all private sector sizes are associated with relative dependency reduction. Nevertheless, countries with a larger private sector adjust faster towards dependency reduction on natural resources compared to other sizes. A possible interpretation of this result is that the larger the size of the private sector, the more jobs would be provided, and as such, more revenue from taxes would be collected.

Mean Indicator Values by Degree of Dependency

The mean values of the degree of dependency on natural resources in Table 5.26 show that regardless of the level of dependency, countries adjust towards dependency reduction. However, countries with less dependency adjust faster than those with other degrees of dependency towards a more diversified economy.

However, the figure reports that countries with higher dependency have slower adjustment towards dependency reduction. The justification of this result is that the contribution of natural resources in the economy of those countries is undoubtedly large. As such, less attention is being paid to develop other areas of the economy. Nonetheless, during the past few decades, the trend of volatile economies in these countries has given reasons to adjust to find new sources of revenue. Saudi Arabia, for example, as one of the high-dependency countries has announced some development plans to overcome the problem of dependency on natural resources.

Table 5.26 Mean value of dependency reduction by degree of dependency

Degree of dependency	Observed	Optimal	Delta
Higher dependency	3.276	8.257	0.006
Upper middle dependency	13.442	7.115	0.068
Middle dependency	20.772	8.714	0.147
Lower middle dependency	27.584	9.156	0.230
Less dependency	46.522	14.678	0.239

5.5 Results of Natural Resource Dependency Reduction

Mean Indicator Values by Year

The adjustment parameter in Table 5.27 shows the movement of the degree of dependency over the sampled periods. The reported figure indicates that the mean adjustment parameter (δ) has very slow movement (upward and downward) reflecting the global economy, opportunities and country-specific characteristics. This reflects in the gap between observed to optimal dependency reduction present in Fig. 5.4. According to the reported figures, the mean adjustment parameter in 1991 starts with a relatively high rate of improvement towards less dependency on natural resource as a response to the initial stage of the second wave of privatisation. There is, then, a continuous fluctuation of the adjustment mostly decreasing to reach the lowest value within the sample accounting for 1.5% in 2016. This is possibly due to the consequences of some of the financial crises which occurred around the world such as the Swedish and Finish Banking crisis of 1990–1993, and the Mexican financial crisis in 1994.

Interestingly, the Asian financial crises in 1997 had a much smaller effect on natural resource rich countries. The adjustment parameter while small in comparison to future years, is relatively better than the previous years.

In 1997 it was only 2%, then increased to 8.5% in 1998 and 9.3% in 1999. This increase shows slow improvement towards less dependency on natural resources. From the year 2000 onward, while there was a decline in economic activity mainly in developed countries, the oil price per barrel doubled from 30 US dollars in 2003 to reach 60 dollars by 2005 and peaked at 147 dollars in 2008. This relative increase in revenue from rents saved the natural resource countries from the effects of the decline in economic activity as well as the global financial crisis. However, the relative development of the adjustment speed towards both privatisation and taxation during the same period, caused further improvement in the adjustment parameter towards more diversified economies. In 2009, privatisation had the fastest adjustment towards its optimal (Table 5.13) with the value of 14.7% and adjustment towards optimal taxation was the third fastest value of 10.5% (Table 5.20). As such, the relative global economic recovery, faster adjustment towards more privatisation and a tax base with high oil prices led the adjustment parameter towards dependency reduction to reach at peak of 14% in 2009. Later, the sharp decline in oil prices in 2014 caused adjustment to decline to 3.2% from 3.8% in 2013.

Nevertheless, this rapid decline in the oil and gas prices encouraged the resource rich countries to search for new sources of income by improving the mean adjustment parameter value to 8.8% in 2015.

Mean Indicator Value by Country[10]

The mean indicator values related to speed of adjustment by country are presented in Table 5.28. The gap between actual and optimal dependency reduction varies

---

[10] A complete list of country mean values is presented in Appendix Table A.16.

Table 5.27 Development of mean indicator of dependency reduction by year

Year	Observed	Optimal	Delta
1991	8.663	8.756	0.087
1992	9.526	8.272	0.029
1993	9.386	7.892	0.044
1994	9.964	7.229	0.053
1995	10.596	7.731	0.028
1996	10.912	8.284	0.022
1997	9.794	8.351	0.022
1998	7.713	8.499	0.085
1999	8.298	8.072	0.093
2000	10.301	9.707	0.106
2001	9.017	9.506	0.052
2002	8.913	10.536	0.020
2003	10.319	11.099	0.050
2004	11.432	10.431	0.064
2005	13.132	11.115	0.051
2006	14.231	10.699	0.026
2007	14.041	10.834	0.052
2008	14.956	10.813	0.035
2009	10.746	9.498	0.140
2010	12.257	9.283	0.065
2011	14.459	8.710	0.059
2012	13.374	8.520	0.036
2013	12.358	8.109	0.038
2014	11.129	6.838	0.032
2015	8.420	6.144	0.088
2016	9.380	5.946	0.015
2017	8.739	5.066	0.040

across countries within a year, and as such there is a variation in the adjustment parameter. The larger the speed of adjustment, the closer the country moves towards its optimal dependency reduction. The countries with the fastest adjustment listed in the table below, show that the majority are African countries which emphasises the development of African resource rich countries towards diversifying the economy.

Angola with the value of 38% has the fastest adjustment speed towards dependency reduction. Previously, it performed well in having a faster adjustment parameter towards both privatisation and taxation. While the gap from observed to the optimal is large, indicating that it is hard to address, the faster adjustment towards the diversified factor of privatisation and taxation led Angola to quickly adjust towards dependency reduction. With regard to natural resources, oil contributes to 90% of export and has a

5.5 Results of Natural Resource Dependency Reduction

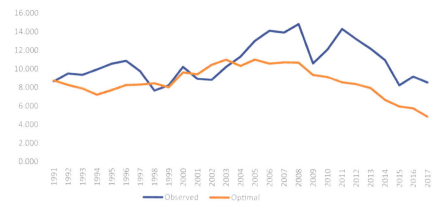

Fig. 5.4 Mean of observed and optimal of dependency reduction by year

large share of GDP. The government of Angola has made a reform to transform state-led economy to private-led economic growth. Initially, it started from the privatisation of several SOEs from public utility to state-oil companies. As such, the country, in accordance with improvement in monetary and fiscal policy has experienced relative macroeconomic stability (Carpenter, 2017).

As for Equatorial Guinea which has relatively faster adjustment, the government emphasised on economic diversification through public investment towards the development of new strategic economic sectors including agriculture, tourism and finance (Appel, 2017). An overview of the country was provided in Sect. 5.2.2.

Botswana is among the resource rich countries that recorded less dependence on natural resources. It was identified as one of the success stories in diversifying the economy. Botswana, which had the world's highest rate of economic growth in Sub-Saharan African rich resources over the past 50 years, has emphasised quality public investment projects. It is the second Sub-Saharan African country that managed to graduate from the least developed countries in 2017 (Gylfason & Nganou, 2016). Entrepreneurship in Botswana has been at the heart of national economic development. Pansiri and Yalala (2017) discussed the evolution of entrepreneurship and small-to-medium enterprises through several policies such as creating funding opportunities and enhancing training for entrepreneurs, research innovation and technical assistance and creating market access.

The economic diversification drive strategy in 2010, mainly in infrastructure and financial development, was also critical in driving further economic development and less dependency on natural resources (Pansiri & Yalala, 2017; Wiebe et al., 2016). A number of large oil exporters are among those in the medium adjustment group, including Mauritania, Iraq, Saudi Arabia, Venezuela, the United Arab Emirates, Qatar and Russia. The drop in commodity prices, especially during the last oil shock of 2014, made direct effects through trade and indirect effects through weakening investment in the economy of these countries. As such, being relatively fast towards

Table 5.28 Mean of dependency reduction by country

Level	Country	Observed	Optimal	Delta
Faster Adjustment ≥ 0.2	Angola	39.955	25.656	0.380
	Congo, Republic	43.527	42.615	0.376
	Vietnam	7.287	1.000	0.363
	Botswana	2.808	24.278	0.334
	China	3.709	1.000	0.297
	Liberia	46.490	13.504	0.295
	Chili	11.361	1.000	0.285
	Equatorial Guinea	30.117	18.850	0.282
	Libya	28.839	1.000	0.264
	Azerbaijan	24.511	2.866	0.244
0.1 ≥ Medium Adjustment < 0.2	Mauritania	23.024	1.000	0.197
	Iraq	24.917	2.526	0.192
	Saudi Arabia	34.497	1.000	0.183
	Venezuela, RB	14.253	1.000	0.170
	Mongolia	19.019	14.620	0.153
	Suriname	16.347	12.537	0.149
	Congo, Dem. Rep	28.038	30.231	0.145
	United Arab Emirates	18.725	3.667	0.143
	Qatar	29.648	1.000	0.107
	Russian Federation	13.236	6.285	0.088
0.1 < Slow Adjustment > 0	Haiti	0.906	1.000	0.002
	Senegal	3.760	4.825	0.003
	Armenia	1.679	6.447	0.003
	Georgia	0.897	4.115	0.003
	Thailand	1.495	19.376	0.005
	Cabo Verde	0.578	6.015	0.006
	Sri Lanka	0.229	4.165	0.006
	Croatia	0.704	9.244	0.006
	Rwanda	7.893	9.040	0.012
	Philippines	1.575	5.390	0.014
No Adjustment = 0	Bhutan	4.370	29.995	0.000
	Kuwait	41.075	1.000	0.000

dependency reduction indicates the need to satisfy the desire of these countries to develop non-resource revenue.

Haiti is among the slowest to adjust towards less dependency on natural resources. The economy relies on agriculture, manufacturing, services, trade and mining with underdeveloped but extensive oil and gas reserves. The oil and gas reserves are estimated to be amount to 941 million barrels of crude oil and about 1.2 trillion cubic feet of natural gas. While a number of oil sites have already been identified for drilling (Sawe, 2020), oil and gas have not yet contributed to the economic development in the country. Therefore, it is reasonable that the country scored one of the slowest adjustments to reduce dependency on natural resources. The country has experienced poverty, corruption and vulnerability to natural disasters and political uncertainty (Dupuy, 2019). Political instability has seriously undermined the effectiveness of public finance and institutions. As such, in terms of economic freedom the country is ranked the 143rd freest out of 194 countries in the 2019 Index (Economic Freedom, 2019a, 2019b).

The results for Bhutan and Kuwait show that the countries per se have no adjustment towards natural resources dependency reduction. Kuwait's economy largely relies on oil and gas which accounts for almost 60% of GDP. Every year, the government saves 10% of resource revenue to protect against possible oil shocks (Almujamed et al., 2017; Economic Freedom, 2020).

5.6 Summary

This chapter identified and examined the determining factors of optimal levels of diversification and their speed of adjustment towards the desired level. The determinants of reaching an optimal level of reduction of dependency on natural resources with its adjustment speed were investigated. By examining the effects of the diversification factors of private sector development, privatisation and taxation to reduce the degree of dependency on revenue from natural resources, a number of estimation methods were applied including static linear regression model, traditional dynamic model and dynamic flexible adjustment model in a single equation and system of equations.

The results indicated that the traditional static and dynamic model were not satisfactory in studying resource dependency reduction due to the failure to capture the possible non-linear influences of private and public sector development. The dynamic model, including flexible adjustment speed, made a key difference compared to the static model. The coefficient signs and significance of some of the exogenous variables changed and improved slightly. The flexible dynamic model had more explanatory power than the traditional static model. In addition, the model performance of the estimations was evaluated using F-test statistics and other goodness of fit indices. The result showed the superiority of the dynamic adjustment model over the static model and the better performance of system of equations over single equation.

As for the determinants of the PSD in natural resource rich countries, low levels of taxation, credit to the private sector, economic growth, and human development with effective levels of governance and relative political stability may help develop the private sector. The findings reveal that it is not only organisational success that largely depends on the quality of human capacity, but also the country level of the PSD is extremely reliant on human development. An appealing result was found when the impact of credit to the private sector on the PSD was examined. The financial resource curse effect on the PSD was observed.

Natural resource rent could foster the development of the private sector. As the results found positive effects of natural resource rents on PSD, the speed of adjustment in countries with oil and gas is higher than countries without these resources. This suggests better adjustment towards the optimal level in such countries, compared to those without oil and gas resources.

Moreover, the study found that several crises including the oil shocks of 2014 had an effect on the speed of adjustment of the PSD confirming the key role of oil and gas rents in the development of the private sector.

With regard to public sector reforms, the public sector can be developed to lead diversification either through privatisation of public services, or through development of a national taxation system that reduces government dependency on revenue from natural resources. Concerning the privatisation in natural resource wealthy countries, the findings confirm the importance of institutions in the progress of privatisation in these countries that are highly vulnerable to market prices. An essential result that confirmed previous findings from the literature, was the role of institutions in explaining economic growth, thereby the finding indicated that natural resource rents might support privatisation only in those countries that have quality institutions. Thus, the appealing result could be that more developed institutional environments moderate the positive effect of natural resource rents on privatisation. Therefore, it is recommended that resource rich countries which have a weak institutional capacity, should delay privatisation until institutions are improved.

By using several policy variables such as interest rate policy, openness policy and credit to finance policy, the speed of adjustment towards optimal privatisation was estimated. The level of commitment of the resource rich countries to privatisation varies across them. However, the speed of adjustment based on level of income indicated that regardless of their income level, natural resource countries adjusted towards optimal privatisation, meaning that attempts had been made to focus on diversification which in turn reduces resource dependency. However, to check for resource type role in speeding adjustment of privatisation, the finding indicated that resource type (Oil & Gas) per se had no effect on privatisation.

In addition to public sector reform, the development of a national taxation system was examined. The significant variables affecting the level of taxation were governance, privatisation, dependency on natural resources, development and tax capacity including country-specific proxy and dummy variables. The policy variables significantly impacting changes in the condition of taxation are investment policy, rule of law, tax capacity and credit to private sector including relevant proxy and dummy

5.6 Summary

variables. While these factors reflect improvements in tax capacity and a broadening tax base, taxation is a highly regulated aspect of the state's fiscal policy.

Regarding the control variables that capture the effect of country-specific factors, the findings suggest that countries with high resource revenue dependency which have lower-middle income tend to adjust towards optimal levels of taxation to reduce dependency on natural resources faster than other countries. Model estimation results suggest that it may take almost 12 years to stabilise the economy of the lower-middle natural resource revenue-dependent countries.

The negative correlation between taxation and oil revenue as a consequence of oil price fluctuation, explains the relative slow adjustment of speed towards optimal taxation during the different sub-periods studied. However, it is critical that the resource rich countries focus on avoiding the potential resource curse. This analysis suggests, in turn, that high resource-dependent countries attend to reduce their vulnerability of revenue through diversifying revenue sources. This model estimation concludes that tax capacity contributes to better performance in tax collection. While it may well be true that the strength of a tax system is a sign of overall governance capability, the impact of natural resources on taxation might vary with the level of governance and its effectiveness.

It is recommended that resource revenue-dependent countries rely on national taxation as an effective policy to reduce revenue volatility and strengthen accountability of governance which in turn will reduce dependency on natural resources.

Natural resource dependence might be reduced through private sector development, public sector reforms and some non-economic factors. When the effects of these diversified factors are estimated, the results confirm that the factors contributing to natural resource dependence reduction are the privatisation of SOEs, a national taxation system, institutional quality, human development and manufacturing production.

PSD was expected to have a resource dependency reduction effect as it is a critical factor in shaping economic growth, job creation and revenue diversification. However, a positive relationship between natural resource dependence and PSD was found, meaning that the more revenue from resources, the faster private sector development is. The reduced effectiveness of the PSD may be due to challenges facing the private sector in natural resource rich countries especially issues related to institutional quality and structure of the economy. Therefore, it is recommended for the resource rich countries to work on the improvement of both the market and its institutions.

The effect of public sector reforms including privatisation of SOEs and a national taxation system is found to reduce the degree of dependency on natural resources. Public sector reforms across the privatisation process raise substantial cash for governments, Zambia and Saudi Arabia are examples of this. The former promotes industrialisation through a number of liberalised polices, in particular, privatisation. The latter develops the degree of privatisation to generate revenue to diversify the heavily oil-dependent economy.

With regard to the national taxation system, the result suggests a positive impact of establishing a national taxation system to reduce long-term resource revenue dependency in resource rich countries. While the private sector may provide a normal rate of return to the resource wealth countries in the form of taxes, the privatisation process may also widen the tax system in many natural resource economies.

In estimating dependency reduction, the result suggests that public sector reforms can have better performance in reducing natural resource dependency than private sector development. Another factor that contributes to effective reduction of the relative dependency on natural resource revenue is human development. Human development has been identified as the core objective of development (Mehrotra & Gandhi, 2012; Suri et al., 2011). Natural resource rich countries have opportunities to use resource rents to improve the country level of human development. While human development was found as a transmission mechanism to derive industrial development of resource rich countries, the findings of this study indicated that human capital has a direct diversification effect of resource dependency reduction.

While literature confirms that commodity price volatility effects pose a major threat to the development of manufacturing through the 'resource movement effect', the engagement of the private sector and public investment would lead the backward and forward linkage from resource commodity to manufacturing, thereby speeding the industrialisation of resource revenue dependent countries. The result reported for the relationship between natural resource dependency and manufacturing showed that manufacturing decreases revenue dependency in natural resource rich countries.

As for the non-economic factors, the relationship between institutional quality and natural resources dependence showed that the more a government is institutionalised in natural resource rich countries, the lesser the degree of natural resource dependence. Hence, the result of this research confirms the importance of improving the quality of institutions in promoting economic diversification of natural resource rich countries.

Whereas this research found the effect of several crises including oil shocks, the speed of adjustment of optimal dependency reduction based on periods as well as time trend improved over time confirmed a continuous improvement towards less dependency on natural resources. This indicates improvement in the economy as well as in institutions of the natural resource rich countries towards diversifying the economy by promoting privatisation policy and improving taxation systems.

Nevertheless, revenue diversification should be a policy priority for resource rich countries. It requires improvement in the institutions and the introduction of a policy that could engage all economic activities of the private sector and public investment towards manufacturing, this in turn would affect the relative degree of dependency on natural resources. The introduction of new taxes at a later time, might improve resource revenue diversification.

Bibliography

Abor, J., & Quartey, P. (2010). Issues in SME development in Ghana and South Africa. *International Research Journal of Finance and Economics, 39*(6), 215–228.

Afonso, W. B. (2013). Diversificaiton toward stability? The effect of local sales taxes on own source revenue. *Journal of Public Budgeting, Accounting & Financial Management, 25*(4), 649–674.

Aftab, N., Jebran, K., & Ullah, I. (2016). Impact of interest rate on private sector credit; Evidence from Pakistan. *Jinnah Business Review, 4*(1), 47–52.

Agrawal, A. K., & Matsa, D. A. (2013). Labor unemployment risk and corporate financing decisions. *Journal of Financial Economics, 108*(2), 449–470.

Ait-Laoussine, N., & Gault, J. (2017). Nationalisation, privatisation and diversification. *The Journal of World Energy Law & Business, 10*(1), 43–54.

Ajaz, T., & Ahmad, E. (2010). The effect of corruption and governance on tax revenues. *The Pakistan Development Review, 49*(2), 405–417.

Akinyemi, B. (2011). An assessment of human resource development climate in rwanda private sector organizations. *International Bulletin of Business Administration, 12*(1), 66–78.

Ali, O., Elbadawi, I., & Selim, H. (2016). *The political economy of public sector employment in resource dependent countries*. Cambridge University Press.

Alimov, A. (2015). Labor protection laws and bank loan contracting. *The Journal of Law and Economics, 58*(1), 37–74.

Almujamed, H., Tahat, Y., Omran, M., & Dunne, T. (2017). Development of accounting regulations and practices in Kuwait: An analytical review. *Journal of Corporate Accounting & Finance, 28*(6), 14–28.

Appel, H. (2017). Toward an ethnography of the national economy. *Cultural Anthropology, 32*(2), 294–322.

Arezki, R., & Van der Ploeg, F. (2011). Do Natural resources depress income per capita? *Review of Development Economics, 15*(3), 504–521.

Atkinson, G., & Hamilton, K. (2003). Savings, growth and the resource curse hypothesis. *World Development, 31*(11), 1793–1807.

Auty, R. (1993). *Sustaining development in mineral economies: The resource curse thesis*. Routledge.

Auty, R. (2001). *Resource abundance and economic development*. Oxford University Press.

Auzer, K. A. (2017). *Institutional design and capacity to enhance effective governance of oil and gas wealth: The case of Kurdistan region*. Springer.

Bakari, S. (2018). The Impact of domestic investment on economic growth new policy analysis from Algeria. *Bulletin of Economic Theory and Analysis, 3*(1), 35–51.

Balza, L., Jiménez, R. A., & Mercado Díaz, J. E. (2013). *Privatisation, institutional reform, and performance in the Latin American electricity sector*. Retrieved from Washington, DC.

Baunsgaard, T., & Keen, M. (2010). Tax revenue and (or?) trade liberalisation. *Journal of Public Economics, 94*(9–10), 563–577.

Beck, T., Demirgüç-Kunt, A., & Levine, R. (2010). Financial institutions and markets across countries and over time: The updated financial development and structure database. *The World Bank Economic Review, 24*(1), 77–92.

Beck, T., & Hesse, H. (2006). *Bank efficiency, ownership, and market structure: Why are interest spreads so high in Uganda?* The World Bank.

Bennett, J., Estrin, S., & Urga, G. (2007). Methods of privatisation and economic growth in transition economies. *Economics of Transition, 15*(4), 661–683.

Bernstein, S., Lerner, J., & Schoar, A. (2013). The investment strategies of sovereign wealth funds. *Journal of Economic Perspectives, 27*(2), 219–238.

Besley, T., & Persson, T. (2011). The logic of political violence. *The Quarterly Journal of Economics, 126*(3), 1411–1445.

Besley, T., & Persson, T. (2014). Why do developing countries tax so little? *Journal of Economic Perspectives, 28*(4), 99–120.

Bhattacharyya, S., & Hodler, R. (2014). Do natural resource revenues hinder financial development? The role of political institutions. *World Development, 57,* 101–113.

Bodart, V., Candelon, B., & Carpantier, J.-F. (2012). Real exchanges rates in commodity producing countries: A reappraisal. *Journal of International Money and Finance, 31*(6), 1482–1502.

Bortolotti, B., & Pinotti, P. (2008). Delayed privatisation. *Public Choice, 136*(3–4), 331–351.

Bouët, A., & Debucquet, D. L. (2012). Food crisis and export taxation: the cost of non-cooperative trade policies. *Review of World Economics, 148*(1), 209–233.

Brown, J. D., Earle, J. S., Shpak, S., & Vakhitov, V. (2019). Is privatisation working in Ukraine? New estimates from comprehensive manufacturing firm data, 1989–2013. *Comparative Economic Studies, 61*(1), 1–35.

Bruhn, M. (2011). *Reforming business taxes: What is the effect on private sector development?* (Public policy for the private sector: View point [330]).

Busse, M., & Gröning, S. (2013). The resource curse revisited: Governance and natural resources. *Public Choice, 154*(1–2), 1–20.

Cabrales, A., & Hauk, E. (2011). The quality of political institutions and the curse of natural resources. *The Economic Journal, 121*(551), 58–88.

Cammett, M., Diwan, I., & Leber, A. (2019). *Is oil wealth good for private sector development?* (Economic research forum working paper [1299]).

Cantore, N., Clara, M., Lavopa, A., & Soare, C. (2017). Manufacturing as an engine of growth: Which is the best fuel? *Structural Change and Economic Dynamics, 42,* 56–66.

Carmignani, F. (2013). Development outcomes, resource abundance, and the transmission through inequality. *Resource and Energy Economics, 35*(3), 412–428.

Carpenter, C. (2017). Angola: Does recent change mean economic development? *Journal of Petroleum Technology, 69*(10), 48–50.

Castells-Quintana, D. (2017). Malthus living in a Slum: Urban concentration, infrastructure and economic growth. *Journal of Urban Economics, 98,* 158–173.

Charles, K. K., Hurst, E., & Schwartz, M. (2019). The transformation of manufacturing and the decline in US employment. *NBER Macroeconomics Annual, 33*(1), 307–372.

Chen, Y., Igami, M., Sawada, M., & Xiao, M. (2018). *Privatisation and productivity in China.* Available at SSRN 2695933.

Cook, P. (2006). Private sector development strategy in developing countries. In *Privatisation and market development: Global movements in public policy ideas* (pp. 78–93). Edward Elgar.

Crivelli, E. (2013). Fiscal impact of privatisation revisited: The role of tax revenues in transition economies. *Economic Systems, 37*(2), 217–232.

Crivelli, E., & Gupta, S. (2014). Resource blessing, revenue curse? Domestic revenue effort in resource-rich countries. *European Journal of Political Economy, 35,* 88–101.

Deacon, R. T. (2011). The political economy of the natural resource curse: A survey of theory and evidence. *Foundations and Trends in Microeconomics, 7*(2), 111–208.

Deng, T. (2013). Impacts of transport infrastructure on productivity and economic growth: Recent advances and research challenges. *Transport Reviews, 33*(6), 686–699.

Dinh, H. T., Palmade, V., Chandra, V., & Cossar, F. (2012). *Light manufacturing in Africa: Targeted policies to enhance private investment and create jobs.* World Bank Publications.

Drucker, P. (2012). *Post-capitalist society.* Routledge.

Dupuy, A. (2019). *Haiti in the world economy: Class, race, and underdevelopment since 1700.* Routledge.

Economic Freedom. (2019a). *Index of economic freedom, Algeria: Center for international trade and economics & environment.* Retrieved November 25, 2019, from Heritage Foundation.

Economic Freedom. (2019b). Index of economic freedom, Haiti: Center for international trade and economics & environment. Retrieved February 9, 2020, from The Heritage Foundation.

Economic Freedom. (2020). Index of economic freedom, Kuwait: Center for international trade and economics & environment. Retrieved February 9, 2020, from The Heritage Foundation.

Estrin, S., & Pelletier, A. (2018). Privatisation in developing countries: What are the lessons of recent experience? *The World Bank Research Observer, 33*(1), 65–102.

Bibliography

Feder, G., Anderson, J. R., Birner, R., & Deininger, K. (2010). Promises and realities of community-based agricultural extension. In *Community, market and state in development* (pp. 187–208). Springer.

Fenochietto, M. R., & Pessino, M. C. (2013). *Understanding countries' tax effort* (IMF working paper 13 [244]).

Fessehaie, J., Rustomjee, Z., & Kaziboni, L. (2016). *Can mining promote industrialisation? A comparative analysis of policy frameworks in three Southern African countries* (WIDER working paper [83]).

Firman, T., & Fahmi, F. Z. (2017). The privatisation of metropolitan Jakarta's (Jabodetabek) urban fringes: The early stages of "post-suburbanisation" in Indonesia. *Journal of the American Planning Association, 83*(1), 68–79.

Frankel, J. A. (2012). *The natural resource curse: A survey of diagnoses and some prescriptions* (HKS faculty research working paper series RWP12-014, John F. Kennedy School of Government, Harvard University).

Ghosh, R., Siddique, M., & Gabbay, R. (2017). Tourism, ecotourism and economic development: An overview. In *Tourism and economic development* (pp. 1–7). Routledge.

Gonza, G., & Burger, A. (2017). Subjective well-being during the 2008 economic crisis: Identification of mediating and moderating factors. *Journal of Happiness Studies, 18*(6), 1763–1797.

Grigoli, F., Herman, A., & Swiston, A. (2019). A crude shock: Explaining the short-run impact of the 2014–16 oil price decline across exporters. *Energy Economics, 78*, 481–493.

Gylfason, T., & Nganou, J.-P.N. (2016). Diversification, Dutch disease and economic growth: Options for Uganda. In S. Mahroum & Y. Al-Saleh (Eds.), *Economic diversification policies in natural resource rich economies* (1st ed., pp. 118–147). Routledge.

Gylfason, T., & Zoega, G. (2003). Inequality and economic growth: Do natural resources matter? *Inequality and Growth: Theory and Policy Implications, 1*, 255.

Gylfason, T., & Zoega, G. (2006). Natural resources and economic growth: The role of investment. *World Economy, 29*(8), 1091–1115.

Han, L. (2012). Strategic privatization and trade policies in an international mixed oligopoly. *The Manchester School, 80*(5), 580–602.

Haouas, I., Yagoubi, M., & Heshmati, A. (2002). *Labour-use efficiency in Tunisian manufacturing industries: A flexible adjustment model* (WIDER discussion paper).

Hasanov, F. (2013). Dutch disease and the Azerbaijan economy. *Communist and Post-Communist Studies, 46*(4), 463–480.

Hendrick, R., & Crawford, J. (2014). Municipal fiscal policy space and fiscal structure: Tools for managing spending volatility. *Public Budgeting & Finance, 34*(3), 24–50.

Hodge, G. A. (2006). *Privatisation and market development: Global movements in public policy ideas*. Edward Elgar.

International Finance Institutions, I. F. C. (2011). *International finance institutions and development through the private sector*. Retrieved from Washington, DC. https://www.adb.org/sites/default/files/publication/29108/ifi-development-private-sector.pdf

Jensen, A. D. (2011). State-building in resource-rich economies. *Atlantic Economic Journal, 39*(2), 171–193.

Jensen, N., & Johnston, N. P. (2011). Political risk, reputation, and the resource curse. *Comparative Political Studies, 44*(6), 662–688.

Jensen, N., & Wantchekon, L. (2004). Resource wealth and political regimes in Africa. *Comparative Political Studies, 37*(7), 816–841.

Ji, K., Magnus, J. R., & Wang, W. (2014). Natural resources, institutional quality, and economic growth in China. *Environmental and Resource Economics, 57*(3), 323–343.

Jiang, C., Yao, S., & Feng, G. (2013). Bank ownership, privatisation, and performance: Evidence from a transition country. *Journal of Banking & Finance, 37*(9), 3364–3372.

Jiang, Y., Peng, M. W., Yang, X., & Mutlu, C. C. (2015). Privatisation, governance, and survival: MNE investments in private participation projects in emerging economies. *Journal of World Business, 50*(2), 294–301.

Kardaş, Ş, & Macit, F. (2015). Turkey-Azerbaijan relations: The economic dimension. *Journal of Caspian Affairs, 1*(1), 23–46.

Kay, J. A., & Thompson, D. J. (1986). Privatisation: A policy in search of a rationale. *The Economic Journal, 96*(381), 18–32.

Kidd, M., & Crandall, W. J. (2006). *Revenue authorities: Issues and problems in evaluating their success*. International Monetary Fund.

Klemm, A., & Van Parys, S. (2012). Empirical evidence on the effects of tax incentives. *International Tax and Public Finance, 19*(3), 393–423.

Knack, S. (2009). Sovereign rents and quality of tax policy and administration. *Journal of Comparative Economics, 37*(3), 359–371.

Kuczynski, P.-P. (1999). Privatisation and the private sector. *World Development, 27*(1), 215–224.

Kurtishi-Kastrati, S. (2013). The effects of foreign direct investments for host country's economy. *European Journal of Interdisciplinary Studies, 5*(1), 26.

Le, T. M., & Viñuela, L. (2012). *The political economy of natural resource taxation: Building credibility and investing in tax administration capacity*. Retrieved from Washington, DC. http://documents.worldbank.org/curated/en/888451468167353276/The-political-economy-of-natural-resource-taxation-building-credibility-and-investing-in-tax-administration-capacity

Lee, J., & Chinn, M. D. (2006). Current account and real exchange rate dynamics in the G7 countries. *Journal of International Money and Finance, 25*(2), 257–274.

Lewis, B. D. (2014). Urbanization and economic growth in Indonesia: Good news, bad news and (possible) local government mitigation. *Regional Studies, 48*(1), 192–207.

Lin, M. H., & Matsumura, T. (2018). Optimal privatisation and uniform subsidy policies: A note. *Journal of Public Economic Theory, 20*(3), 416–423.

Malawi, A. I., & Bader, M. (2010). The impact of interest rate on investment in Jordan: A cointegration analysis. *Journal of King Abdulaziz University: Economics and Administration, 105*(3055), 1–26.

Marcelin, I., & Mathur, I. (2015). Privatisation, financial development, property rights and growth. *Journal of Banking & Finance, 50*, 528–546.

Martinez-Vazquez, J., & McNab, R. M. (2000). The tax reform experiment in transitional countries. *National Tax Journal*, 273–298.

Mason, L., Prior, T., Mudd, G., & Giurco, D. (2011). Availability, addiction and alternatives: Three criteria for assessing the impact of peak minerals on society. *Journal of Cleaner Production, 19*(9–10), 958–966.

Mazaheri, N. (2016). *Oil booms and business busts: Why resource wealth hurts entrepreneurs in the developing world*. Oxford University Press.

Mazalto, M. (2009). Environmental liability in the mining sector: Prospects for sustainable development in the Democratic Republic of the Congo. In *Mining, society, and a sustainable world* (pp. 289–317). Springer.

McGuirk, E. F. (2013). The illusory leader: Natural resources, taxation and accountability. *Public Choice, 154*(3–4), 285–313.

McMillan, M. S., & Rodrik, D. (2011). *Globalization, structural change and productivity growth* (0898-2937).

Mehrotra, S., & Gandhi, A. (2012). India's human development in the 2000s: Towards social inclusion. *Economic and Political Weekly*, 59–64.

Mikesell, J. (2013). *Fiscal administration* (9th ed.). Wadswort Cengage Learning.

Mohan, T. R. (2001). Privatisation: Theory and evidence. *Economic and Political Weekly*, 4865–4871.

Muradian, R., Walter, M., & Martinez-Alier, J. (2012). Hegemonic transitions and global shifts in social metabolism: Implications for resource-rich countries. Introduction to the special section. *Global Environmental Change, 22*(3), 559–567.

Mzumara, M., Chingarande, A., & Karambakuwa, R. T. (2012). An analysis of the revealed comparative advantage in Southern African development community member states. *Journal of Sustainable Development in Africa, 14*(8), 53–74.

Nasser, A. (2019). *Introduction to ARAMCO initial public offering.*

Nellis, J. (1998). *Privatization in transition economies: An update* (World Bank discussion papers, 13–22).

Nellis, J. (2003). *Privatization in Africa: What has happened? What is to be done?* (Center for global development working paper, 25).

Nikolić, I., & Kovačević, M. (2014). The impact of privatization: Empirical analysis and results in Serbian industry. *Industrija, 42*(1), 63–86.

Odhiambo, O., & Olushola, O. (2018). Taxation and economic growth in a resource-rich country: The case of Nigeria. In J. Iwin-Garzynska (Ed.), *Taxes and taxation trends.* IntechOpen.

OECD. (2009, January). *Privatisation in the 21st century: Recent experiences of OECD countries, report on good practices.* Retrieved from https://www.oecd.org/daf/ca/corporategovernanceof state-ownedenterprises/48476423.pdf

Okafor, R. G. (2012). Tax revenue generation and Nigerian economic development. *European Journal of Business and Management, 4*(19), 49–56.

Osmundsen, P. (2009). *Time consistency in petroleum taxation: Lessons from Norway* (USAEE-IAEE WP, 09-031).

Ossowski, R., & Gonzáles, A. (2012). *Manna from heaven: The impact of nonrenewable resource revenues on other revenues of resource exporters in Latin America and the Caribbean.*

Otchia, C. S. (2014). Agricultural modernization, structural change and pro-poor growth: Policy options for the democratic Republic of Congo. *Journal of Economic Structures, 3*(1), 8.

Pagano, M. A., & Hoene, C. (2010). States and the Fiscal policy space of cities. In B. Michael, B. David, & Y. Joan (Eds.), *The property tax and local autonomy* (pp. 243–284). Puritan Press Inc.

Pansiri, J., & Yalala, A. T. (2017). The evolution of entrepreneurship and emall-to-medium business development in Botswana. *Botswana Journal of Business, 10*(1), 53–79.

Percoco, M. (2014). Quality of institutions and private participation in transport infrastructure investment: Evidence from developing countries. *Transportation Research Part A: Policy and Practice, 70*, 50–58.

Piketty, T., & Qian, N. (2009). Income inequality and progressive income taxation in China and India, 1986–2015. *American Economic Journal: Applied Economics, 1*(2), 53–63.

Popov, A. (2014). Credit constraints and investment in human capital: Training evidence from transition economies. *Journal of Financial Intermediation, 23*(1), 76–100.

Pradhan, R. P., & Bagchi, T. P. (2013). Effect of transportation infrastructure on economic growth in India: The VECM approach. *Research in Transportation Economics, 38*(1), 139–148.

Ragasa, C., Ulimwengu, J., Randriamamonjy, J., & Badibanga, T. (2016). Factors affecting performance of agricultural extension: Evidence from democratic Republic of Congo. *The Journal of Agricultural Education and Extension, 22*(2), 113–143.

Rodrik, D. (2016). An African growth miracle? *Journal of African Economies, 27*(1), 10–27.

Ross, M. (2001). Does oil hinder democracy? *World Politics, 53*(3), 325–361.

Ross, M. (2012). *The oil curse: How petroleum wealth shapes the development of nations.* Princeton University Press.

Ross, M. (2015). What have we learned about the resource curse? *Annual Review of Political Science, 18*, 239–259.

Sachs, J. D., & Warner, A. M. (1995). *Natural resource abundance and economic growth* (National Bureau of Economic Research [No. w 5395]).

Sachs, J. D., & Warner, A. M. (1997). Sources of slow growth in African economies. *Journal of African Economies, 6*(3), 335–376.

Sachs, J. D., & Warner, A. M. (2001). The curse of natural resources. *European Economic Review, 45*(4–6), 827–838.

Sawe, B. E. (2020). *What are the major natural resources of Haiti?*

Schoneveld, G., & Zoomers, A. (2015). Natural resource privatisation in sub-Saharan Africa and the challenges for inclusive green growth. *International Development Planning Review, 37*(1), 95–118.

Sekwati, L. (2010). Botswana: A note on economic diversification. *Botswana Journal of Economics, 7*(11), 79–85.

Shaban, M., & James, G. A. (2018). The effects of ownership change on bank performance and risk exposure: Evidence from Indonesia. *Journal of Banking & Finance, 88,* 483–497.

Shi, Y., & Tao, J. (2018). 'Faulty' fiscal illusion: Examining the relationship between revenue diversification and tax burden in major US cities across the economic cycle. *Local Government Studies, 44*(3), 416–435.

Sinha, N., & Kalayakgosi, K. A. (2018). Government size and economic growth in Botswana: An application of non-linear Armey curve analysis. *VISION: Journal of Indian Taxation, 5*(1), 60–90.

Sinha, S., Beijer, A., Hawkins, J., & Teglund, A. (2001). Approach and organization of Sida support to private sector development. *Sida Evaluation Report, 1,* 14.

Su, D., & Yao, Y. (2017). Manufacturing as the key engine of economic growth for middle-income economies. *Journal of the Asia Pacific Economy, 22*(1), 47–70.

Su, Y., & Liu, Z. (2016). The impact of foreign direct investment and human capital on economic growth: Evidence from Chinese cities. *China Economic Review, 37,* 97–109.

Subramanian, K., & Megginson, W. (2018). Employment protection laws and privatization. *The Journal of Law and Economics, 61*(1), 97–123.

Suri, T., Boozer, M. A., Ranis, G., & Stewart, F. (2011). Paths to success: The relationship between human development and economic growth. *World Development, 39*(4), 506–522.

Suslova, E., & Volchkova, N. (2012, October 1). *Human capital, industrial growth and resource curse.* Industrial Growth and Resource Curse.

Sverdrup, U., Ringen, S., & Jahn, D. (2016). *Norway report: Sustainable governance indicators 2016.*

Swanson, B. E., & Rajalahti, R. (2010). *Strengthening agricultural extension and advisory systems* (ARD discussion paper 20).

Tanzi, V. (2011). *Government versus markets: The changing economic role of the state.* Cambridge University Press.

Thomas, M. A. H., & Trevino, M. J. P. (2013). *Resource dependence and fiscal effort in Sub-Saharan Africa.* International Monetary Fund.

Thompson, B. K. (2007). *Foreign direct investments and their effect on an embryonic private sector in the economic development of Ghana* (PhD, Walden University, Ghana).

Tran, N. M., Nonneman, W., & Jorissen, A. (2015). Privatization of Vietnamese firms and its effects on firm performance. *Asian Economic and Financial Review, 5*(2), 202.

Trushin, E. (2017). Uzbekistan: Problems of development and reform in the agrarian sector. In B. Z. Rumer & S. Zhukov (Eds.), *Central Asia: Challenges of independence* (pp. 259–291). Routledge.

UNDP. (2019). *Human development reports: Human development indicators.* Retrieved October 15, 2019, from http://hdr.undp.org/en/countries/profiles/ZMB

United Nations. (2011). *Partnering public and private investment for development.* Paper presented at the United Nations Conference on Trade and Development Geneva.

Van der Ploeg, F. (2011). Natural resources: Curse or blessing? *Journal of Economic Literature, 49*(2), 366–420.

Venables, A. J. (2016). Using natural resources for development: Why has it proven so difficult? *Journal of Economic Perspectives, 30*(1), 161–184.

Von Haldenwang, C., & Ivanyna, M. (2018). Does the political resource curse affect public finance? The vulnerability of tax revenue in resource-dependent countries. *Journal of International Development, 30*(2), 323–344.

WDI. (2018). *Natural resource contribution to GDP.* Retrieved January 23, 2019, from World Bank.

WDI. (2019). *Domestic credit to the private sector.* Retrieved January 23, 2019, from World Bank.

Bibliography

WDI. (2020a). *Poland: Ease of doing business, total natural resource rents and economic fitness.* Retrieved February 7, from The World Bank.

WDI. (2020b). *World governance indicator.* Retrieved January 1, 2020, from World Bank.

Weber, J. G. (2014). A decade of natural gas development: The makings of a resource curse? *Resource and Energy Economics, 37*, 168–183.

Wiebe, D. J., Ray, S., Maswabi, T., Kgathi, C., & Branas, C. C. (2016). Economic development and road traffic fatalities in two neighbouring African nations. *African Journal of Emergency Medicine, 6*(2), 80–86.

World Bank, W. (2019). *The World Bank in Gambia.*

World Bank, W. (2020). *The World Bank in Algeria. Overview.*

Yu, R., & Lee, S.-H. (2011). Optimal trade and privatization policies in an international mixed market. *Hitotsubashi Journal of Economics, 52*(1), 55–68.

Zaifer, A. (2015). *The acceleration of privatisation in Turkey: Why in the last decade?* SOAS University of London.

Zhao, S. (2013). Privatization, FDI inflow and economic growth: Evidence from China's provinces, 1978–2008. *Applied Economics, 45*(15), 2127–2139.

Zinnes, C., Eilat, Y., & Sachs, J. (2001). The gains from privatization in transition economies: Is "Change of ownership" enough? *IMF Staff Papers, 48*(1), 146–170.

Zoomers, A. (2013). A critical review of the policy debate on large-scale land acquisitions: Fighting the symptoms or killing the heart? In S. T. M. Evers, C. Seagle, & F. krijtenburg (Eds.), *Africa for sale? Positioning the state, land and society in foreign large-scale land acquisition in Africa* (pp. 55–77). Brill.

Chapter 6
Overall Summary, Hypotheses Tests and Policy Implications

Abstract This chapter presents the conclusion of the book by summarising the estimated model, testing the hypotheses and discussing the implication of the results. This book examined the effects of the determinants of an optimal level of diversified factors of private sector development, privatisation and taxation, and their speed of adjustment towards the minimum level of natural resource revenue dependency. In examining such effects, several estimation methods were used, including static linear regression model, traditional dynamic model and dynamic flexible adjustment model in the form of a single equation and a system of equations. The dynamic flexible adjustment model and the better performance of system of equations made a key difference compared to the other estimation models. The finding indicated that economic diversification to reduce resource revenue dependency of natural resource rich countries can be achieved through public sector development. This finding should be of interest to natural resource rich countries. Accordingly, there are several ways these countries can reduce their degree of dependency on natural resources revenue. A number of recommendations along with more policies will be offered in accordance with the findings of the study.

Keywords Hypothesis testing · Policy implication · Contribution to the literature · Future research

6.1 Introduction

The problem of natural resource dependency along with providing relevant theories in relation to economic diversification to reduce natural resource dependency was presented. A summary of the previous studies surrounding the relationship between private sector development, public sector privatisation, taxation and the reduction of natural resource dependency was provided. Previous studies have approached the problem of natural resource dependency in various ways. Much of the empirical literature considered natural resource curse and economic growth. However, no empirical investigation has studied the change in the degree of dependency on natural resources in response to private sector development and/or public sector development. This study investigated the relationship between the diversified factors of private sector development, privatisation and taxation to reduce natural resource dependency.

In examining this relationship, several estimation methods were used such as static linear regression model, traditional dynamic model and dynamic flexible adjustment model, which is linear neither in regressors nor in parameters. Then, the research methodology design considered the country heterogeneity and testing for heteroskedasticity. As such, the model specified to test for the interdependence between the four models of PSD, privatisation, taxation and dependency, and thus a complete system of equations with interdependence was estimated.

The analysis presented in Chapter 5 provided an appealing outcome of this relationship. This chapter provides insights into the implications of all these factors affecting the rate of dependency on natural resources revenue. It also provides a summary of the results, along with the main findings, contributions, discussions of the limitations and their implications for future research. Based on the analysis of the results, recommendations for decision-makers are made.

6.2 The Research Questions and Hypotheses Test

6.2.1 The Research Questions

Five key research questions (with to sub-research questions) were raised as follows: (1) How does private sector development affect the degree of dependency on resource revenues in natural resources rich countries, (2) How does public sector development affect the degree of dependency on resource revenue extractions. This research question was further broken down into two sub-research questions: (2.1) Does public sector privatisation affect the degree of dependency on natural resources in resource rich countries, (2.2) Does a national taxation system result in less dependency on resource revenues in natural wealth countries, (3) How do natural resource rents from oil and gas affect the economic diversification factors in natural resources rich countries, (4) How does institutional quality affect the degree of dependency on natural resources in resources rich countries? (5) Does human development affect the degree of dependency on natural resources in resources rich countries?

The corresponding hypotheses for all five research questions were:

Hypothesis 1 RQ_1: There is a positive impact of PSD in reducing the degree of dependency on natural resource revenues.

Hypothesis 2 RQ_{2_1}: Public sector privatisation affects the degree of dependency in natural resource rich countries.

Hypothesis 2 RQ_{2_2}: National taxation system has a relative reduction effect on the degree of resource revenue dependency in natural resource rich countries.

Hypothesis 3 RQ_{3_1}: Natural resource rents from oil & gas positively affect private sector development in natural resource rich countries.

6.2 The Research Questions and Hypotheses Test

Hypothesis 3 RQ_{3_2}: Natural resource rents from oil & gas do not promote public sector privatisation in natural resource rich countries.

Hypothesis 3 RQ_{3_3}: Natural resource rents from oil & gas negatively affect national taxation system in natural resource rich countries.

Hypothesis 4 RQ_4: Natural resource dependency reduction relies on the quality of institutions.

Hypothesis 5 RQ_5: Human development positively affects natural resource revenue dependency reduction.

6.2.2 Hypotheses Testing

In the regression analysis, a variable is highly significant when its p-value is less than 0.01%, significant when its p-value is less 0.05% and weakly significant when its p-value is less than 0.10%. This classification is called the level of significance along with the measure of the coefficient of determination (R^2), a log likelihood ratio, and different specification tests according to the model type, would determine the variables that may be included in the equation (Greene, 2012). This research used different reliable specification tests for the choice of the explanatory variables and their interactions with country-specific characteristics. Theoretical validation and significance levels were used to compare and evaluate these variables.

Table 6.1 presents a summary of hypotheses tests among the estimation of different models. None of the hypotheses are supported in both specifications of static and dynamic models. However, as the analysis is based on the dynamic flexible model, hypothesis $1RQ_1$ is not supported. The coefficient of PSD was positive and significant, indicating a positive relationship between natural resource dependence and PSD. There is evidence of less effectiveness of PSD in natural resource rich countries.

PSD refers to a range of strategies aimed at strengthening the private sector to promote economic growth, sustainability, employment opportunities and improve the

Table 6.1 Hypotheses test among the estimated models

Hypothesis	Model 1	Model 2	Model 3
H1	O	X	X
H2 2 (2–1)	X	X	O
H2 2 (2–2)	O	X	O
H3 (3–1)	-	-	O
H3 (3–2)	-	-	O
H3 (3–3)	-	-	O
H4	X	O	O
H5	O	X	O

Note (X) for rejection and (O) for acceptance of the hypothesis (-) indication that the hypothesis is not applicable to the model

welfare of people (Di Bella et al., 2013; C. Lin et al., 2011). Nevertheless, the natural resource curse literature discussed in Chapter 2 suggested a negative impact of natural resource rents on long-term economic growth. Though it might be true that in a period of resource price boom, natural resource-dependent countries experience economic growth, this growth cannot be sustainable due to commodity price volatility, the undermining of other sectors competitiveness and procyclical government spending.

Generally, there are different models of privatisation, public–private partnership or others applied to enhance the contribution of the private sector in the economy. Nevertheless, natural resource-dependent countries have relative largesse of public sectors. There are citizen expectations of economic opportunities to improve their living conditions, as almost all the national workforce is employed in government sector. This perception has limited such strategies aimed at strengthening the private sector, as the public sector activities per se have dominated the economy of natural resource rich countries.

The effect of public sector reforms including the privatisation of state-owned enterprises and a national taxation system is effective in reducing the degree of dependency on natural resources. The degree of privatisation has been promoted among several natural resource rich countries to generate revenue to diversify the economy. While the private sector may provide a normal rate of return to the resource rich countries in the form of taxes, the privatisation process may widen the tax system in the economy. This supports hypotheses $2RQ_{2_1}$ and $2RQ_{2_2}$ that privatisation of state-owned enterprises and establishing a national taxation system reduces long-term resource revenue dependency in resource rich countries. Thus, the null hypotheses fail to be rejected.

Natural resource rent can be used to promote the development of the private sector (see Sect. 5.2). The results found positive effects of natural resource rents on PSD, the speed of adjustment in countries with oil and gas is faster than countries without these resources. This implies that natural resource rents from oil and gas resources positively affect private sector development in natural resources rich countries, hence, hypothesis $3RQ_{3_1}$ is supported. In other words, the study is failed to reject the null hypothesis.

However, the model specified in Sect. 5.3 found that resource type of oil & gas per se has no effect on privatisation, resulting in hypothesis $3RQ_{3_2}$ of the effect of oil and gas on privatisation development being failed to reject the null hypothesis.

Continuing to measure the effect of oil and gas rents, the findings in Sect. 5.4 showed that natural resource rents from oil and gas do not support the establishment of a national taxation system, accordingly, hypothesis $3RQ_{3_3}$ is supported. This suggests better adjustment towards an optimal taxation level in countries without oil and gas resources.

The findings from Sect. 5.5 showed that the contribution of both institutional quality and human development to economic diversification of natural resource rich countries. Although the literature of natural resource curse such as Adams et al. (2019); S. Bhattacharyya and Collier (2013); Frankel (2012) and Venables (2016) are convinced about the real existence of the curse, S. Bhattacharyya and Hodler (2014); Van der Ploeg (2011) and Venables (2016) believed that these features depend on country-specific conditions such as the quality of institution. Hence, the findings of the research are consistent with the previous findings, confirming the importance of improving the quality of institutions in promoting economic diversification of natural resource rich countries, resulting in hypothesis $4RQ_4$ being failed to reject the null hypothesis.

Human development is a critical factor for the economic diversification of natural resource rich countries. It is a transferable mechanism to diversify the resource rich economies through expanding manufacturing growth. In line with a study by Y. Su and Liu (2016), who found a direct positive impact of human development on economic growth of China, this research reported a direct diversification effect of resource dependency reduction, thus hypothesis $5RQ_5$ is supported.

6.3 Summary of Results

The main results of this study can be summarised as follows:

Firstly, the economy of natural resource rich countries is characterised by weak governance, poor infrastructure, a low degree of political stability and less investment in the non-resource sector. Therefore, in the initial stages of private sector development, the government of natural resources rich countries should offer a tax incentive. The analysis of the results suggests that strong and long-lasting political stability enables the private sector to be effective. Such stability, however, associates with the level of governance, as political stability has implications for transparency and anti-corruption. As such, the private sector in resource rich countries requires effective levels of governance to develop. In addition, human development is positively associated with PSD, suggesting that the country level of PSD largely depends on the quality of human capacity.

An appealing result in favour of the resource rich countries herewith suggests that natural resource rents, in particular oil and gas, can accelerate the adjustment towards the development of private sector. The analysis of the results presents relatively faster adjustment towards private sector development mainly in low middle-income resource wealthy countries.

Second, the results for privatisation suggest that there is a causal relationship between privatisation and taxation. While before privatisation, taxes were levied on state-owned enterprises in a number of countries, these enterprises were inefficient and unproductive. Then, the expansion of privatisation increases the tax rate collection. An important result herewith confirms the necessity of improving institutions and regulatory conditions of the resource rich countries in favour of privatisation, which enables competitors to consider non-resource investment in natural resource rich countries. Therefore, it is recommended that, if they have a weak institutional capacity, resource rich countries should slow down their privatisation. Furthermore, to some extent, the process of privatisation depends on the openness of natural resource rich countries. Trade openness is a mechanism of transmission to improve human development and transfer technology to resource rich countries.

While the analysis indicates the non-role of natural resource rents in general in the privatisation process, these factors, caused a positive trend of privatisation over the period of the study.

Third, while the effectiveness of taxation in natural resource rich countries is equivocal, the result for the optimal taxation model confirms a positive relationship between privatisation and taxation in such countries. There are opportunities for these countries to improve the tax base and tax revenue through the support of the privatisation process. The relationship between optimal taxation and natural resource dependence indicates that countries generating revenue from natural resource rents are unlikely to rely on taxes. In other words, an increase in the share of natural resource rents leads to lower revenue from taxes. Although the theory of tax suggests that high-income countries raise more taxes than low-income countries, the result presents a negative correlation between tax share and level of income in natural resource rich countries. This result confirms the resource curse claim, in which, resource rents reduce the government's need to tax its citizens. Therefore, it is critical for the resource rich countries to consider taxation to reduce the degree of dependency on natural resources. In doing so, another factor to improve tax revenue, according to the findings of this study, is tax capacity. The analysis of the result indicates that taxation is proportional to tax capacity. The analysis for trade measure indicates that natural resource countries may still be reliant on trade tax revenue. Although trade liberalisation cut such taxes, it is recommended for these countries not to apply trade liberalisation unless revenue sources are diversified.

Fourth, a number of factors that have been related to natural resource dependency reduction are presented. The results suggest that public sector reforms can have better performance in reducing natural resource dependence than private sector development. Private sector development is a critical factor in the revenue diversification of natural resource rich countries. However, the positive relationship of PSD with natural resource dependence indicates that PSD might not be effective in reducing natural resource dependency. It is suggested to slow down PSD until privatisation occurs with improvement in institutions. The effect of public sector reforms, including privatisation of state-owned enterprises and a national taxation system, is found to be reducing the degree of dependency on natural resources. The privatisation process while raising substantial cash for governments, develops the remaining public enterprises. Accordingly, the private sector engages in the economic activity, and thereby provides a normal rate of return to the resource wealth countries in the form of taxes. Therefore, there is a positive impact of establishing a national taxation system to reduce long-term resource revenue dependence in resource rich countries, as the results suggest. A further economic factor is manufacturing productions which contribute to the diversification of natural resource revenues. As a result, it downsizes revenue dependency in natural resource rich countries.

Fifth, the non-economic factor of institutional quality indicates that the more institutionalised an economy of natural resource rich countries is, the less degree of natural resource dependence they have. A further critical factor in overcoming the problem of resource revenue dependency is human development. The progress of human capacity is a means of transfer to influence the industrial development of

6.3 Summary of Results

those countries that are rich in natural resources, hence it is a transferable mechanism to diversify their economies. These two factors play a critical role in affecting the adjustment of the sampled countries towards dependency reduction (see Table 6.2). These two appealing findings are in line with natural resource curse literature.

Sixth, the result of the mean indicator values by country shows that only two countries, namely Kuwait and Bhutan, have no attempts to adjust towards less dependency on natural resources ($\delta_{it} = 0$). However, several countries such as Angola, the Republic of Congo, Vietnam, Botswana, China, Liberia, Chile, Equatorial Guinea, Libya, Azerbaijan Mauritania, Iraq, Saudi Arabia, Venezuela, Mongolia, The United Arab Emirates, Qatar and Russia have shown their desire to adjust towards less dependency. While the majority of these countries are oil exporters, some of them have significantly gained from natural resources over long periods and others have experienced economic growth possibly at the expense of institutional improvement. This is probably a response of radical changes in general economic policy, starting from import substitution to liberalisation, which resulted in increased capital mobilisation, privatisation and investment in education and infrastructure.

The result reported in Table 6.3 shows that Angola is the fastest country adjusting towards less dependency with a 38% adjustment speed. As explained in Chapter 4, the country is progressing towards private-led economic growth.

Surprisingly, Iraq is the second country that has a medium adjustment towards less dependency on natural resources with the value of 19%. Iraq had a command economy with a distribution of wealth through food programme. After the invasion of Kuwait in 1990, the US-led coalition attacked Iraq. Following the attack economic sanctions were introduced. As such, Iraq's economy was enormously weakened and relied mostly on United Nations' oil for food programme and illegal trading in the market. Later changes took place in the aftermath of the collapse of Saddam Hussein's regime in 2003. In 2005 elections were held, a new constitution was approved and then the people's representative government was established in 2006 (Ellison & Pino, 2012).

Iraq's economy is heavily characterised by oil production, macroeconomic instability, mass unemployment and lack of infrastructure. Iraq has the potential to grow with an advantage of oil prices to invest in the country's damaged infrastructure. Higher spending, particularly in public investment, together with reasonable oil prices will result in further development of the country. Improvement in the governance indicator of the country is a further advantage; the governance growth has recorded 1660% since 1996, yet the country is scored 9 out of one hundred (Table 6.2). However, several factors have resulted in a governance gap and the failure to achieve its full potential of growth such as political instability executed public investment projects, conflict destruction of the accumulated human capital and a decrease in education, and massive corruption (Diwakar, 2015; Gunter, 2013; Sassoon, 2016).

Armenia is another resource rich country that on the production side the sectors of service, manufacturing, agriculture and mining are the main drivers of economic growth. It is one of the post-socialist countries that has struggled to transition to a market-oriented economy due to limited private-led projects and its command system (Otto & Chobotova, 2013). Armenia has the slowest adjustment speed towards less

Table 6.2 Country Adjustment in Comparison to Human Development and Governance Indicators

Country	Delta	HDI 2016	HDI Improvement %	Governance Rank 2016	Governance Improvement %
Angola	0.380	0.570	50	13	−30
Congo, Republic	0.376	0.613	15	12	8
Vietnam	0.363	0.685	45	54	60
Botswana	0.334	0.719	27	71	2
China	0.297	0.749	50	67	57
Liberia	0.295	0.463	29	9	296
Chili	0.285	0.843	20	79	−10
Equatorial Guinea	0.282	0.592	13	8	−60
Oman	0.276	0.834	18	62	−8
Norway	0.275	0.951	12	99	0.13
Libya	0.264	0.690	0.04	1	−91
Gabon	0.263	0.696	13	21	−57
Azerbaijan	0.244	0.749	18	48	156
Iran	0.209	0.799	38	45	36
Mauritania	0.197	0.519	39	22	−57
Iraq	0.192	0.672	19	9	1660
Saudi Arabia	0.183	0.857	23	63	27
Venezuela, RB	0.170	0.752	15	8	−77
Mongolia	0.153	0.730	25	50	−0.7
Suriname	0.149	0.726	0.08	40	16
Congo, Dem. Rep	0.145	0.453	21	7	26
United Arab Emirates	0.143	0.863	19	91	18
Uzbekistan	0.128	0.701	19	32	321
Kazakhstan	0.126	0.808	18	51	212
Chad	0.119	0.398	35	6	−80
Syria	0.118	0.539	−0.03	2	−89
Qatar	0.107	0.847	11	75	6
Russian Federation	0.088	0.817	11	45	35

Source Author's own construction, 2020

6.3 Summary of Results

Table 6.3 Country Level Adjustment towards Dependency Reduction

Country	Delta	Level	Country	Delta	Level	Country	Delta	Level	Country	Delta	Level
Angola	0.380	Fast	Mauritania	0.197	Medium	Albania	0.034	Slow	Mexico	0.032	Slow
Congo, Republic	0.376		Iraq	0.192		Armenia	0.003		Macedonia, FYR	0.052	
Vietnam	0.363		Saudi Arabia	0.183		Burkina Faso	0.026		Mali	0.016	
Botswana	0.334		Venezuela, RB	0.170		Bolivia	0.032		Mozambique	0.034	
China	0.297		Mongolia	0.153		Brazil	0.015		Malawi	0.037	
Liberia	0.295		Suriname	0.149		Colombia	0.045		Malaysia	0.035	
Chili	0.285		Congo, Dem. Rep	0.145		Cabo Verde	0.006		Namibia	0.009	
Equatorial Guinea	0.282		United Arab Emirates	0.143		Algeria	0.053		Philippines	0.014	
Oman	0.276		Uzbekistan	0.128		Egypt, Arab Rep	0.073		Poland	0.025	
Norway	0.275		Kazakhstan	0.126		Georgia	0.003		Romania	0.015	
Libya	0.264		Burundi	0.120		Ghana	0.056		Russian Federation	0.088	
Gabon	0.263		Chad	0.119		Guinea	0.029		Rwanda	0.012	
Azerbaijan	0.244		Syria	0.118		Guinea-Bissau	0.058		Senegal	0.003	
Yemen	0.216		Ecuador	0.110		Guyana	0.091		Togo	0.054	
Iran	0.209		Sierra Leone	0.110		Croatia	0.006		Thailand	0.005	
			Qatar	0.107		IDN	0.019		Tunisia	0.045	
						Jordan	0.045		Tanzania	0.029	
						Kyrgyz Republic	0.017		Uganda	0.064	
						Lao PDR	0.011		Ukraine	0.030	
						Sri Lanka	0.006		United States	0.010	
						Madagascar	0.011		South Africa	0.036	

dependency on natural resources with the value of 0.3%. This slowest adjustment is perhaps due to the promotion of the intensification of natural resource production with the objective of poverty reduction (Burns et al., 2017).

Seventh, by using several policy variables, the speed of adjustment towards optimal privatisation, optimal taxation and optimal dependency reduction was estimated. The level of commitment of the resource-wealthy countries to each diversified factor is differed across countries. However, the speed of adjustment based on level of income indicated that natural resource countries, regardless of their income level, adjusted towards the optimal privatisation, meaning that attempts have been made to focus on diversification which in turn reduces resource dependency.

Eighth, knowledge of the speed of adjustment in each optimal dependent variable is helpful for resource revenue-dependent countries to design a stabilisation policy through the substitution of resources revenue with economic diversification sourced privatisation or tax revenues. It is difficult for resource rich countries to rapidly adjust towards privatisation or taxation as sudden changes in generating revenues can have significant political and economic costs affecting economic growth negatively.

Finally, estimating dynamic flexible adjustment models in investigating natural resource dependency reduction is econometrically challenging. This is because (1) macro data on resource rich countries are typically unbalanced panel data, (2) the dynamic model is adjusting over time (i.e., a lagged dependent variable is included as a regressor), (3) the empirical model imposes no restrictions by allowing the speed of adjustment to be flexible (δ_{it}) and (4) in estimating the relationship between each diversified factor of PSD, privatisation and taxation with natural resource dependency, two-ways or multiple-ways of causality between each pair and all dependent variables are introduced. In such a relationship where the system is interdependent, therefore, (5) the dynamic flexible adjustment model is estimated as a system of equations.

6.4 Policy Implications

The findings of this book should be of interest to natural resource rich countries. Accordingly, there are several ways these countries can reduce their degree of dependency on natural resources revenue. For example, public sector development might generate many changes concerning sources of income. Another way is that many countries have enhanced their privatisation to deepen their economic reforms and increase private investment in public enterprises. Privatisation may provide substantial revenues for the government which may lead to a reduction in natural resource dependency.

Furthermore, the private sector may provide a normal rate of return to the resource rich countries in the form of taxes. The establishment of a national taxation system is the second aspect of public sector development. Taxation may provide relatively long-lasting economic stability to reduce long-term resource revenue volatility. The empirical results of this study concluded better performance of public sector reforms in reducing natural resource dependency. Policymakers and stakeholders may take these opportunities into account when considering economic diversification to reduce natural resource dependency.

The empirical results of this research present the increasing opportunities of natural resource dependency reduction, when the country is involved in improving institutional quality and human capacity building. The result of this research confirms the importance of improving the quality of institutions in promoting the economic diversification of natural resource rich countries. Therefore, the government of natural resource rich countries should strengthen the capacity of the state and its institutions to have a better position in diversification of its production base to reduce natural resource dependency.

Finally, human capital may have a direct diversification effect of resource dependency reduction through transferring those countries that are rich in natural resources to the industrial development. It is advisable to policymakers of these countries that utilise natural resource revenue to increase investment in human capital. This accelerates the private sector's engagement in economic activities in which it may lead the backward and forward linkage from resource commodity to manufacturing, thereby speeding the industrialisation of resource revenue-dependent countries.

6.5 Final Conclusion and Contributions to the Literature

6.5.1 Final Conclusion

This book identified and examined the effects of the determinants of an optimal level of diversified factors of private sector development, privatisation and taxation, and their speed of adjustment towards a desired level of dependency reduction. In examining such effects, a number of estimation methods are used, including static linear regression model, traditional dynamic model and dynamic flexible adjustment model in the form of a single equation and a system of equations. The dynamic flexible adjustment model and the better performance of system of equations made a key difference compared to the other estimation models.

The results concluded that private sector development does not have a dependency reduction effect in natural resource rich countries. Although natural resource rents could foster the development of the private sector, the speed of adjustment in countries with oil and gas was higher than countries without these resources.

The finding indicated that economic diversification to reduce resource revenue dependency of natural resource rich countries can be achieved through public sector development. The public sector can be developed to lead diversification either through the privatisation of public services, or through the development of a national taxation system. The finding concluded the importance of institutions in the progress of privatisation in resource rich countries that are highly vulnerable to market prices. In examining the determinants of a national taxation system, the significant variables affecting the level of taxation were governance, privatisation strategy of resource rich countries and tax capacity improvements.

Nevertheless, beside the effect of the diversified factors, institutional quality and human development improve the performance of economic diversification to reduce natural resource dependency reduction. Therefore, countries that experienced improvement on institutions and human capacity have adjusted faster towards less dependency.

6.5.2 Contributions to the Literature

The current research examined the importance of various factors of diversification in reducing the degree of dependency on natural resource revenues, namely private sector development, privatisation and taxation. The aim was to quantitatively examine the diversified factors of the economy that contribute to reduce dependency on natural resources.

In the empirical work of this research, the dynamic flexible adjustment model in a system of equations was estimated on an unbalanced panel data of 110 natural resource rich developed, developing and emerging countries of different sizes and of different political systems, observed from 1990–2017. The flexible adjustment model in the study of private sector development, privatisation and taxation to reduce natural resource dependency reduction was first used in which restrictions were not imposed by allowing the speed of adjustment to be flexible. The adjustment parameter was specified in terms of factors affecting the speed of adjustment.

The estimated model of this research accounted for unobserved fixed effects, by introducing a set of proxy and dummy variables and their interactions. Complete accounting for a fixed effect or a random effect model in the current estimated model was not possible due to the presence of the flexible dynamic adjustment model and over-parametrisation of the model. However, the models were estimated as a complete system of four interdependent equations, accounting for endogeneity and simultaneity, as well as controlling for country characteristics, heterogeneity effects and dynamics. In addition to the abovementioned, the main contributions of this book to the literature can be summarised as follows:

The initial contribution of this research is to build a large database of aggregate country level for resource rich countries, which would also be very useful for future analyses. The data set used in this study is in the form of unbalanced panel data, covering natural resource producers in developed, developing and emerging countries of different sizes and of different political systems from 1990 to 2017.

In order to shed light on economic diversification with the objective of natural resource dependency reduction, the research first, established a relationship between private sector development and natural resource dependency. Second, it established a relationship between public sector development including privatisation and taxation with natural resource dependency. Finally, a relationship between the diversified factors of private sector development and public sector development in natural resource-dependent countries to reduce dependency on natural resource revenues was established.

A further contribution of this book is the development of an appropriate analytical framework to identify the key macroeconomic factors affecting private sector development and public sector development in natural resource rich countries. This is believed to be imperative, especially in addressing how government policies can stimulate private and public sector development that will in turn boost the economic diversification of natural resource rich countries. This book reviewed the non-economic determinant factors of development such as institutional quality, human development and other factors that impact the speed of adjustment of the private and public sector development.

An empirical contribution of this book is that, to date, no previous studies have applied the dynamic flexible adjustment model to investigate factors affecting natural resource dependency reduction in the economy. This contributes in two important ways, first it provides comprehensive and precise policy recommendations for natural resource rich countries, and second, it will attract further research in the area. Then, this research can be considered as an input for analysing the relationship between the diversified factors and their determinants.

Finally, there are contributions of this book in terms of empirics. First, a dynamic adjustment model was employed at country level in order to capture the flexible adjustment of the effective level of the PSD, privatisation, taxation and reducing the degree of dependency on natural resources. Second, it empirically identified the determinants of the optimal level of PSD, privatisation and taxation in resource rich countries to reduce the degree of dependency on resource revenue. Third, an adjustment model was flexibly specified, in which, country- and time-specific policy factors determining the speed of adjustment were identified. Fourth, the gap between observed and optimal levels of the PSD, privatisation, taxation and dependency was estimated. Fifth, the performance of countries in attaining target levels and speed of changes towards target was compared. Finally, the PSD, privatisation, taxation and resources dependency were estimated as a system accounting for endogeneity and simultaneity.

6.6 Limitations and Recommendations for Further Research

This research has some limitations. First, the result of unavailability of data is well known, especially in a sample of this size where many of them are from developing countries. The data unavailability caused a number of critical macroeconomic variables to be excluded from the estimations, such as non-resource taxes revenue types, and number of firms privatised. As a result, this research was unable to identify suitability of different types of taxation to resource rich countries, such as proportional and flat taxes, state and local income taxes, capital gains taxes and other payroll taxes, to determine which tax policy has the most influence on income diversification to reduce natural resource dependency. In addition to number of firms privatised, the limitations of the data imposed restrictions to measure whether partially or fully privatised firms are in favour of resource rich countries.

Additionally, most of the dependent and independent variables included in the research have a lack of long-term time-series data for these variables. As data availability is an essential attribute for panel data either to be balanced or unbalanced, the unbalanced nature of sample data is attributed to limited data availability.

Furthermore, it might be true that to some extent, all have a level of natural resources, but not all of them are resource-dependent countries. Although attempts have been made to examine all countries that have natural resources, this was not always possible, as several numbers of sampled countries have very limited resource revenues. Despite the fact that these countries are intended to have similar content and structure as resource rich countries, the variation in the studied sampled countries enhanced the generalisation of the findings.

While this research found the effect of privatisation and taxation on economic diversification with the objective of natural resource dependency reduction, these effects are varied with the different methods of privatisation, either fully or partially privatised and the type of taxation. Hence, doing research on the effect of the type of privatisation and taxation might provide new insights for further research and more effective policies for economic diversification to reduce natural resource dependency.

Finally, to provide new insights in future research, studies may measure the effects of the diversified factor of PSD, privatisation and taxation to reduce natural resource dependency using the third generation of dynamic factor demand models introduced by Prucha and Nadiri (1986) and recently used by Khayyat (2017).

Bibliography

Adams, D., Adams, K., Ullah, S., & Ullah, F. (2019). Globalisation, governance, accountability and the natural resource 'curse': Implications for socio-economic growth of oil-rich developing countries. *Resources Policy, 61*, 128–140.

Bhattacharyya, S., & Collier, P. (2013). Public capital in resource rich economies: Is there a curse? *Oxford Economic Papers, 66*(1), 1–24.

Bhattacharyya, S., & Hodler, R. (2014). Do natural resource revenues hinder financial development? The role of political institutions. *World Development, 57*, 101–113.

Burns, S. L., Krott, M., Sayadyan, H., & Giessen, L. (2017). The world bank improving environmental and natural resource policies: Power, deregulation, and privatization in (Post-Soviet) Armenia. *World Development, 92*, 215–224.

Di Bella, J., Grant, A., Kindornay, S., & Tissot, S. (2013). *Mapping private sector engagements in development cooperation.*

Diwakar, V. (2015). The effect of armed conflict on education: Evidence from Iraq. *The Journal of Development Studies, 51*(12), 1702–1718.

Ellison, G., & Pino, N. (2012). *Globalization, police reform and development: Doing it the Western way?* Springer.

Bibliography

Frankel, J. A. (2012). The natural resource curse: A survey of diagnoses and some prescriptions. *HKS Faculty Research Working Paper Series RWP12–014, John F. Kennedy School of Government, Harvard University*.

Greene, W. H. (2012). *Econometric analysis*. Pearson Education

Gunter, F. R. (2013). *The political economy of Iraq: Restoring balance in a post-conflict society*. Edward Elgar Publishing.

Khayyat, N. T. (2017). *ICT investment for energy use in the industrial sectors*. Springer.

Lin, C., Lin, P., Song, F. M., & Li, C. (2011). Managerial incentives, CEO characteristics and corporate innovation in China's private sector. *Journal of Comparative Economics, 39*(2), 176–190.

Otto, I., & Chobotova, V. (2013). Opportunities and constraints of adopting market governance in protected areas in Central and Eastern Europe. *International Journal of the Commons, 7*(1), 34–57.

Prucha, I. R., & Nadiri, M. I. (1986). A comparison of alternative methods for the estimation of dynamic factor demand models under non-static expectations. *Journal of Econometrics, 33*(1–2), 187–211.

Sassoon, J. (2016). Iraq's political economy post 2003: From transition to corruption. *International Journal of Contemporary Iraqi Studies, 10*(1–2), 17–33.

Su, Y., & Liu, Z. (2016). The impact of foreign direct investment and human capital on economic growth: Evidence from Chinese cities. *China Economic Review, 37*, 97–109.

Van der Ploeg, F. (2011). Natural resources: Curse or blessing? *Journal of Economic Literature, 49*(2), 366–420.

Venables, A. J. (2016). Using natural resources for development: Why has it proven so difficult? *Journal of Economic Perspectives, 30*(1), 161–184.

Appendix 1
Country Classification and Coefficient Correlations

See Tables A.1, A.2, A.3, and A.4.

Table A.1 Country classification

No	Countries	Degree of dependency	Income group
1	Albania	Very Low	Middle
2	Algeria	Medium	Middle
3	Angola	Medium	Middle
4	Armenia	Very Low	Middle
5	Australia	Very Low	Higher
6	Azerbaijan	Medium	Middle
7	Bangladesh	Very Low	Lower
8	Belarus	Very Low	Upper Middle
9	Benin	Very Low	Lower
10	Bhutan	Very Low	Lower Middle
11	Bolivia	Very Low	Lower Middle
12	Botswana	Very Low	Upper Middle
13	Brazil	Very Low	Upper Middle

(continued)

© The Editor(s) (if applicable) and The Author(s), under exclusive license to Springer Nature Singapore Pte Ltd. 2023
G. M. Muhamad, *Reducing Natural Resource Dependency for Economic Growth in Resource Rich Countries*, Perspectives on Development in the Middle East and North Africa (MENA) Region, https://doi.org/10.1007/978-981-99-3640-3

Table A.1 (continued)

No	Countries	Degree of dependency	Income group
14	Burkina Faso	Low	Lower
15	Burundi	Medium	Lower
16	Cabo Verde	Very Low	Middle
17	Cambodia	Very Low	Lower
18	Cameroon	Very Low	Lower Middle
19	Canada	Very Low	Higher
20	Chad	Medium	Lower
21	Chile	Low	Higher
22	China	Very Low	Middle
23	Colombia	Very Low	Upper Middle
24	Comoros	Very Low	Lower Middle
25	Congo, Dem. Rep	High	Lower
26	Congo, Rep	Very High	Lower Middle
27	Cote d'Ivoire	Very Low	Lower Middle
28	Croatia	Very Low	Higher
29	Ecuador	Low	Upper Middle
30	Egypt, Arab Rep	Very Low	Middle
31	El Salvador	Very Low	Middle
32	Equatorial Guinea	Very High	Higher
33	Eswatini	Very Low	Middle
34	Fiji	Very Low	Middle
35	Gabon	High	Upper Middle
36	Gambia, The	Very Low	Lower
37	Georgia	Very Low	Middle
38	Ghana	Low	Lower Middle
39	Guatemala	Very Low	Middle
40	Guinea	Low	Lower
41	Guinea-Bissau	Low	Lower
42	Guyana	Medium	Middle
43	Haiti	Very Low	Lower
44	Honduras	Very Low	Lower Middle
45	Hungary	Very Low	Higher
46	India	Very Low	Lower Middle
47	Indonesia	Very Low	Middle

(continued)

Appendix 1: Country Classification and Coefficient Correlations

Table A.1 (continued)

No	Countries	Degree of dependency	Income group
48	Iran	Medium	Upper Middle
49	Iraq	Very High	Upper Middle
50	Japan	Very Low	Higher
51	Jordan	Very Low	Middle
52	Kazakhstan	Low	Upper Middle
53	Kenya	Very Low	Lower
54	Kuwait	Very High	Higher
55	Kyrgyz Republic	Very Low	Lower
56	Lao PDR	Very Low	Lower Middle
57	Lebanon	Very Low	Upper Middle
58	Liberia	Medium	Lower
59	Libya	Very High	Higher
60	Macedonia	Very Low	Upper Middle
61	Madagascar	Very Low	Lower
62	Malawi	Very Low	Lower
63	Malaysia	Low	Upper Middle
64	Mali	Very Low	Lower
65	Mauritania	Low	Lower Middle
66	Mauritius	Very Low	Upper Middle
67	Mexico	Very Low	Higher
68	Moldova	Very Low	Lower Middle
69	Mongolia	Low	Middle
70	Mozambique	Low	Lower
71	Namibia	Very Low	Upper Middle
72	Nepal	Very Low	Lower
73	Nicaragua	Very Low	Lower Middle
74	Niger	Low	Lower
75	Nigeria	Low	Lower Middle
76	Norway	Very Low	Higher
77	Oman	High	Higher
78	Pakistan	Very Low	Lower Middle

(continued)

Table A.1 (continued)

No	Countries	Degree of dependency	Income group
79	Panama	Very Low	Upper Middle
80	Peru	Very Low	Upper Middle
81	Philippines	Very Low	Lower Middle
82	Poland	Very Low	Higher
83	Qatar	High	Higher
84	Romania	Very Low	Upper Middle
85	Russian Federation	Low	Upper Middle
86	Rwanda	Very Low	Lower
87	Saudi Arabia	Very High	Higher
88	Senegal	Very Low	Lower Middle
89	Seychelles	Very Low	Higher
90	Sierra Leone	Low	Lower
91	South Africa	Very Low	Upper Middle
92	Sri Lanka	Very Low	Middle
93	Suriname	Low	Upper Middle
94	Syrian Arab Republic	Medium	Lower Middle
95	Tanzania	Very Low	Lower
96	Thailand	Very Low	Middle
97	Togo	Low	Lower
98	Tunisia	Very Low	Middle
99	Turkey	Very Low	Higher
100	Uganda	Low	Lower
101	Ukraine	Very Low	Middle
102	United Arab Emirates	Medium	Higher
103	United Kingdom	Very Low	Higher
104	United States	Very Low	Higher
105	Uruguay	Very Low	Higher
106	Uzbekistan	Low	Lower Middle
107	Venezuela, RB	Medium	Upper Middle
108	Vietnam	Very Low	Lower Middle
109	Yemen, Rep	High	Lower Middle
110	Zambia	Low	Lower Middle

Appendix 1: Country Classification and Coefficient Correlations

Table A.2 Pearson correlation coefficients (PSD)

	psd	tax	dep1	cps	inf	A04	A10	A15	A16	A20	A21	A25	C19	C20	trn
psd	1														
tax	0.127	1													
dep	−0.044	−0.220	1												
cps	0.158	0.147	−0.232	1											
inf	0.272	0.181	−0.122	0.495	1										
A04	0.252	0.100	0.133	−0.051	−0.034	1									
A10	0.207	−0.031	0.108	−0.033	−0.041	0.169	1								
A15	0.163	0.256	−0.294	0.635	0.541	−0.086	0.010	1							
A16	0.173	0.261	−0.186	0.367	0.347	0.006	0.025	0.666	1						
A20	0.294	0.251	−0.087	0.585	0.885	−0.013	−0.012	0.662	0.463	1					
A21	−0.081	−0.065	−0.024	−0.029	−0.121	0.008	0.001	−0.061	−0.037	−0.075	1				
A25	0.312	0.234	0.163	0.025	0.095	0.353	0.181	0.018	0.210	0.150	−0.020	1			
C19	−0.275	−0.279	0.027	−0.408	−0.656	0.043	−0.049	−0.526	−0.373	−0.743	0.023	−0.186	1		
C20	0.064	−0.008	−0.235	0.262	0.276	−0.066	−0.053	0.224	0.075	0.212	−0.019	−0.161	−0.140	1	
trn	0.187	0.052	0.045	0.175	0.110	0.109	0.064	−0.013	−0.063	0.256	0.006	0.125	−0.197	−0.083	1

Abbreviations: Private sector development (psd), Taxation (tax), Natural Resource Dependence (dep), PCA Credit to the private sector (cps), PCA Infrastructure (inf) FDI inward (A04), Economic Growth (A10), Governance (A15), Political stability (A16), Human development (A20), Trade Openness (A25), Agricultural Production (C19), Manufacturing Production (C20) and Time Trend (trn)

Table A.3 Pearson correlation coefficients (privatisation)

	pusd	tax	dep	iq	cps	C05	C08	C17	C19	C20	A10	A25	A33	trn
pusd	1													
tax	0.436	1												
dep	−0.050	−0.220	1											
iq	0.341	0.276	−0.340	1										
cps	0.177	0.147	−0.232	0.592	1									
C05	0.271	0.420	−0.048	0.058	−0.017	1								
C08	−0.242	−0.089	0.000	0.007	0.061	−0.052	1							
C17	0.314	0.275	−0.143	0.342	0.299	0.079	−0.462	1						
C19	−0.403	−0.279	0.027	−0.445	−0.408	−0.223	0.107	−0.307	1					
C20	−0.165	−0.008	−0.235	0.223	0.262	0.050	0.372	−0.047	−0.140	1				
A10	−0.131	−0.031	0.108	−0.026	−0.033	−0.049	0.014	−0.050	−0.049	−0.053	1			
A25	0.122	0.234	0.163	−0.031	0.025	0.058	−0.069	−0.009	−0.186	−0.161	0.181	1		
A33	0.035	0.148	0.045	0.082	0.107	0.006	−0.030	0.121	−0.265	0.064	0.350	0.476	1	
trn	−0.022	0.052	0.045	−0.009	0.175	−0.066	0.008	0.145	−0.197	−0.083	0.064	0.125	0.126	1

Abbreviations: Privatiasation (pusd), Taxation (tax), Natural Resource Dependence (dep), PCA Institutional quality (inq) PCA Credit to the private sector (cps), Unemployment (C05), Wage & Salary (C08), Subsidy (C17), Agricultural Production (C19), Manufacturing Production (C20), Economic Development (A10), Trade Openness (A25), and Time Trend (trn)

Appendix 1: Country Classification and Coefficient Correlations

Table A.4 Pearson correlation coefficients (taxation)

	tax	pusd1	pusd2	dep1	A10	A15	C01	C02	D01	trn
tax	1									
pusd1	−0.162	1								
pusd2	0.436	−0.225	1							
dep1	−0.220	0.562	−0.050	1						
A10	−0.031	0.081	−0.131	0.108	1					
A15	0.256	−0.594	0.334	−0.294	0.010	1				
C01	0.169	0.078	0.105	0.232	0.128	0.128	1			
C02	0.251	0.115	0.098	0.079	0.199	−0.063	0.653	1		
D01	0.339	−0.241	−0.169	−0.049	0.006	0.296	−0.018	−0.095	1	
trn	0.052	0.012	−0.022	0.045	0.064	−0.013	0.143	0.089	0.083	1

Abbreviations: Taxation (tax), Diversification (pusd1), Privatisation (pusd2), Natural Resource Dependence (dep), Economic Development (A10), Governance (A15), Export (C01), Import (C02), Tax capacity (D01), and Time Trend (trn)

Appendix 2
Single Equation Model

See Tables A.5, A.6, A.7, and A.8.

Table A.5 Static and dynamic model parameters estimates (PSD)

Model	Static model		Restricted dynamic		Unrestricted dynamic	
Variables	Estimate	Std error	Estimate	Std error	Estimate	Std error
A. Determinants of optimal PSD						
Intercept	13.462[a]	2.460	−1.707	10.547	10.661[c]	6.040
Taxation	−0.039	0.039	−0.148	0.153	−0.561[a]	0.079
NR dependency	−0.041[b]	0.013	−0.048	0.061	0.106[b]	0.037
Credit to private sector	−0.577[c]	0.230	−2.267[c]	1.027	0.711	0.821
Infrastructure quality	2.992[a]	0.576	0.992	2.033	3.274[b]	1.069
FDI inward	0.043[c]	0.024	0.091	0.092	0.042	0.033
Economic growth	0.256[a]	0.053	1.139[a]	0.228	0.276[b]	0.093
Governance	0.028[c]	0.017	0.054	0.059	0.078[c]	0.037

(continued)

Table A.5 (continued)

Model	Static model		Restricted dynamic		Unrestricted dynamic	
Variables	Estimate	Std error	Estimate	Std error	Estimate	Std error
Political Stability	0.020[c]	0.011	0.027	0.042	0.044	0.027
Human development	−2.931	4.773	27.133	16.887	14.041	10.057
Monetary policy	−0.018[b]	0.007	−0.044	0.034	0.019[c]	0.009
Trade openness	0.020[b]	0.006	0.023	0.022	0.009	0.014
Agricultural Production	0.004	0.021	0.045	0.123	−0.090[c]	0.055
Manufacturing production	−0.015	0.010	0.031	0.064	0.036	0.055
Trend	0.114[b]	0.032	0.036	0.116	0.161[c]	0.078
Low middle income			−1.493	3.438	−8.737[b]	2.600
Middle income			−3.690	4.314	−6.365[b]	2.502
Upper middle income			−5.099	4.817	−17.149[a]	3.320
Higher income			−6.179	5.316	−17.848[a]	3.063
B. Determinant of speed of adjustment						
Intercept			0.121[a]	0.014	0.435[a]	0.079
Development policy					−0.012[a]	0.003
Human development					0.003[b]	0.001
Openness policy					0.000	0.000
Rule of law					−0.001	0.001
Credit to private sector					0.035[c]	0.016
Speed of privatisation					−0.003[c]	0.001
Trend					−0.002	0.002
Distance					0.014[a]	0.002
OG dummy					0.009	0.024
Low middle income					−0.453[a]	0.067
Middle income					−0.393[a]	0.065
Upper middle income					−0.458[a]	0.071
Higher income					−0.456[a]	0.070
Observations	1373		1309		1191	
Adjusted R-squared	0.195		0.807		0.820	
RMSE	6.624		3.298		3.156	

Note The dependent variable is PSD and the p value is: [a]$p \leq 0.001$, [b]$p \leq 0.05$, [c]$p \leq 0.10$

Appendix 2: Single Equation Model 181

Table A.6 Static and dynamic model parameter estimate (privatisation)

Model	Static model		Restricted dynamic		Unrestricted dynamic	
Variables	Estimate	Std error	Estimate	Std error	Estimate	Std error
A. Determinants of privatisation						
Intercept	15.892[a]	1.061	10.885[c]	6.383	4.735	3.668
Taxation	0.586[a]	0.059	0.196	0.185	0.459[a]	0.086
Dependency	−0.003	0.012	−0.015	0.058	0.214[a]	0.035
Institutional quality	1.191[b]	0.318	2.009	1.246	4.018[a]	0.734
Credit to private sector	−0.130	0.228	0.270	0.959	2.414[b]	0.680
Unemployment	0.189[a]	0.039	0.200	0.153	−0.329[b]	0.086
Salary & wages	−0.032[a]	0.006	−0.047	0.036	−0.138[a]	0.027
Subsidies	0.005	0.016	0.021	0.055	−0.020	0.033
Agricultural productions	−0.124[a]	0.020	−0.021	0.126	−0.009	0.072
Manufacturing productions	−0.093[a]	0.011	−0.114	0.074	0.071	0.063
Economic development	−0.188[b]	0.050	−0.196	0.198	0.009	0.095
Trade openness	−0.013[c]	0.005	0.006	0.023	0.015	0.011
Total investment	−0.012	0.013	−0.036	0.054	0.031	0.030
Trend	−0.053[c]	0.027	0.224[c]	0.117	0.059	0.070
Lower middle income			1.301	3.443	−2.123	2.110
Middle income			3.539	3.957	−1.908	2.837
Upper middle income			4.829	4.539	−5.341[c]	3.169
Higher income			4.919	4.716	−4.226	3.385
B. Determinants of adjustment speed						
Intercept			0.094[a]	0.012	0.046	0.054
Rule of law					−0.001	0.001
Openness policy					0.000	0.000
Subsidy policy					−0.001[c]	0.000
Interest rate policy					−0.001[a]	0.000
Credit to the private sector (PCA)					0.001	0.009
Oil & gas dummy variable					0.001	0.001
Trend					0.013	0.001
distance					0.012[a]	0.020

(continued)

Table A.6 (continued)

Model	Static model		Restricted dynamic		Unrestricted dynamic	
Variables	Estimate	Std error	Estimate	Std error	Estimate	Std error
Lower middle income					0.041	0.050
Middle income					−0.159	0.043
Upper middle income					−0.163	0.043
Higher income					−0.141	0.047
Observation	1267		1188		1188	
Adjusted R-squared	0.401		0.907		0.923	
RMSE	6.425		2.476		2.184	

Note The dependent variable is privatisation and the p value is: [a]$p \leq 0.001$, [b]$p \leq 0.05$, [c]$p \leq 0.10$

Table A.7 Static and dynamic model parameter estimate (taxation)

Model	Static model		Restricted dynamic		Unrestricted dynamic	
Variables	Estimate	Std error	Estimate	Std error	Estimate	Std error
A. Determinants of taxation						
Intercept	−0.799	0.753	−1.574	4.533	−0.833	2.768
Diversification	0.018[c]	0.006	0.024	0.025	−0.031[c]	0.015
Privatisation	0.423[a]	0.020	0.291[b]	0.102	0.189[b]	0.061
Dependency	−0.069[a]	0.014	−0.123[c]	0.060	−0.064[b]	0.022
Economic growth	0.139[a]	0.034	0.676[b]	0.202	0.332[a]	0.067
Governance	−0.020[b]	0.007	0.015	0.045	0.058[c]	0.028
Export	−0.045[a]	0.011	−0.088	0.057	−0.013	0.026
Import	0.070[a]	0.012	0.183[b]	0.059	0.000	0.027
Tax capacity	0.210[a]	0.013	0.242[a]	0.053	−0.067	0.046
Trend	−0.013	0.020	0.005	0.110	0.366[b]	0.106
Lower middle income			−2.535	2.876	−2.040	1.853
Middle income			−3.154	2.806	−1.423	1.875
Upper middle income			−1.576	3.185	−4.167[c]	2.415
Higher income			−5.189	3.713	−0.492	2.465
B. Determinants of adjustment speed						
Intercept			0.064[a]	0.010	−0.121[b]	0.042

(continued)

Appendix 2: Single Equation Model

Table A.7 (continued)

Model	Static model		Restricted dynamic		Unrestricted dynamic	
Variables	Estimate	Std error	Estimate	Std error	Estimate	Std error
Investment policy					−0.002[a]	0.001
Rule of law					0.001[b]	0.001
Tax capacity					−0.006[a]	0.001
Credit to private sector					0.017[c]	0.009
Trend					0.003[c]	0.002
Distance					−0.015[a]	0.003
OG dummy					0.014	0.018
Lower middle income					0.042	0.031
Middle income					0.034	0.028
Upper middle income					0.011	0.037
Higher income					0.092[c]	0.042
Observation	1349		1295		950	
Adjusted R-squared	0.477		0.935		0.908	
RMSE	4.378		1.558		1.479	

Note The dependent variable is Taxation and the p value is: [a]$p \leq 0.001$, [b]$p \leq 0.05$, [c]$p \leq 0.10$

Table A.8 Static and dynamic model parameters estimates (dependency)

Model	Static		Dynamic restricted		Dynamic unrestricted	
Variables	Estimate	Std error	Estimate	Std error	Estimate	Std error
A. Determinants of optimal dependency						
Intercept	45.421[a]	4.637	95.395[a]	19.484	66.035[a]	6.676
PSD	−0.375[a]	0.081	0.993	0.483	0.617[a]	0.146
Privatisation	0.025	0.063	−0.046	0.346	−0.530[a]	0.113
Taxation	−0.344[a]	0.081	−0.176	0.497	−0.442[b]	0.154
Institutional quality	−6.204[a]	0.472	−3.183	3.530	6.443[a]	1.453
Political stability	0.001	0.018	−0.010	0.117	−0.072	0.047
Human development	1.643	3.412	−33.111	36.079	−44.772[b]	13.394
Public investment	0.162[c]	0.069	−0.806[c]	0.402	−0.665[a]	0.122
Manufacturing production	−0.094[a]	0.021	−0.044	0.175	−0.218[c]	0.104

(continued)

Table A.8 (continued)

Model	Static		Dynamic restricted		Dynamic unrestricted	
Variables	Estimate	Std error	Estimate	Std error	Estimate	Std error
Real exchange rate	−0.164[a]	0.036	−0.335[a]	0.079	−0.151[a]	0.015
Trend	−0.029	0.051	−0.401	0.324	0.163	0.124
Low middle income			−22.540[c]	9.339	−6.373[c]	3.688
Middle income			−11.924	10.308	5.576	3.387
Upper middle income			−9.845	11.952	13.354[b]	3.813
Higher income			−12.312	13.285	5.837	4.358
B. Determinants of speed of adjustment						
Intercept			0.047[a]	0.008	−0.101[b]	0.037
Development policy					0.010[a]	0.002
Stability policy					0.001[c]	0.000
Openness policy					−0.001[b]	0.000
Investment policy					0.000	0.000
Tax capacity improvement policy					0.000	0.001
Institution improvement policy					−0.056[a]	0.014
Trend					0.002[c]	0.001
Distance					0.006[a]	0.001
OG dummy					−0.007	0.019
Low middle income					0.067[c]	0.032
Middle income					0.010	0.022
Upper middle income					0.075[b]	0.025
Higher income					0.084[b]	0.029
Observations	1267		1217		1207	
Adjusted R-squared	0.274		0.947		0.953	
RMSE	12.86		3.470		3.269	

Note The dependent variable is Dependency and the p value is: [a]$p \leq 0.001$, [b]$p \leq 0.05$, [c]$p \leq 0.10$

Appendix 3
The Determinants of Speed of Adjustment

See Tables A.9, A.10, A.11, and A.12.

Table A.9 The determinants of speed of adjustment (PSD)

Model	Static model		Restricted dynamic		Unrestricted dynamic	
Variables	Estimate	Std error	Estimate	Std error	Estimate	Std error
Intercept	…	…	0.145[a]	0.016	0.561[a]	0.087
Development policy	…	…	…	…	−0.022[a]	0.003
Human development	…	…	…	…	−0.001[c]	0.000
Openness policy	…	…	…	…	0.000	0.000
Rule of law	…	…	…	…	−0.003[a]	0.001
Credit to private sector	…	…	…	…	−0.010	0.015
Speed of privatisation	…	…	…	…	−0.003[b]	0.002
Trend	…	…	…	…	−0.006[b]	0.002
Distance	…	…	…	…	0.015[a]	0.002
OG dummy variable	…	…	…	…	0.196[a]	0.035
Low middle income	…	…	…	…	−0.227[b]	0.069
Middle income	…	…	…	…	−0.277[a]	0.063
Upper middle income	…	…	…	…	−0.377[a]	0.072

(continued)

Table A.9 (continued)

Model	Static model		Restricted dynamic		Unrestricted dynamic	
Variables	Estimate	Std error	Estimate	Std error	Estimate	Std error
Higher income	...	...	...	...	−0.417[a]	0.069
Observations	937		937		937	
Adjusted R-squared	0.188		0.814		0.847	
RMSE	6.633		3.176		2.877	

Note The dependent variable is PSD and the p value is: [a]$p \leq 0.001$, [b]$p \leq 0.05$, [c]$p \leq 0.10$

Table A.10 The determinants of speed of adjustment for privatisation

Model	Static model		Restricted dynamic		Unrestricted dynamic	
Variables	Estimate	Std error	Estimate	Std error	Estimate	Std error
Intercept			0.088[a]	0.014	−0.104[c]	0.045
Rule of law					0.001	0.001
Openness policy					0.000[c]	0.000
Subsidy policy					0.000	0.001
Interest rate policy					0.001	0.000
Credit to the private sector (PCA)					−0.021[c]	0.009
Oil & gas dummy variable					0.009	0.021
Trend					0.001	0.001
Lower middle income					0.044	0.036
Middle Income					0.022	0.035
Upper middle income					0.039	0.041
Higher income					0.042	0.043
distance					0.103[a]	0.006
Observation	937		937		937	
Adjusted R-squared	0.5461		0.9235		0.9496	
RMSE	5.1121		2.099		1.7034	

Note The dependent variable is Privatisation and the p value is: [a]$p \leq 0.001$, [b]$p \leq 0.05$, [c]$p \leq 0.10$

Appendix 3: The Determinants of Speed of Adjustment

Table A.11 The determinants of speed of adjustment (taxation)

Model	Static model		Restricted dynamic		Unrestricted dynamic	
Variables	Estimate	Std error	Estimate	Std error	Estimate	Std error
Intercept			0.085[a]	0.015	−0.036	0.036
Rule of law					0.000	0.001
Investment policy					0.000	0.001
Tax capacity					0.001	0.001
Credit to private sector					−0.013	0.011
OG dummy					−0.017[c]	0.020
Trend					−0.001	0.001
Lower middle income					−0.014	0.034
Middle Income					−0.008	0.026
Upper middle income					−0.059[c]	0.034
Higher income					−0.001	0.035
distance					0.120[a]	0.008
Observation	937		937		937	
Adjusted R-squared	0.4955		0.9004		0.9382	
RMSE	3.4706		1.5417		1.2149	

Note The dependent variable is Taxation and the p value is: [a]$p \leq 0.001$, [b]$p \leq 0.05$, [c]$p \leq 0.10$

Table A.12 The determinants of speed of adjustment (dependency reduction)

Model	Static		Dynamic restricted		Dynamic unrestricted	
Variables	Estimate	Std error	Estimate	Std error	Estimate	Std error
Intercept			0.043[a]	0.009	−0.065[b]	0.025
Stability policy					0.000	0.000
Openness policy					0.000	0.000
Investment policy					0.000	0.000
Tax capacity improvement policy					−0.001	0.001
Institution improvement policy					0.022[c]	0.012
OG dummy variable					0.010	0.014
Trend					0.000	0.001
Low middle income					0.005	0.024
Middle income					0.030[c]	0.015

(continued)

Table A.12 (continued)

Model	Static		Dynamic restricted		Dynamic unrestricted	
Variables	Estimate	Std error	Estimate	Std error	Estimate	Std error
Upper middle income					0.012	0.019
Higher income					0.012	0.022
Distance					0.044[a]	0.003
Observations	937		937		937	
Adjusted R-squared	0.2579		0.9486		0.9654	
RMSE	13.4364		3.5352		2.9003	

Note The dependent variable is dependency and the p value is: [a]$p \leq 0.001$, [b]$p \leq 0.05$, [c]$p \leq 0.10$

Appendix 4
Country Mean Indicator Values

See Tables A.13, A.14, A.15, and A.16.

Table A.13 Country mean indicator value of PSD

Country	Observed	Optimal	Delta
Angola	8.344	16.149	0.107
Albania	20.895	23.755	0.087
United Arab Emirates	12.591	29.670	−0.029
Armenia	23.833	24.615	−0.215
Azerbaijan	27.060	27.949	0.349
Burundi	5.450	11.431	0.467
Benin	15.143	20.800	0.047
Burkina Faso	11.313	19.888	0.217
Bangladesh	18.416	22.789	0.278
Belarus	26.163	27.871	0.148
Bolivia	8.358	21.135	0.226
Brazil	15.054	7.123	−0.061
Bhutan	40.844	29.955	−0.114
Botswana	18.328	22.828	0.310
Cote d'Ivoire	7.868	15.019	0.286
Congo, Dem. Rep	10.077	15.821	0.664

(continued)

© The Editor(s) (if applicable) and The Author(s), under exclusive license to Springer Nature Singapore Pte Ltd. 2023
G. M. Muhamad, *Reducing Natural Resource Dependency for Economic Growth in Resource Rich Countries*, Perspectives on Development in the Middle East and North Africa (MENA) Region, https://doi.org/10.1007/978-981-99-3640-3

Table A.13 (continued)

Country	Observed	Optimal	Delta
Congo, Rep	17.342	20.125	0.074
Cabo Verde	24.530	22.296	−0.076
Algeria	18.378	18.578	0.110
Egypt, Arab Rep	7.970	21.396	0.123
Fiji	13.033	19.822	−0.215
Georgia	17.086	26.816	0.074
Gambia, The	13.154	24.115	0.268
Equatorial Guinea	28.630	9.241	0.188
Guatemala	13.478	16.195	0.023
Honduras	19.467	14.590	−0.044
Croatia	17.573	16.163	−0.177
Indonesia	24.832	23.745	0.136
Iran, Islamic Rep	20.525	28.336	0.148
Iraq	8.937	24.691	−0.011
Jordan	19.145	23.235	−0.136
Japan	18.978	16.829	−0.145
Kazakhstan	20.849	25.293	0.147
Kyrgyz Republic	15.631	26.202	0.099
Cambodia	10.335	21.382	0.106
Lao PDR	19.852	27.106	−0.051
Lebanon	21.898	13.871	−0.186
Liberia	12.580	22.428	0.237
Sri Lanka	20.541	24.094	−0.128
Moldova	16.503	25.393	0.211
Madagascar	11.798	20.805	0.454
Mexico	17.049	15.757	0.007
Macedonia, FYR	16.126	13.657	−0.026
Mali	11.824	18.587	0.152
Mongolia	23.558	26.546	0.033

(continued)

Appendix 4: Country Mean Indicator Values

Table A.13 (continued)

Country	Observed	Optimal	Delta
Mozambique	10.015	21.367	0.161
Mauritius	16.459	22.688	−0.318
Malawi	7.169	22.768	0.193
Malaysia	16.810	15.772	−0.125
Namibia	20.259	18.472	−0.371
Nicaragua	18.485	22.588	0.030
Nepal	16.590	22.165	0.184
Oman	6.439	28.182	−0.041
Pakistan	10.399	20.488	0.316
Peru	16.375	30.060	0.150
Philippines	18.035	22.683	0.125
Poland	15.392	23.169	−0.229
Romania	20.331	22.449	−0.069
Russian Federation	17.367	18.854	−0.007
Rwanda	8.222	15.771	0.200
Senegal	17.315	18.352	0.050
Sierra Leone	8.217	15.737	0.305
El Salvador	14.073	19.886	−0.035
Suriname	26.229	18.618	−0.175
Swaziland	10.095	13.986	−0.009
Seychelles	22.679	17.522	−0.356
Syria Arab Rep	11.202	14.472	0.004
Togo	12.404	20.382	0.262
Thailand	20.999	18.819	0.016
Tunisia	17.990	21.609	0.028
Turkey	5.198	11.537	−0.048
Uganda	16.185	21.870	0.261
Ukraine	18.596	23.259	0.108
Uruguay	12.881	16.196	−0.369
United States	16.992	16.486	−0.159
Uzbekistan	18.356	22.906	−0.131
South Africa	15.125	10.941	−0.062
Zambia	10.721	−18.440	−0.077

Note The Mean values of some countries are not presented due to missing data

Table A.14 Country mean indicator values of privatisation

Country	Observed	Optimal	Delta
Angola	25.352	26.654	0.366
Albania	23.955	28.248	0.115
United Arab Emirates	4.818	33.568	−0.022
Armenia	21.931	29.670	0.089
Azerbaijan	21.414	20.828	0.226
Burundi	19.373	13.068	0.101
Benin	12.600	20.470	0.005
Burkina Faso	13.132	15.910	0.023
Bangladesh	8.932	16.248	−0.031
Belarus	29.190	21.622	0.088
Bolivia	21.468	21.976	0.029
Brazil	27.884	27.785	0.230
Bhutan	19.546	19.667	0.123
Botswana	30.109	30.289	0.232
Cote d'Ivoire	14.763	22.720	0.069
Congo, Dem. Rep	9.526	11.503	0.089
Congo, Rep	22.962	25.224	0.274
Cabo Verde	23.684	28.168	0.196
Algeria	22.982	22.617	0.144
Egypt, Arab Rep	29.116	24.595	0.121
Fiji	22.671	27.607	0.060
Georgia	20.519	28.822	0.155
Gambia, The	13.341	18.124	0.032
Equatorial Guinea	6.367	25.940	0.029
Guatemala	11.252	21.624	−0.013
Honduras	22.407	24.232	−0.001
Croatia	36.131	32.356	0.034
Indonesia	15.683	19.366	0.008
Iran, Islamic Rep	16.733	14.234	0.068
Iraq	25.308	18.915	0.007
Jordan	33.269	28.052	0.121
Japan	16.563	29.655	0.009
Kazakhstan	15.083	21.879	0.033
Kyrgyz Republic	25.413	25.212	0.155
Cambodia	10.291	21.993	−0.017

(continued)

Appendix 4: Country Mean Indicator Values   193

Table A.14 (continued)

Country	Observed	Optimal	Delta
Lao PDR	13.214	20.067	0.088
Lebanon	27.886	27.480	0.079
Liberia	21.695	23.282	0.101
Sri Lanka	20.496	24.185	0.088
Moldova	31.254	27.654	0.180
Madagascar	11.007	12.531	0.062
Mexico	16.824	25.318	0.025
Macedonia, FYR	17.145	12.106	0.044
Mali	12.434	21.199	0.000
Mongolia	21.473	27.071	0.128
Mozambique	23.358	21.771	0.027
Mauritius	19.830	28.999	0.116
Malawi	19.068	21.473	0.096
Malaysia	18.632	32.083	0.034
Namibia	29.660	31.966	0.139
Nicaragua	14.975	24.697	0.073
Nepal	16.051	15.181	−0.013
Oman	29.619	24.293	0.201
Pakistan	16.863	23.130	0.059
Peru	17.791	21.675	0.057
Philippines	15.158	22.599	0.005
Poland	32.898	35.880	0.190
Romania	31.732	27.380	0.126
Russian Federation	23.684	26.115	0.242
Rwanda	16.350	15.880	0.054
Senegal	18.425	24.661	0.141
Sierra Leone	15.604	16.640	0.153
El Salvador	21.196	24.966	0.118
Suriname	24.451	23.958	0.150
Seychelles	36.287	31.523	0.162
Syria Arab Rep	17.615	19.503	0.058
Togo	18.794	19.721	0.090
Thailand	15.897	22.705	0.049
Tunisia	29.144	24.269	0.027
Turkey	27.399	25.175	0.211
Uganda	13.300	18.995	0.044
Ukraine	35.540	26.141	0.179
Uruguay	28.516	31.029	0.125
United States	11.126	0.220	0.030

(continued)

Table A.14 (continued)

Country	Observed	Optimal	Delta
Uzbekistan	18.935	25.676	0.004
South Africa	30.389	32.731	0.034
Zambia	19.069	18.902	0.620

Note The Mean values of some countries are not presented due to missing data

Table A.15 Country mean indicator values of taxation

Country	Observed	Optimal	Delta
Angola	13.672	15.37	0.315
Albania	9.534	7.377	0.131
United Arab Emirates	0.245	4.079	−0.053
Armenia	9.214	9.264	0.016
Azerbaijan	8.484	7.521	0.430
Burundi	6.862	4.904	0.099
Benin	9.47	8.128	0.006
Burkina Faso	8.032	8.483	0.053
Bangladesh	4.953	8.421	−0.010
Belarus	18.32	15.08	0.171
Bolivia	7.873	5.894	−0.005
Brazil	13.201	11.567	0.047
Bhutan	9.427	14.492	0.085
Botswana	15.938	14.989	0.173
Cote d'Ivoire	9.75	9.164	0.062
Congo, Dem. Rep	5.536	8.098	0.111
Congo, Rep	9.187	9.894	0.127
Cabo Verde	4.608	0.1	0.145
Algeria	33.498	16.369	0.295
Egypt, Arab Rep	14.66	16.144	0.058
Fiji	16.787	0.1	−0.004
Georgia	12.729	13.2	0.100
Gambia, The	4.117	5.963	0.175
Equatorial Guinea	4.062	0.1	0.210
Guatemala	10.1	14.204	0.014
Honduras	8.573	10.953	0.021
Croatia	17.333	11.469	0.031
Indonesia	9.946	16.181	0.032
Iran, Islamic Rep	6.439	5.675	0.006

(continued)

Appendix 4: Country Mean Indicator Values 195

Table A.15 (continued)

Country	Observed	Optimal	Delta
Iraq	0.242	1.293	−0.030
Jordan	3.65	4.35	−0.028
Japan	10.309	14.455	−0.017
Kazakhstan	6.975	8.539	0.073
Kyrgyz Republic	2.636	2.556	−0.007
Cambodia	6.406	8.922	0.031
Lao PDR	4.461	4.884	−0.019
Lebanon	11.346	11.459	−0.012
Liberia	9.334	9.391	0.125
Sri Lanka	13.997	0.1	0.023
Moldova	14.199	0.1	0.215
Madagascar	5.842	3.782	0.107
Mexico	7.543	8.401	0.056
Macedonia, FYR	8.307	5.958	−0.029
Mali	8.691	9.873	0.033
Mongolia	15.067	13.9	0.276
Mozambique	6.362	2.699	0.284
Mauritius	16.883	0.1	0.060
Malawi	5.138	6.79	0.072
Malaysia	12.536	18.529	0.057
Namibia	27.847	0.1	0.162
Nicaragua	13.244	13.592	0.092
Nepal	10.859	5.043	0.029
Oman	3.93	7.129	0.108
Pakistan	5.862	7.821	0.046
Peru	14.286	5.494	0.032
Philippines	13.747	14.117	0.030
Poland	18.013	13.687	0.018
Romania	17.702	14.759	0.032
Russian Federation	9.596	7.161	0.108
Rwanda	2.875	2.022	0.014
Senegal	9.951	6.481	0.003
Sierra Leone	8.772	11.53	0.082
El Salvador	10.921	12.965	0.039
Suriname	8.809	7.622	0.198
Swaziland	16.427	0.1	0.272

(continued)

Table A.15 (continued)

Country	Observed	Optimal	Delta
Syria Arab Rep	10.663	5.448	0.136
Togo	9.168	8.021	0.062
Thailand	15.263	17.144	−0.011
Tunisia	19.76	17.421	0.003
Turkey	11.18	8.309	0.101
Uganda	1.071	1.46	0.039
Ukraine	11.593	13.316	0.124
Uruguay	17.998	11.199	0.049
United States	10.591	14.494	0.025
Uzbekistan	4.54	3.727	−0.015
South Africa	24.609	20.454	0.014
Zambia	2.802	3.33	0.288

Note The Mean values of some countries are not presented due to missing data

Table A.16 Country mean indicator values of dependency

Country	Observed	Optimal	Delta
Angola	39.955	25.656	0.380
Albania	2.279	9.306	0.034
United Arab Emirates	18.725	3.667	0.143
Armenia	1.679	6.447	0.003
Azerbaijan	24.511	2.866	0.244
Burundi	22.077	22.558	0.120
Benin	5.817	11.668	−0.007
Burkina Faso	11.693	22.590	0.026
Bangladesh	0.905	7.961	−0.029
Belarus	1.723	17.233	−0.011
Bolivia	6.945	6.723	0.032
Brazil	3.120	23.644	0.015
Bhutan	4.370	29.995	0.000
Botswana	2.808	24.278	0.334
Chili	11.361	1.000	0.285
China	3.709	1.000	0.297
Cote d'Ivoire	5.275	5.838	−0.003
Cameron	8.124	1.000	−0.013

(continued)

Appendix 4: Country Mean Indicator Values

Table A.16 (continued)

Country	Observed	Optimal	Delta
Congo, Dem. Rep	28.038	30.231	0.145
Congo, Rep	43.527	42.615	0.376
Colombia	4.608	1.000	0.045
Comoros	2.711	1.000	−0.051
Cabo Verde	0.578	6.015	0.006
Algeria	15.922	5.751	0.053
Ecuador	9.253	1.000	0.110
Egypt, Arab Rep	8.403	13.030	0.073
Fiji	1.620	2.405	−0.025
Gabon	30.877	1.000	0.263
Georgia	0.879	4.115	0.003
Ghana	12.229	1.000	0.056
Guinea	16.674	1.000	0.029
Gambia, The	4.872	11.752	−0.024
Guinea-Bissau	17.685	1.000	0.058
Equatorial Guinea	30.117	18.850	0.282
Guatemala	1.753	31.019	−0.010
Guyana	19.494	1.000	0.091
Honduras	2.334	12.980	−0.006
Croatia	0.704	9.244	0.006
Haiti	0.906	1.000	0.002
IDN	3.094	15.370	0.019
Iran, Islamic Rep	23.150	23.848	0.209
Iraq	24.917	2.526	0.192
Jordan	0.977	1.569	0.045
Japan	0.150	11.277	−0.013
Kazakhstan	17.604	10.178	0.126
Kenia	4.090	1.000	−0.028
Kyrgyz Republic	4.327	1.000	0.017
Cambodia	3.968	6.344	−0.017
Kuwait	41.075	1.000	0.000

(continued)

Table A.16 (continued)

Country	Observed	Optimal	Delta
Lao PDR	9.846	5.328	0.011
Lebanon	0.150	7.237	−0.019
Liberia	46.490	13.504	0.295
Libya	28.839	1.000	0.264
Sri Lanka	0.229	4.165	0.006
Moldova	0.244	1.291	−0.014
Madagascar	7.389	11.009	0.011
Mexico	3.815	15.655	0.032
Macedonia, FYR	1.992	1.000	0.052
Mali	8.145	9.264	0.016
Mongolia	19.019	14.620	0.153
Mozambique	11.557	4.915	0.034
Mauritania	23.024	1.000	0.197
Mauritius	0.150	25.640	−0.007
Malawi	9.027	8.307	0.037
Malaysia	10.163	9.527	0.035
Namibia	2.033	12.869	0.009
Niger	10.689	1.000	−0.005
Nigeria	26.107	1.000	−0.006
Nicaragua	2.588	5.994	−0.009
Norway	7.727	1.000	0.275
Nepal	1.210	4.814	−0.027
Oman	33.546	14.556	0.276
Pakistan	1.690	4.001	−0.023
Panama	0.189	1.000	−0.012
Peru	74.000	24.410	−0.004
Philippines	1.575	5.390	0.014
Poland	1.181	1.528	0.025

(continued)

Table A.16 (continued)

Country	Observed	Optimal	Delta
Qatar	29.648	1.000	0.107
Romania	2.455	9.139	0.015
Russian Federation	13.236	6.285	0.088
Rwanda	7.893	9.040	0.012
Saudi Arabia	34.497	1.000	0.183
Senegal	3.760	4.825	0.003
Sierra Leone	15.385	29.992	0.110
El Salvador	0.627	13.025	−0.009
Suriname	16.347	12.537	0.149
Swaziland	3.550	26.966	−0.017
Seychelles	0.152	15.899	−0.028
Syria Arab Rep	12.935	14.916	0.118
Chad	19.108	1.000	0.119
Togo	14.143	13.580	0.054
Thailand	1.495	19.376	0.005
Tunisia	3.923	17.978	0.045
Turkey	0.363	10.773	−0.003
Tanzania	7.871	1.000	0.029
Uganda	15.488	2.252	0.064
Ukraine	4.671	5.249	0.030
Uruguay	0.928	18.051	−0.001
United States	0.959	1.000	0.010
Uzbekistan	18.465	2.807	0.128
Venezuela, RB	14.253	1.000	0.170
Vietnam	7.287	1.000	0.363
Yemen, Rep	24.011	1.000	0.216
South Africa	5.107	18.335	0.036
Zambia	8.565	1.609	0.013

Note The Mean values of some countries are not presented due to missing data

Printed in the United States
by Baker & Taylor Publisher Services